"Bob Greene is a virtuoso of the things that bring journalism alive: literary talent, hard reporting, a taste for mixing it up haunch-to-paunch, shank-to-flank, and elbow-to-rib with people of all sorts, and a willingness to let out a barbaric yawp now and again." —*Tom Wolfe*

"Instant replay access to the crazy-quilt times through which we have been passing, while allowing future generations to know what it was like to be an American as we begin our final approach to the 21st Century." —*Chicago Tribune*

"The best national columnist in his weight class . . . Think of his column as the back seat of a taxi. You never know who's going to turn up next, or what will come out of his conversation with the driver." —*Pittsburgh Press*

"Deliciously diverse . . . Revealing the skills of a beat reporter as well as a sure and graceful literary voice . . . Greene writes with humor, poignancy, and amazing empathy that makes situations and people come alive. . . . As irresistible as a Lay's potato chip—that is, it's impossible to read just one . . . A superb example of a writer at the top of his form" —*Seattle Times*

"Going through the book is like visiting old friends. . . . Greene seems to be after the texture of our times, the events of daily life that shape our experience. . . . Refreshingly warm, compassionate, interested, amused, and amusing . . . Read Bob Greene. He is talking about our lives." —*San Francisco Chronicle*

PENGUIN BOOKS

AMERICAN BEAT

Bob Greene is a syndicated columnist for the *Chicago Tribune* whose column appears in more than 150 newspapers in the United States. He is a contributing editor of *Esquire* magazine, in which his "American Beat" column appears each month, as well as a contributing correspondent for "ABC News Nightline." He has written five previous books: *Ragtime* (with Paul Galloway); *Johnny Deadline, Reporter: The Best of Bob Greene*; *Billion-Dollar Baby*; *Running: A Nixon-McGovern Campaign Journal*; and *We Didn't Have None of Them Fat Funky Angels on the Wall of Heartbreak Hotel, and Other Reports from America.*

AMERICAN BEAT

by Bob Greene

PENGUIN BOOKS

Penguin Books Ltd, Harmondsworth,
Middlesex, England
Penguin Books, 40 West 23rd Street,
New York, New York 10010, U.S.A.
Penguin Books Australia Ltd, Ringwood,
Victoria, Australia
Penguin Books Canada Limited, 2801 John Street,
Markham, Ontario, Canada L3R 1B4
Penguin Books (N.Z.) Ltd, 182–190 Wairau Road,
Auckland 10, New Zealand

First published in the United States of America by
Atheneum 1983
First published in Canada by
McClelland and Stewart Limited 1983
Published in Penguin Books 1984

LIBRARY OF CONGRESS CATALOGING IN PUBLICATION DATA
Greene, Bob.
American beat.
Reprint. Originally published: New York: Atheneum,
1983.
I. Title.
PN4874.G679A25   1984   814'.54   84-283
ISBN 0 14 00.7320 5

Printed in the United States of America by
R. R. Donnelley & Sons Company, Harrisonburg, Virginia
Set in CRT Baskerville

For Rob Fleder and Marilyn Johnson

Contents

AMERICAN BEAT

Introduction

I HAVE A job that I like. I make my living by going out and seeing things. Then I write stories about what I saw. If that sounds like an enviable line of work . . . well, I agree. I'm lucky to be doing it.

The stories that appear here were written between the middle of the 1970s and the present. They originally appeared three different places: in my "American Beat" column in *Esquire* magazine; in the *Chicago Tribune*, where my syndicated newspaper column has been based since 1978; and in the *Chicago Sun-Times*, where I worked before that.

I am neither a pundit nor a political philosopher. I try to be a storyteller; I try to go out and explore something that interests me, and then—after hanging around and watching and listening and asking questions—I try to give the reader some sense of what it was like to have been there.

Some of the stories here were written "off the news," in the course of covering breaking events. The Atlanta murders, the Super Bowl, the death of Elvis Presley—on those stories I was one of many reporters on the scene, trying to carve out a piece of the action for myself.

Much more often, I was the only writer around, trying to tell a story that otherwise wouldn't get told. A lone conscientious teacher in an Arizona classroom, a young woman who got fired from her job because she dropped her pants and sat on a Xerox machine, two fifteen-year-old boys growing up in a sprawling suburban shopping mall, a father begging someone to help his wayward son before it became too late . . . those are the kinds of things that don't really qualify as "news," but that seem to me to have as much to do with the way we live as most of the events that warrant bold banner headlines.

Sometimes I visited someone with whom I just felt like spending time. Once in a while it was a person who was a prime target for other journalists, as in the case of Richard Nixon. Most of the time, though, it was someone who, at the time I made my call, was not especially sought after by the rest of the press: Fess Parker twenty years after "Davy Crockett"; Ingemar Johansson; Frank Sinatra, Jr. I was seldom in search of news; what exactly drew me is hard for me to define. I hope it shows up in the stories.

I found myself on the road much of the time. The experiences I came across differed widely; but whether I was flying across the country watching Ella Fitzgerald trying to perform on a DC-10, or picking out the prettiest girl in Kanawha County, West Virginia, or sitting with mass murderer Richard Speck in his prison cell, all of those experiences eventually translated into stories.

In a strange way, though, the stories weren't the main reason for the journeys; the journeys themselves were the reason. One of the men I write about in this book—Bob Seger, the singer—once wrote a song that included the line: "Such a fine memory, I think I'm going to take it with me." That's what all of this has been about: a never-ending trip in search of memories, all of them there for the taking.

Before we get on with the book itself, I'd like to say thank you to a few people.

At *Esquire*, Phillip Moffitt enthusiastically embraced the idea of "American Beat," and gave me the encouragement, the resources, and the forum to expand the newspaper reporting I had been doing for years into a format without editorial limits, with the entire country as my "hometown."

At the *Chicago Tribune*, the people with whom I work most closely every day have given me a genuine sense of family. No matter where I may travel in pursuit of my stories, the *Tribune* is where I return to sort them out and to write them; the people who work with me—they are my bosses, my colleagues, and my friends—make coming to work a pleasure. I am indebted to Jim

Squires, Max McCrohon, the late Bill Jones, Dick Ciccone, Colleen Dishon, Mike Argirion, and Randy Curwen; and at the Tribune Company Syndicate, Bob Reed, Walter Mahoney, Don Michel, and Evelyn Smith.

At the *Chicago Sun-Times*, where the earliest pieces in this book first appeared, some of my fondest thoughts still reside. Of Jim Hoge—editor while I was at the paper, now publisher—I can only say: outside of my own family, no one has been more important to my life.

BOB GREENE
March 1983

That's Entertainment

STEVE CAUDILL, A twenty-three-year-old airfreight handler, bled from his nose, mouth, and eyes. The blood formed a mask over his face; with each breath he took, the bleeding grew worse. As he moved to avoid getting hit one more time, a paper cup full of beer dropped from the darkness and splashed his legs.

"Kill somebody!" came a voice from high in the arena, but it was hard to make out individual voices amid the animal chant. More beer was thrown into the ring. Caudill's opponent—David Guidugli, twenty-six, a construction worker—was also losing blood, but the sound of the crowd seemed to make him afraid to stop.

This was in a place called Hara Arena, a converted ice rink on the outskirts of Dayton, Ohio. The evening had not been promoted as a boxing match, and indeed it was something . . . different. These two contestants were not boxers; neither were the thirty-four other local men who were providing the entertainment for the audience of almost four thousand.

The crowd was excited to see Caudill and Guidugli spill their blood, yes, but if the truth be told, they had been even happier several minutes earlier, when Stanton Long, a machine operator, had staggered to the side of the ring and, in great pain, vomited the entire contents of his stomach onto the concrete floor below. And they had laughed mightily when Raymond Morris, a forty-five-year-old bartender, had convulsed on the mat after taking a beating from a man twenty-two years his junior.

The arena had been chilly before the people had arrived, but now it was steaming. You could feel the heat.

Three weeks earlier, the posters had gone up in the bars and factories around Dayton. "HOW TOUGH ARE YOU?" read the headline that stood next to a large drawing of a man's fist. The subhead: "We're looking for the toughest man in the Southwest Ohio area. Could it be you?"

The poster solicited "bar bouncers, construction workers, bar brawlers, truck drivers, policemen, factory workers, firemen, farmers, etc., etc." Professional boxers were not welcome. Tickets for the two evenings would be scaled from $6 to $10. The winner would receive $1,000, the runner-up $500. The others would receive nothing.

This was the Toughman Contest. If you live in New York or Chicago or Los Angeles, you may have never heard of this phenomenon; it does not travel to most major metropolitan areas. But virtually every weekend of the year, a Toughman Contest is held somewhere in the United States—in Wheeling, West Virginia; in Savannah, Georgia; in Grand Rapids, Michigan; in Green Bay, Wisconsin.

The premise—as devised by Arthur Dore, the entrepreneur from Bay City, Michigan, who invented Toughman in 1979—is simple. People in towns that have not been able to support professional boxing for years will pack the nearest arenas and fairgrounds coliseums to see the local braggarts and barroom bullies try to hurt one another. And the meanest men in these towns will fight—most of them for free—out of some vague dream of glory.

The word *boxing* is almost never used in promoting the Toughman Contest. It's too tame a phrase and would turn off potential customers; besides, it doesn't come close to describing what goes on in the Toughman ring. Sure, there are boxing gloves and three two-minute rounds and a panel of judges to select a winner if both contestants go the distance. But almost no one does. Most matches end with one contestant either on the floor or begging for someone to stop the beating. There is fear and cruelty and humiliation in that ring. There are 300-pound men punching 175-pound men to the canvas and then snorting aloud as they punch them some more. There are men who, finding themselves unable to back up the bravado that brought them there in the first place, weep as they are repeatedly slammed against the ropes. There are painfully out-of-shape men being tortured by men tough enough to maim them. On the final night, a contestant who continues to win his matches may be required to fight four different opponents. These elimination bouts go on until there is only one man left.

No, *boxing* doesn't cover it. The Toughman competition has more to do with professional wrestling, except that this is not the illusion of blood and violence but the fact of blood and violence; it has more to do with *The Music Man*, except that the local pride that Art Dore has come to town to exploit comes from a darker side of the human spirit.

"This is what people want to see," Dore said. A bearded man of forty-three, he was sitting in a room in the concrete bowels of Hara Arena a few hours before the Dayton show was to begin. "It's a macho thing. It's for real. They know it's not fake. There's no bobbing or weaving or dancing. These people want action. They want to see a guy who's always boasting that he can whip someone's ass go out and prove it.

"I don't try to analyze it," Dore said with a shrug. "I just try to sell it."

And the men who would do the bleeding? They had sent résumés to the arena, listing their physical dimensions and their occupations: carpenter, Frigidaire worker, city parks maintenance man, Pepsi delivery agent. Many had simply noted "Unemployed." For two nights they would step into the ring with strangers, while other strangers screamed at them from the seats and Art Dore, at the microphone, egged them on with insults and exhortations.

Between elimination bouts they waited in a small room on the arena's first floor. The men wore cut-off Levi's and tank tops, T-shirts and swimming trunks. Some looked like motorcycle gang members; others would have seemed more at home next to a gas station pump. Here was a man with a ring in his left ear; there was another with an obscenity tattooed on the back of his hand. Most of the Toughman contestants waiting backstage could not precisely define what made them want to do this. They seemed to be drawn by the promise of the one thing that had eluded them all their lives: success. They were all small-town, small-job boys; none had attempted to make it in the larger world. They had accepted that, and lived with it. Since grade school they had known they had certain . . . limitations. And then Art Dore had come to town with his promise: You don't need talent. You don't need grace. You don't need ambition. All you need is the meanness that has been your little secret all your life, and if you're mean enough, you're going to be a star. Success? Bleed for it, and it can finally be yours.

"I don't know," said Harlan Glassburn, a twenty-five-year-old construction worker, whose entry form listed him at six feet five inches and 245 pounds. "I just want to see what I can do in there. I've been in a few barroom brawls, but you get hit with a pool stick and you ain't going to be standing up too long. I know I ain't going to make it all the way to the end of this, but at least I got more guts than the people sitting up in the stands. They just want to see blood, and I ain't afraid to bleed."

Stanton Long, the twenty-three-year-old machine operator who would later vomit before the delighted crowd, said, "All my buddies at work were talking about this. You know, there's a lot of crazy people walking around Dayton, a lot of people carrying guns. I've beat up many guys with my fists, but I don't carry a gun. I'm a pretty mellow guy, but if there's a fight, someone's got to do the fighting."

After winning his first-round match, Bruce Niles, thirty-two years old and 330 pounds, a stockman for International Harvester, came into the room. The noise from the crowd followed him in.

"The fights I've been in on the street, there's been a lot of kicking and biting," he said. "You know, you drink a lot of beer and your head gets all buzzed up. Out there just now, I knocked the guy over the ropes, and I don't know what got into me . . . I wanted to kill him. The referee kept pulling me off, but I got on top of the guy. I don't know what it is . . . when you get excited . . . you just want to blow it out of your gourd . . . finish the job. . . ."

High in the arena, fueled by beer, the crowd was on its feet and screaming. This was the second night of the Toughman

Contest. Although the fighters were being led into the ring one pair after another, the pace was not fast enough for some members of the audience. "Bring on the meat!" a voice called out. A number of fistfights had broken out in the stands, the frequency of these brawls increasing as the night grew longer.

"Those are everyday people out there," said Jerry Johnson, a carpenter who had paid his way into both nights of the contest. "They're people just like us, mashing each other's noses and mouths up. There's no rules, just good action."

Johnson's tone was flat and even, betraying not a trace of irony. He seemed to be enjoying a casual night out. If another visitor to Hara Arena felt a different set of emotions—a sick creeping in the pit of the stomach, an unclean film on the soul that seemed to grow thicker with each new roar from the crowd, with each new bloodletting—that visitor was clearly in the minority. The people in the arena seemed to feel no revulsion. They felt only an urgent tingling.

The crowd was mostly male, but the women who were in the audience seemed to be enjoying the show even more than the men. "I think it must be exciting to hit someone like that," said Rosa Ginter, thirty-three, a nursing-home employee. "I don't think it's true that women don't like violence. I'd like to see even more action, if you want to know the truth."

About halfway back on the main floor, a twenty-year-old woman named Tonya Hopkins—a cashier at a local K mart—sat with her husband, watching a particularly bloody exchange. Her eyes were alive. Asked if she wanted to sit at ringside, she left her husband to accompany a reporter to the card table that had been set up against the ring. Up close, she could hear each punch tear at flesh, watch each spurt of blood spatter from the mouths and noses of the fighters. She did not take her eyes away from them; her breathing became irregular, and her chest heaved.

"I like it," she said, her eyes still on the men. "I really like it. These guys can really take a lot of stuff. I didn't realize . . . I like the way they look in each other's eyes. It's so physical . . . I think it's more the taking that gets to me than the giving. I can't stop looking in their faces. It's so beautiful."

"There's almost seven hundred pounds of men in that ring," Art Dore shouted into the ringside microphone as two huge contestants belted each other toward the end of the evening.

The Dayton Toughman Contest was nearly over. It had played itself out almost without incident. Oh, there was one problem when a group of men from the audience lured an arena security guard into a men's rest room, where their companions waited for him, split his head open, beat him, and left him on the floor. But generally, Dore was happy with the way the two evenings had gone.

David Guidugli won the title of Toughest Man in Southwest Ohio; he was presented with a check for $1,000, and Dore played a cassette tape of the theme from *Rocky* into the microphone as Guidugli stood, cut and weary, in the center of the ring.

Hara Arena emptied as quickly as it had filled. Several of the Toughman contestants stayed around, as if there might be something else waiting for them, but when no one spoke to them they quietly departed.

The heat was gone, too. Once again, the arena was just a chilly ice rink that for some reason had a boxing ring set up in the middle. Streaks of blood remained on the white floor of the ring, but other than that there was no reminder of what had occurred during the past two nights.

Art Dore closed his briefcase. He walked toward the box office of the arena to check the night's receipts. In the morning he would be on a plane; he had work to do. Dayton was over; he was on his way to find the toughest man in Sioux City, Iowa.

A Wolf in Wolf's Clothing

I<small>T IS NEARING</small> midnight in the $800,000 condominium of Nick Nickolas. We are on the sixty-eighth floor of an elegant highrise near Lake Michigan in Chicago.

Nickolas, who is forty-one, drinks a Stolichnaya with an orange peel. Across the room, banging balls across the brown felt top of Nickolas's pool table, is one Claudia Mendron. Miss Mendron has been a Playboy Bunny, a Chicago Bears Honey Bear, and a model in a *Playboy* magazine layout entitled "Pro Football's Main Attractions." She is twenty-five and very tan; her blond hair cascades to her shoulders, which are bare. She wears a pair of tight white jeans and a tighter white top. Nickolas pays no attention to her. He is telling a story.

"People talk about women aging worse than men," Nickolas says. "It's the truth! I went back to Oakland, to my twenty-three-year high school reunion. My date happened to be a young lady who was Miss California. And I got to the reunion, and I saw the girl I took to the senior prom back when I was in high school. She looked terrible! I was so embarrassed, I wouldn't even introduce my date to her. I didn't want to admit that I ever actually went out with her. She looked terrible, and me—I never looked better."

Nickolas directs his eyes across the room at Miss Mendron.

"Let's face it," he says. "I wouldn't be with Claudia here if she weighed a hundred and sixty-five pounds. I don't care how pretty she is or how pretty she kisses."

Miss Mendron stops shooting pool and gazes over at Nickolas.

"Right?" Nickolas says.

"Right," she says, beaming.

The nation's social fabric has been embellished in recent years by the arrival of something called the New American Man. In his extreme and exotic form, the New American Man drinks white wine and cries a lot and is so achingly sensitive that he often finds himself quivering. He is constantly searching for the feminine side of his own personality. He is a staunch supporter of feminist theology; in many cases, his wife has left him, but he is secretly proud that she was able to show such strength.

It is instructive and somehow perversely comforting, then, to know that in isolated pockets of male America, men like Nick Nickolas exist. Nickolas is not the New American Man. To be blunt, he is a dinosaur. If the feminine side of Nickolas's personality were ever to reveal itself, Nickolas would probably stomp on it until it was dazed and bleeding.

Nickolas owns a chain of high-ticket fish restaurants, each called Nick's Fishmarket, in Beverly Hills, Honolulu, and Chicago, with another under construction in Houston. He is a burly man (six feet two inches, 225 pounds) with dark hair and brown eyes; he favors western clothes, cowboy hats, and gold jewelry. In a time when even Hugh Hefner supports the Equal Rights Amendment and is showing signs of something of a feminist consciousness, Nickolas is a total throwback to the days of leering playboys and ladies' men; the fantasy he is living out is one that millions of men once openly embraced but have since forsaken out of resignation or what they perceive as heightened awareness. Nickolas seems stuck in the 1950s, and yet his approach appears to be working to perfection for him.

He is constantly surrounded by stunning young women, most of them in their early twenties (Nickolas estimates the number of women he has been romantically involved with to be in the "high hundreds"). He lives in limousines and mirror-walled homes and first-class airplane cabins. He is fond of saying such things as "The reason I like my women young is that the older ones are offended if you call them at three in the morning and say 'Let's go to Hawaii.' "

Men like Nickolas aren't supposed to exist anymore. When he asks a young woman out, he will often put her in his limousine first, give her $500, and tell her to buy some new clothes. ("So she doesn't embarrass me or herself," Nickolas explains. What happens when an outraged modern woman turns him down on such an offer? "It's never happened yet.")

Nickolas is a man with a fifteenth-century sense of honor and a rather wicked temper. If someone insults a woman in his presence, Nickolas has been known to deck the offender, and unfriendly food critics foolish enough to step into a Nick's Fishmarket after writing a negative review have found themselves dragged across their dinner by Nick himself and tossed out into the street. But Nickolas prides himself on being gentle with his women. "I never need to meet another woman in my life," he says. "I get enough new ones coming in just on referrals."

None of this would be of interest, perhaps, if women felt unanimous scorn for Nickolas or simply found him pathetic. But all evidence indicates that plenty of women do not. The women around Nick Nickolas—almost all of them beautiful and, by most objective standards, desirable—seem to want nothing to do with the New American Man, at least as long as Nick is around. On paper, none of Nickolas's routine should work in the new age; in reality, it seldom fails.

"Half of the people who hear about me don't like me," Nickolas says. "We are dealing with envy here. Let's face it, a man who hears about me isn't going to say, 'That Nick Nickolas is a hell of a guy.' "

We are having a late-afternoon drink in Nickolas's condominium. Johnny Paycheck is blasting out of speakers that are built into the walls. Nickolas has gone into his closet (sixty suits, ninety shirts, five hundred ties) and changed from a business suit to jeans, a western shirt open to the waist, and hand-tooled leather cowboy boots that have been cut into bedroom slippers.

"The modern man is a sissy," Nickolas says. "He is defensive, he can't feel good inside about himself, so he becomes afraid of women. He's come to the point where he can't even walk up to a woman and say, 'Hey, how you doin'?' He feels so bad about himself that a little rejection from a woman is going to defeat him.

"You see what I mean? The modern man takes a wimpy approach. He comes on soft, like he's going to get shot down. So he will.

"I'll be in one of my restaurants, and I'll see a pretty lady at the bar. I'll say to the bartender, 'Hi, David, anyone here *Nick* should meet?' I only say it so the woman will know I'm Nick, and I'll see the people who work for me smiling at each other and saying, 'All right! Here he comes! Watch out!' "

Nickolas understands that this kind of talk will generally bring raised eyebrows from people who did not believe that men with his attitudes still exist at this late date. He enjoys eliciting that reaction, and once he is rolling it is difficult to slow him down.

Nickolas on romance: "I don't let a woman move in with me, but I'm not afraid to tell 'em I love 'em. Hell, I've told a woman I love her four hours after I met her. And it's true. What are you supposed to do, wait a year before you tell her? Are you supposed to tell her you 'like her a lot'? We've suppressed the phrase 'I love you' because we're afraid of it. It's one of the prettiest, nicest things you can say to a woman."

Nickolas on the way women gravitate to him: "They hear about me. One of their friends says, 'You may not fall in love with him, but you'll have a good time. You'll go first class, he'll treat you nice, and if you don't want him to jump in your skivvies, he won't.' I've never won any beauty contests, but women tell me, 'When I first met you I never thought I'd end up in the sack with you, but here I am.' I hear that a lot."

Nickolas on the oft-repeated charge that he is afraid of bright women: "Bring 'em on. What am I supposed to do, ask them to fill out a questionnaire before I take them to dinner? I'll admit it, the first thing I'm attracted to is beauty. My life is not centered around what I think. I'm not afraid to say it: I don't need a whole lot of mental stimulation from a woman. Who needs the pressure? You want to debate about Southeast Asia? I don't give a —— about Southeast Asia. Come on, baby, we're going to Greece for two weeks."

And what about the times when Nickolas makes a mistake, when he brings a woman home only to find that they're not hitting it off, that his efforts have been wasted?

" 'Sorry, darling, aloha,' " Nickolas says. " 'You want to go somewhere, Frankie here will take you in the car. Later.' "

It is considered correct these days to reflexively criticize the world of Nick Nickolas, but it is questionable how wise such a reaction is. In a society that has apparently rejected his values, Nickolas appears to have found delirious happiness. It is easy to denounce Nickolas's way of life and to condemn him for going against the grain of every ideal that enlightened people have come to embrace. It is another thing to admit grudgingly that maybe he has something here. In today's social atmosphere, where everything, at times, seems to have gone wrong between the sexes, most men and women would automatically say that Nickolas does not have the answers—but do *they*?

A more reasonable response to Nickolas is probably a sort of puzzled ambivalence. Yes, he seems too basic and simple to be real, a kind of cutout doll, ready to be propped up to receive the assaults of the people he offends. But how many men can deny—in all honesty—that they would welcome the company of the women to be found at Nickolas's side? And how many women can deny—when no one's listening—that they feel a sort of fascination at the idea of stepping, however briefly into Nickolas's strange world, where all the rules are reversed? Sure, it's safe to claim these days that you are repelled by Nickolas's excesses and extremes; it is a little chancier to admit that, after all, you wouldn't mind sharing in some of the things he's managed to give himself. What Nickolas has finally given himself is a private universe that shouldn't work at all but does. And how many people who rail against that are really doing so out of a genuine sense of moral outrage and not out of a frustrated desire to have their share of the pleasures he gets?

Claudia Mendron, the Playboy Bunny and NFL cheerleader, is a woman who has been asked out perhaps a thousand times a year since she was a teenager. Turning men down is a way of life for her. Of Nickolas she says, "I love him the way he is. He's a man's man. He's handsome and gallant and charming and playful and a conglomeration of everything put together.

"Yes, he's macho and aggressive. He's the leader in the relationship. Deep down, I think every woman wants a man like Nick Nickolas. If he were like Phil Donahue or Alan Alda, I don't think I would be interested."

Someone who knows Nickolas well says, "People who hear about Nick thirdhand can be very critical of the way he is. But it's funny: you go into one of his restaurants, and all the men who work there—the waiters, the bartenders—they all seem to be imitating him. I think it's unconscious: they walk the way he walks, talk the way he talks . . . it's as if they're all trying to be little Nicks."

There are people who say that Nickolas really hates women. "Hate them?" he replies. "Women are the greatest motivation in my life. The woman I base all my relationships on is my mother. The way I was raised, in my house the woman was always superior. I wanted my mother to have all the niceties. I had the greatest respect for my mother, and that's carried over to the way I feel about women today."

And now we are at a party in the condominium, given by Nickolas for guests at the National Restaurant Show. Nickolas is in a chocolate-brown tuxedo, with no tie; the ever-present cowboy boots are on his feet.

A woman, slightly tipsy, makes her way across the room until she is at Nickolas's side. It is clear that they have met before.

"I've thought about it, Nick, and I've decided it's worth the ten pounds," she says.

"Hey," Nickolas says with a smile, "great."

"I mean it," she says. "It's absolutely worth the ten pounds."

"Terrific," Nickolas says.

Someone else, overhearing this, looks puzzled.

"Nick told me that I could stay here with him some night," the woman explains. "But he said that I'd have to lose ten pounds first."

There is, for the moment, total silence.

"So I'm going to lose the ten pounds, Nick," she says.

"Hey," Nickolas says with a shrug and the flash of a grin. "Make it eight."

Song of the
Powder Room

IT WAS EARLY in the evening, still before the dinner hour. The place is called Zorine's, a fancy private club that gets regular mention in the gossip columns. On this, a weeknight, business was slow; the crowds would come later, after nine o'clock, when the solid wall of sound caused by disco dancing records would wash over the club.

Now, though, it was almost deserted. At a piano by the bar, a musician named Jim Burke played cocktail music. He, too, would leave when it was time for the disco records to begin.

A visitor, who had never been inside Zorine's before, sat nursing a drink at the bar. He looked over the empty tables, trying to decide whether to stay and wait for the throngs. And then it happened.

A woman came out of the ladies' room. She was wearing a uniform and an apron; it was obvious that she was the washroom attendant. She looked around the club, as if to confirm that there weren't too many people she might bother.

She whispered something to the piano player. He nodded. He began to play a light jazz tune. The washroom attendant started to sing along with him. Softly at first, and then she picked up his rhythm and began to sing louder. The song was "It Ain't

Necessarily So," and by the middle of the first chorus she was standing with her feet spread apart, her arms stretched outward, and she was belting out the lyrics in a most astonishing manner.

There is only one word to describe the purity and sweetness of that lady's voice: perfect. The visitor at the bar had heard Ella Fitzgerald in live performance once, and he had heard Billie Holiday on records. Outside of Miss Fitzgerald and Miss Holiday, though, he had never heard a voice in a class with this washroom lady who was wailing out her song in the empty club.

She completed the song, and said something quietly to the piano player. He hit a note, and she began "Summertime." It was the same thing all over again; beyond her raw talent there was something else; there was that artist's sense of what it means to be a star. She wasn't merely singing, she was performing. The range and authority and clarity of her voice were astounding. She sang "Summertime," and "Georgia on My Mind," and "Bye Bye Blackbird," and "God Bless the Child," and as the magnificence of her voice rebounded off the walls in the vacant club, the only thing to do was to stare at her and wonder how this could be happening.

After about fifteen minutes, she halted. She thanked the piano player, and headed back toward the washroom.

The visitor at the bar stopped her and introduced himself. He thanked her for her songs.

"Oh, that was just for myself," she said. "I do it sometimes if it's not crowded, before the dance records start."

The visitor asked her who she was.

"I'm Millie Gay," she said. "I hope I didn't bother you. It's just that sometimes I'll be sitting there in the ladies' room, and I'll hear the piano and I'll have to come out. I really can't help it."

She talked some more with the visitor, and she looked as if she was weighing whether to tell him something. Finally she did, and her story came pouring out.

Back in the early 1950s, Millie said, she and her sister Evelyn were under contract to Savoy Records. They were gospel singers, and they put out a dozen singles and one album.

"In 1951, I performed in Carnegie Hall," she said. "It was the first time gospel singers had ever sung in Carnegie Hall. I was on the bill with Mahalia Jackson and the Clara Ward Singers. It was quite an evening. I'll never forget it."

Like many black performers in those days, however, Millie Gay never received the money that was due her. She is forty-seven years old now, and when her husband—who was working as a doorman in the Rush Street area—heard about the opening of Zorine's, he arranged for Millie to get the 6:30 P.M.-to-1:00 A.M. job as ladies' room attendant.

"It's a nice job," she said. "My responsibilities are to keep the ladies' room straight, all neat and tidy for the girls who come in. I keep the toilet tissues in order, and make sure that there are towels nice and handy, and make sure that the toilets are tidy."

She noticed that some people were beginning to come into the club.

"I'd better get back to the ladies' room," Millie said. "It's going to be crowded soon, and I'm supposed to stay in there. The records will be playing before too long, and the people are going to want to start dancing."

The visitor asked Millie how she passed the hours and hours when the disco records were playing and she was sitting in the ladies' room.

She looked out over the dance floor.

"It's all right," she said. "When they're dancing out here, I'm singing in there."

Something Blue

SHE WAS SUPPOSED to get married. This was the afternoon. She had planned it all. The ceremony, the guests, the reception—Jeannie was going to be a bride, and as corny as it may sound these days, that is all she ever wanted to be.

Then he walked out on her. His name was John; he was a medical student, and she had come to Chicago six years ago to be with him. "When I get done with school," he had said, and she had waited. She had gone to work at Sears, as a copywriter for the catalog, and although she was not in love with Chicago, she was in love with John. Everything she did pointed to this day.

So the afternoon was here, and Jeannie was not in a church. Instead, she was in her one-room studio apartment on the fifth floor of an apartment building in New Town. It was a sultry day; she had pulled the white shades down, to keep out the heat and to block out the view of Broadway to the west.

"It was supposed to be kind of funny," Jeannie said.

That's what it was supposed to be. She had sent out invitations to her closest women friends at Sears, saying that she "requests the humiliation of your presence" on the occasion of her "jilting at the altar. . . . There will be a reception only, as the church ceremony originally scheduled at this time has been canceled."

Explaining it later, she would say, "It seemed like a good way to avoid being by myself and crying all afternoon. . . . I know it sounds like kind of a sick idea, but I thought maybe I could laugh about it. If I made fun of it, I wouldn't have time to cry."

The guests had arrived; Kim was there, and Louise, and Zahava, and Jo, and Sheila. They were all, like Jeannie, in their mid-twenties (Jeannie was twenty-four); she greeted them at the door wearing a bridal bonnet. New York State pink champagne was in Jeannie's refrigerator.

Linda Ronstadt, on Jeannie's stereo, sang "I Guess It Doesn't Matter Anymore." The women arranged themselves on the couch, on the chairs, on the floor. One, Zahava, was wearing a bridesmaid's dress, and flowers in her hair. There was a wedding cake, with figurines of a bride and groom; the head of the groom had been cut off. It had seemed funny, during the planning.

The women drank.

"Here," said Kim, handing Jeannie a gift-wrapped package.

"You weren't supposed to do this," Jeannie said, but all of the women had.

She started to open the present.

"If you break the ribbon, that's how many kids you're going to have," Kim said.

"You're supposed to line your drawers with this paper," one of the other women said.

"You guys . . ." Jeannie said.

There were more presents. Each had a card attached. "In the Loss of Your Loved One," said one card. "Thoughts of Sympathy." "Wedding Wishes for the Bride Not to Be," the word "Not" written in with ball-point pen.

"I had to cancel my subscription to *Bride's Magazine* . . ." Jeannie said.

"Oh, Jeannie," said Sheila.

". . . but it was too late," Jeannie said. She lifted up her champagne glass. "Here's to my poor mother. She had to cancel her subscription to *Bride's Magazine*, too. My mother feels like such a loser."

For the first hour or so, there were plenty of laughs, as the presents were opened. Then the laughter died as the women stayed together in the little room.

"When did he leave town?" Jo asked.

"John?" Jeannie said. "He left on Tuesday. But he called me this morning."

"He did?" three of the women said at once.

Jeannie nodded.

"What did he say?" Louise said.

Jeannie shrugged, and began talking about something else.

There were more Ronstadt songs: "When Will I Be Loved," "You're No Good," "Time Heals." Zahava, the only married woman in the room, said:

"Being married is fun, in its own way. Being single is fun, in its own way too."

"You guys don't have to say that," Jeannie said.

"No, really," Zahava said.

Jeannie went to the kitchen to bring out some food. By the wall telephone was a list of numbers: "John's Folks," "John's Hospital." Taped to the refrigerator was a picture of an attractive woman in a bikini, with the handwritten notation, "Soon! You Can Resemble This!!! Stop, Think, and Don't Eat!"

Jeannie went back to the main room, where the other women were waiting with a serious present for her, complete with a serious card:

"He's the fool. He doesn't know what he's missing. Maybe someday he'll realize his BIG error."

"You guys have made this one of the nicest days of my life," Jeannie said.

"We're going to miss you," Louise said.

"I'll miss you, too," Jeannie said. "I can't really believe I'm leaving."

"Well, Jeannie," Louise said, "when you marry some famous senator, we'll all come down to Washington for the wedding."

"Really," Jeannie said. "I don't want to let you guys down twice."

"It's too hot today for a wedding, anyway," Kim said.

There was silence.

"You know, I was born and raised to be an independent woman, a career woman," Jeannie said. "But who wants to be alone for the rest of their lives?"

"Stop it, Jeannie," Zahava said. "You'll get married."

The women toasted one another.

"I heard there's a good Gary Cooper movie on tonight," Jeannie said.

Limo

SOMEWHERE ON THE Indiana Toll Road, heading east, the sound of the FM radio station began to fade. This was a disappointment; the disc jockey for WVPE in Elkhart had just been exhorting his listeners to send in ten dollars each in an effort to help the station go stereo, and I was listening for an address so I could mail my money.

"Julius, we'd better find another station," I said.

My voice echoed in the vast back seat of the double-length, jet-black Lincoln Continental limousine. Outside the windows of the limo, the cornfields of Indiana were whizzing by.

"Yes, sir," came the voice of Julius Person, my chauffeur. A Toyota pulled up next to us, like a Cessna buzzing a 747, and its occupants tried to stare into our window. But I did not look back; I just read my *Wall Street Journal* while Julius searched for another rock station.

It had started as one of those dares that you give to yourself.

The air traffic controllers' strike was in its first days; I had a reporting trip scheduled to central Ohio, and getting there from Chicago in the confusion of the strike's beginning was not an appetizing thought.

It was to be a four-day trip; an eight-hour drive from Chicago. The situation called for something to break the monotony of the Indiana Toll Road and the Ohio Turnpike. My idea of the greatest luxury in this life has always been the chauffeured limousine; once in a while I would even treat myself to a limo ride to O'Hare International Airport. But a limousine for eight straight hours through heartland Illinois, Indiana, and Ohio? And for four days in central Ohio during the trip?

The owners of Chicago Limousine Service said the tariff would be $1,200, plus the chauffeur's hotel and meal expenses in Ohio, plus a suitable tip.

You live once.

Julius Person, fifty-five, was a dapper, compact man in a black suit and a chauffeur's cap who would have looked perfect as a host at Harlem's Cotton Club in the Twenties. He had my newspaper waiting on the back seat when I came out the door of my apartment building. He opened the trunk; his own suitcase was already there.

The car was enormous; it had been lengthened at a custom body shop that specializes in stretch limousines. If you lay down with your head against the back seat, your feet would not reach

all the way to the front seat. All during our drive out of Chicago
we were the object of gapers. But it was not until we hit the
Indiana Toll Road—"Main Street of the Midwest," as its slogan
goes—that the delirious ridiculousness of this excess became clear.
Virtually every car on the road tried to check us out; it was as
if Lyndon Johnson had suddenly been set down on the pavement
of northern Indiana.

I looked out the windows, and the scenery told me that this
was something out of *Penrod*. Pure farmland all around; two
lanes this way, two lanes that way, and the Knute Rockne Service
Area looming up ahead. But Julius's radio jarred me back to the
Eighties. A disc jockey had asked his listeners to suggest a name
for the station's women's softball team, and those listeners, on
an open line, were responding:

"The Bush Leaguers."

"The Ball Busters."

"The Pitching Mounds."

"The Periods."

Julius turned around in the front seat. "That air conditioning
cool enough for you, Mr. Greene?" he said.

If you have never pulled up for lunch at the Holiday Inn in
Perrysburg, Ohio, with your chauffeur at the wheel of your limo,
there is no preparing you for it.

The folks at the front desk lined up and stared as Julius and
I made our way into the dining room. All during the trip thus
far, Julius had been as silent as possible; I understood instinctively that part of his professionalism was maintaining the psychic
distance between himself and his passenger. And he was even
extending this to our lunch; we might be sharing a table, but he
was not going to impose himself unless asked.

Finally I realized this was getting absurd. "So Julius," I said.
"How is that tuna fish sandwich?"

"It's very good," Julius said. He nodded for emphasis.

I asked him if an out-of-town assignment like this one was
unusual for him.

"I do it once in a while," he said. "The last one was taking
Pearl Bailey down to St. Louis, and then over to Indianapolis."

"Was she singing or something?" I said.

"No," Julius said. "She was promoting a movie. I believe she played a duck."

We passed through Fostoria, Ohio, on Route 23. Ace's Body Shop and the Fraternal Order of Eagles lodge and Ron Smith Realty came lazily into view; Julius had slowed down to heed the speed limit. There was some construction on the road. The flagman was a teenage girl; she saw us and said something into a hand radio, and when we reached the end of the construction three minutes later the other flagman—also a girl—was smiling and waving at us.

We were going to be coming close to the place where my parents live. I had Julius detour to their neighborhood. He carefully backed the limousine into their driveway. He waited in the car while I visited inside.

Later, I would learn that one of my parents' neighbors had telephoned another:

"Is everything all right at the Greene house? No, I know everything's not all right at the Greene house. There's a hearse in the driveway, and young Bob is in from Chicago looking very grim."

Why I will never be a good rich person, Part One:

Every time a carful of people would look in the back seat to see whose limo it was, I would feel guilty for letting them down. Of all the people they might have hoped for, I felt it was my fault that it was only me.

Why I will never be a good rich person, Part Two:

When we reached our destination and stopped for the night, Julius dropped me at the Hyatt Regency and told me that he was going to go get a room at a cheap hotel that I knew to be in a seedy part of town. He told me he would call me in my room as soon as he got there. I watched him drive away in that big limo, and all I could think about all evening was what a crummy deal it was that I got to stay at the Hyatt and Julius had to look for a dump. It was clearly what he was used to on trips like these; he accepted it, and if I really belonged in a limousine, I would have too.

In the morning Julius was waiting outside the Hyatt with the *Wall Street Journal* and the local newspaper in the back seat. He was smiling.

"Mr. Greene," he said, "I believe I have found us the hardest rock station in the entire United States." And as we cruised through central Ohio, the sound of Foreigner singing "Women" reverberated inside the car.

In the course of my reporting, I met two working mothers named Elaine Shayne and Beanie Weiss. They were admiring the limousine; Mrs. Shayne said she had to go to the K mart, and Julius and I exchanged glances. Why not?

So it was that Mrs. Shayne and Mrs. Weiss pulled up to the local K mart in the Lincoln Continental limousine. Julius stopped at the front door of the store. He fairly leapt from the driver's seat, circled around to the back seat, opened the door, and, with a flourish, helped the women alight from the car.

A crowd was gathering. For a moment they were silent, but soon shouts broke out.

"Where are you from?" a voice demanded.

" 'Queen for a Day,' " said Beanie Weiss. The two of them entered the store.

Julius stood sentinel by the limo. "Those women don't own this limousine," someone said. "If they could afford a limousine like this, they wouldn't shop at the K mart."

Julius smiled. "The reason they can afford a limousine like this is that they shop at the K mart," he said.

I don't know what the best moment of the four days was. It may have been when I was dropping in at the local newspaper office and there was a commotion at the window of the city room. I thought that someone must have dropped dead on the street down below, but when I joined the others at the window I saw that everyone was looking out at Julius, who was being interviewed by a young reporter the city editor had sent.

It may have been at a bar late at night when, at closing time, I walked out with the other customers and Julius was waiting—in that suit and cap—with the back door open.

It may have been when a local cop cruised by Julius's parked car four times, going slower every time. Because Julius was a black stranger in a white Ohio town, I thought he might be in for some petty harassment. But the policeman finally pulled to a stop and, in a voice full of politeness, said:

"Sir, what kind of mileage does that car get?"

"Very good," Julius said, in a serious tone. "Very good."

It was a little like being a kid at an amusement park. I suppose if you got to ride the roller coaster every day, you would get jaded by it. But when you're new at it, you think the kick will never go away. I suppose, somewhere, there are men who step into their limousines every morning and truly don't give it a second thought. And I suppose I will never be one of them.

On the way back to Chicago, Julius said from the front seat:

"Did you see that pretty girl back there who was hitchhiking?"

For a moment I considered it. But we had a long way to go through Indiana, and this was supposed to be my fantasy, not hers.

I had to call my office. So, at a truck stop outside of Indianapolis, Julius pulled up to a phone booth and, beside the highway, I made the call as traffic slowed down to look at the limo.

When I got back in and we were on our way again, I asked Julius if he ever got used to every person he passed gawking at him.

"It doesn't take you long to get used to it," he said. "I've been doing this a long time. And you learn right away that they're not looking at you. They just want to see who's in the back seat."

I asked him if he didn't ever just drive the limo around on his own, so that he could savor in relative privacy some of whatever it was the car gave off.

"I can't do that," he said. "The car doesn't belong to me. It belongs to the company."

"Then you don't drive this on your own?" I asked.

I could only see the back of his head.

"No," he said. "I drive a Gremlin."

The last few hours through Indiana were smooth. Julius's radio continued to provide a sound track; an Indianapolis newscaster informed us that a local man had just been arrested and charged with murdering his wife and children, and then John Lennon was singing "A Day in the Life."

On the outskirts of Chicago, traffic began to back up on the expressway. It was rush hour.

"Julius," I said, "do you ever run into any of your passengers again?"

He was still staring straight ahead. "I just drive wherever they tell me to drive, sir," he said.

We rode in silence to my home; I ran in and dropped off my suitcase, and then Julius headed in the direction of my office. I still had time to check the phone messages.

We both got out in front of the office building. I signed the receipt for the trip, and then Julius and the limousine were back in Michigan Avenue traffic, and soon they were lost. You would think after all these years you would forget what it feels like when the roller-coaster ride is over. You'd be surprised how quickly it comes back to you.

Night Callers

Loneliness is the great American epidemic. More than any disease it insinuates itself into the lives of people wealthy and poor, old and young. It is an affliction of which people are ashamed; they are willing to admit almost anything before they will admit they are lonely.

It makes itself known in many ways, and probably no way is seen more graphically than Audrey Loehr sees it.

Mrs. Loehr is sixty-two years old; she is an employee of one of the giant oil companies—a company with its name on the pumps of gas stations all over the world.

Mrs. Loehr lives and works in Tulsa. Her job is a simple one. It is this:

The oil company has a policy that, on any charge over thirty-five dollars, a gas station attendant must call a toll-free number to get the credit card approved. The attendant has the 800 number posted inside the station; he calls it, and someone on the other end answers, and he reads the card number and the person on the other end punches that number into a computer to make sure the card has not been lost or stolen.

Mrs. Loehr is one of the people on the other end. The credit card center is located in Tulsa; it is open twenty-four hours a day, 365 days a year, so there are always employees—almost all of them women—available to answer the phone when a gas station attendant anywhere in the country has a big charge to check out.

Mrs. Loehr says that there is a pattern to the calls. Most of the time they are straightforward business calls—gas dealers dialing to confirm a charge card.

But on weekends—Fridays, Saturdays, and Sundays—late at night, the obscene calls will begin.

Mrs. Loehr will answer the phone, and, from off in the distance, a man's voice will say something aggressively sexual to her. The voice will make lewd suggestions, will ask improper questions. The voice will say things that most people would never say to other people face-to-face.

She has figured it out:

"At that time of the night, most gas stations are manned by only one person," she said. "It's usually a young man who has been assigned to work all night. He's alone there, and it's dark, and there's no one to talk to."

So what the attendants will do—in Los Angeles, in Houston, in St. Louis, in New York, in Chicago—is call the toll-free number, the one that is posted at the station. And when they hear a woman's voice, they will speak of sex to it.

"It's very sad," she said. "Some of the young girls who work here think it's funny, but I don't think they really understand what loneliness is. When I pick up the phone and hear one of these men start up again, all I can think about is how alone they must be to resort to something like that."

She said there is often a tone of desperation in the men's voices; the men want the female voice to stay on the line.

"They will say, 'Keep talking, keep talking, don't hang up,' " she said. "They know so little about women; the idea of women frustrates them so much that the only contact they can have is to say these things to a stranger's voice.

"If they need professional help, we can't help them. We're just credit-card checkers, and our supervisor has told us to hang up as soon as we know it's that kind of a call. He says that they need guidance, and it would do us no good to try to talk to them, and I know he's probably right."

Mrs. Loehr feels that she has come to understand something about the young men: "They must have so little in their lives; can you imagine standing in a gas station somewhere and dialing that number, just so they can say those things to a female voice?

"I am sixty-two years old, and I don't sound like a young girl. The men must know that. And yet just because I'm a woman, that's enough. It makes you so sad.

"There's nothing humorous about it, and there's nothing sexual, other than the words. It's just such a sign of their loneliness. They are so unimaginative in the things they say, and their voices tell you more than the words do. The voices are voices of men who are so unsure of themselves that they have to resort to this."

She has sometimes thought what the lonely young men might do other than mouth the obscenities: recite a love poem, a proverb from a foreign philosopher, a quote from the Bible. As far as she knows, none ever has; one caller, though, always whispers "I love you" just before he hangs up.

"I'm just sorry about it," she said. "I wish in their own lives they had a way to get a woman's attention. It would be nice if the gas stations could afford to hire couples to work the all-night shifts; it would make me feel glad to think each of those men had a real, live woman to talk to.

"Sometimes they will try to personalize you. One man said to me, 'You sound tall.' I could imagine him, alone in that gas station somewhere, fantasizing about a tall woman who would talk to him."

She said that she fears something has happened to the masculinity of American men; something that makes them so afraid of women that the only way they can deal with them is to make such a call, over the miles.

She said that there is no real answer; loneliness is a part of so many lives, and it is her fate to work in a job where it comes ringing so often. "I just answer the calls," she said. "When I find out that it's one of those calls, I hang up. But I always silently wish that the men find inner peace, and that they somehow get better."

We Will Pay Cash for Your Class Ring

THE ADVERTISEMENT IN the newspaper caught her eye. Perhaps it was the drawing of the high school class ring; perhaps it was the headline:

WANTED . . . 25,000 class rings needed . . . We pay cash! Paying up to $125, all cash!!!

The ad had been placed by the American Gold and Silver Co., Inc., of St. Louis; the company's representatives had come to town and set up shop, for four days, in twelve motels around the city. The rest of the ad copy explained why:

> We have a buyer who has put in an order for 25,000 class rings. We desperately need to fill this order as soon as possible, so for the remaining part of this week and weekend American Gold and Silver will be offering a special premium on all class rings. . . .

She read the ad twice. She is thirty-seven years old; her name is Carol Andrysiak. She went to her closet.

The ring was in an old box, near the bottom of a pile of other boxes. A gold band, with a blue stone surrounded by white mother-of-pearl, and the school crest in the center. Bremen Community High School, Class of '61.

"Sell the old class ring," she said to herself. "A hundred twenty-five bucks. Okey doke."

She put it in her purse.

On the weekend, she drove to the Holiday Inn in a nearby suburb. The desk clerk said the American Gold and Silver people were in room 107.

There were perhaps fifteen people lined up in the corridor. She stood at the end of the line.

The woman in front of her was holding a baby in her arms. They started a conversation. The woman with the baby said that she had been divorced, and now she had to raise the child. She said she had been a pompom girl in high school; "I thought life was going to be a piece of cake," she said.

Up a few feet in the line was a young couple. She talked to them, too; the man had just been laid off his job, and now the two of them were going to sell their class rings. They wanted the rings, they said, but the recession made this day necessary.

She began to roll the ring around in her hand. Slowly she moved closer to the door. All the while she was thinking.

She had had the dream back in high school, too. Back when she had bought that ring, she was going to get married and live in the suburbs and have two children and somehow, in her spare time, become a famous writer.

She had married, but that was long over. There had never

been children. Now she lived alone in a studio apartment in the city. The novels had never quite got written; she worked as a secretary in a busy office building.

She clutched the ring in her palm, and she started to wonder what had happened to all of these people in line. What had happened to the hopeful boys and girls in high school, who had purchased their class rings with such pride? Here they all were, well into the mainstream of their lives, having to sell a piece of yesterday to make it today.

Her thoughts were interrupted. She was first in line. The door to room 107 opened, and she was escorted in. The door closed again behind her.

There was a man at a table, a jeweler's scale in front of him. Another man—a plainclothes security guard—stood to one side.

It took maybe three minutes. The man weighed her ring, then examined it through an eyepiece. He offered her $45.

She asked him about the $125 offer, and he said the ring was not heavy enough.

She took the $45 in cash. The man had her sign a receipt. When she returned to the hallway, the line had grown.

Now that the ring was gone, she couldn't stop thinking of high school. The romantic dreams that all seemed possible; the endless opportunities she had seen ahead . . . she wondered what would become of her ring.

It was a good thing she did not wonder too hard. For the newspaper advertisement had not been quite accurate. "We have a buyer who has put in an order for 25,000 class rings. . . ." Yes, but the buyer did not want to use them to make new class rings.

The rings were going to be melted down. It was as simple as that. Gold has gone up so much in price since the days that people now in their thirties and forties and fifties bought class rings that it is worth it for American Gold and Silver to travel around the country buying them up. This four-day trip to Chicago would bring in some 3,000 class rings; all to be melted, all to be sold to a gold refinery.

Sometimes, the day after a man or woman has sold a ring, they will call the American Gold and Silver offices in St. Louis and say they made a terrible mistake. The memories of the ring meant too much; could they buy it back?

And Irwin J. Reif, the vice-president of the company, would have to tell them that it was not possible. All the rings had been mixed together; they could not be retrieved. Reif himself, who had bought his own high school class ring back in 1932, would never sell his; "I'm too sentimental. To me it means my high school days—the songs, the girls. . . . What a story every one of those rings could tell. But I guess if you need the money . . ."

She walked out of the Holiday Inn. It was a hot summer afternoon. In her car, she tuned the radio to a country and western station. "Oh, I really liked what I was," she thought, and then she didn't think anymore.

Fifteen

"THIS WOULD BE excellent, to go in the ocean with this thing," says Dave Gembutis, fifteen.

He is looking at a $170 Sea Cruiser raft.

"Great," says his companion, Dan Holmes, also fifteen.

This is at Herman's World of Sporting Goods, in the middle of the Woodfield Mall in Schaumburg, Illinois.

The two of them keep staring at the raft. It is unlikely that they will purchase it. For one thing, Dan has only twenty dollars in his pocket, Dave five dollars. For another thing—ocean voyages aside—neither of them is even old enough to drive. Dave's older sister, Kim, has dropped them off at the mall. They will be taking the bus home.

Fifteen. What a weird age to be male. Most of us have forgotten about it, or have idealized it. But when you are fifteen . . . well, things tend to be less than perfect.

You can't drive. You are only a freshman in high school. The girls your age look older than you and go out with upperclassmen who have cars. You probably don't shave. You have nothing to do on the weekends.

So how do you spend your time? In the 1980s, most likely at a mall. Woodfield is an enclosed shopping center sprawling over 2.25 million square feet in northern Illinois. There are 230 stores at Woodfield, and on a given Saturday those stores are cruised in and out by thousands of teenagers killing time. Today two of those teenagers are Dave Gembutis and Dan Holmes.

Dave is wearing a purple Rolling Meadows High School Mustangs windbreaker over a gray M*A*S*H T-shirt, jeans, and Nike running shoes. He has a red plastic spoon in his mouth, and will keep it there for most of the afternoon. Dan is wearing a white Ohio State Buckeyes T-shirt, jeans, and Nike running shoes.

We are in the Video Forum store. Paul Simon and Art Garfunkel are singing "Wake Up Little Susie" from their Central Park concert on four television screens. Dave and Dan have already been wandering around Woodfield for an hour.

"There's not too much to do at my house," Dan says to me.

"Here we can at least look around," Dave says. "At home I don't know what we'd do."

"Play catch or something," Dan says. "Here there's lots of things to see."

"See some girls or something, start talking," Dave says.

I ask them how they would start a conversation with girls they had never met.

"Ask them what school they're from," Dan says. "Then if they say Arlington Heights High School or something, you can say, 'Oh, I know somebody from there.'"

I ask them how important meeting girls is to their lives.

"About forty-five percent," Dan says.

"About half your life," Dave says.

"Half is girls," Dan says. "Half is going out for sports."

An hour later, Dave and Dan have yet to meet any girls. They have seen a girl from their own class at Rolling Meadows High, but she is walking with an older boy, holding his hand. Now we are in the Woodfield McDonald's. Dave is eating a McRib sandwich, a small fries, and a small Coke. Dan is eating a cheese-burger, a small fries, and a medium root beer.

In here, the dilemma is obvious. The McDonald's is filled with girls who are precisely as old as Dave and Dan. The girls are wearing eye shadow, are fully developed, and generally look as if they could be dating the Green Bay Packers. Dave and Dan, on the other hand . . . well, when you're a fifteen-year-old boy, you look like a fifteen-year-old boy.

"They go with the older guys who have the cars," Dan says.

"It makes them more popular," Dave says.

"My ex-girlfriend is seeing a junior," Dan says.

I ask him what happened.

"Well, I was in Florida over spring vacation," he says. "And when I got back I heard that she was at Cinderella Rockefella one night, and she was dancing with this guy, and she liked him, and he drove her home and stuff."

"She two-timed him," Dave says.

"The guy's on the basketball team," Dan says.

I ask Dan what he did about it.

"I broke up with her," he says, as if I had asked the stupidest question in the world.

I ask him how he did it.

"Well, she was at her locker," he says. "She was working the combination. And I said, 'Hey, Linda, I want to break up.' And she was opening her locker door and she just nodded her head yes. And I said, 'I hear you had a good time while I was gone, but I had a better time in Florida.' "

I ask him if he feels bad about it.

"Well, I feel bad," he says. "But a lot of guys told me, 'I heard you broke up with her. Way to be.' "

"It's too bad the Puppy Palace isn't open," Dan says.

"They're remodeling," Dave says.

We are walking around the upper level of Woodfield. I ask them why they would want to go to the Puppy Palace.

"The dogs are real cute and you feel sorry for them," Dan says.

We are in a fast-food restaurant called the Orange Bowl. Dave is eating a frozen concoction called an O-Joy. They still have not met any girls.

"I feel like I'd be wasting my time if I sat at home," Dan says. "If it's Friday or Saturday and you sit home, it's considered . . . low."

"Coming to the mall is about all there is," Dave says. "Until we can drive."

"Then I'll cruise," Dan says. "Look for action a little farther away from my house, instead of just riding my bike around."

"When you're sixteen, you can do anything," Dave says. "You can go all the way across town."

"When you have to ride your bike . . ." Dan says. "When it rains, it ruins everything."

In the J. C. Penney store, the Penney Fashion Carnival is under way. Wally the Clown is handing out favors to children, but Dave and Dan are watching the young female models parade onto a stage in bathing suits.

"Just looking is enough for me," Dan says.

Dave suggests that they head out back into the mall and pick out some girls to wave to. I ask why.

"Well, see, even if they don't wave back, you might see them later in the day," Dan says. "And then they might remember that you waved at them, and you can meet them."

We are at the Cookie Factory. These guys eat approximately every twenty minutes.

It is clear that Dan is attracted to the girl behind the counter. He walks up, and his voice is slower and about half an octave lower than before.

The tone of voice is going to have to carry the day, because the words are not all that romantic:

"Can I have a chocolate-chip cookie?"

The girl does not even look up as she wraps the cookie in tissue paper.

Dan persists. The voice might be Clark Gable's:

"What do they cost?"

The girl is still looking down.

"Forty-seven," she says and takes his money, still looking away, and we move on.

Dave and Dan tell me that there are lots of girls at Woodfield's indoor ice-skating rink. It costs money to get inside, but they lead me to an exit door, and when a woman walks out we slip into the rink. It is chilly in here, but only three people are on the ice.

"It's not time for open skating yet," Dan says. "This is all private lessons."

"Not much in here," Dave says.

We sit on benches. I ask them if they wish they were older.

"Well," Dan says, "when you get there, you look back and you remember. Like I'm glad that I'm not in the fourth or fifth grade now. But I'm glad I'm not twenty-five, either."

"Once in a while I'm sorry I'm not twenty-one," Dave says. "There's not much you can do when you're fifteen. This summer I'm going to caddy and try to save some money."

"Yeah," Dan says. "I want to save up for a dirt bike."

"Right now, being fifteen is starting to bother me a little bit," Dave says. "Like when you have to get your parents to drive you to Homecoming with a girl."

I ask him how that works.

"Well, your mom is in the front seat driving," he says. "And you're in the back seat with your date."

I ask him how he feels about that.

"It's embarrassing," he says. "Your date understands that there's nothing you can do about it, but it's still embarrassing."

Dave says he wants to go to Pet World.

"I think they closed it down," Dan says, but we head in that direction anyway.

I ask them what the difference is between Pet World and the Puppy Palace.

"They've got snakes and fish and another assortment of dogs," Dan says. "But not as much as the Puppy Palace."

When we arrive, Pet World is, indeed, boarded up.

We are on the upper level of the mall. Dave and Dan have spotted two girls sitting on a bench directly below them, on the mall's main level.

"Whistle," Dan says. Dave whistles, but the girls keep talking.

"Dave, wave to them and see if they look," Dan says.

"They aren't looking," Dave says.

"There's another one over there," Dan says.

"Where?" Dave says.

"Oh, that's a mother," Dan says. "She's got her kid with her." They return their attention to the two downstairs.

Dan calls to them: "Would you girls get the dollar I just dropped?"

The girls look up.

"Just kidding," Dan says.

The girls resume their conversation.

"I think they're laughing," Dan says.

"What are you going to do when the dumb girls won't respond," Dave says.

"At least we tried," Dan says.

I ask him what response would have satisfied him.

"The way we would have known that we succeeded," he says, "they'd have looked up here and started laughing."

The boys keep staring at the two girls.

"Ask her to look up," Dan says. "Ask her what school they go to."

"I did," Dave says. "I did."

The two boys lean over the railing.

"Bye, girls," Dave yells.

"See you later," Dan yells.

The girls do not look up.

"Too hard," Dan says. "Some girls are stuck on themselves, if you know what I mean by that."

We go to a store called the Foot Locker, where all the salespeople are dressed in striped referee's shirts.

"Dave!" Dan says. "Look at this! Seventy bucks!" He holds up a pair of New Balance running shoes. Both boys shake their heads.

We move on to a store called Passage to China. A huge stuffed tiger is placed by the doorway. There is a PLEASE DO NOT TOUCH sign attached to it. Dan rubs his hand over the tiger's back. "This would look so great in my room," he says.

We head over to Alan's TV and Stereo. Two salesmen ask the boys if they are interested in buying anything, so they go back outside and look at the store's window. A color television set is tuned to a baseball game between the Chicago Cubs and the Pittsburgh Pirates.

They watch for five minutes. The sound is muted, so they cannot hear the announcers.

"I wish they'd show the score," Dave says.

They watch for five minutes more.

"Hey, Dave," Dan says. "You want to go home?"

"I guess so," Dave says.

They do. We wave goodbye. I watch them walk out of the mall toward the bus stop. I wish them girls, dirt bikes, puppies, and happiness.

Jesus on a Tortilla

IT WAS A hot New Mexico morning. Mrs. Maria Rubio was making burritos for her husband's lunch. The husband, Eduardo, was still in bed.

Mrs. Rubio was working with the tortillas, rolling them around the ingredients. She had rolled two of the tortillas into burritos, and was preparing to roll the third, when she looked down at the tortilla. She gasped and spoke aloud.

"It is Jesus Christ!" she said.

She was referring to a pattern on the tortilla, made by a series of skillet burns. She was convinced that the skillet burns formed a picture of Jesus. She determined that this was a miracle.

She ran to her daughter, Rosie. Rosie looked at the tortilla and said, "It is Jesus."

Mrs. Rubio took the tortilla to her sister, Margarita Porras. Mrs. Porras said, "I think it's Jesus, too."

She took the tortilla to the bedroom. Her husband examined the tortilla and said, "It's Jesus, all right."

Mrs. Rubio called a family friend, Mike Salmon.

"She was crying," Salmon recalls. "She said that there was the image of Jesus on her tortilla, and she thought that perhaps God was punishing her. I had her sister get on the phone, and her sister said, 'I have seen it, and it looks like Jesus.' "

By now the group knew they would have to do something.

They decided to have the tortilla blessed.

Carrying the tortilla very carefully, they walked to the Our Lady of Guadalupe Church, across the street from the Rubios' home. The Rubios live in the small New Mexico town of Lake Arthur, two hundred miles south of Albuquerque. When they got to the church, they found that the pastor was not there; he serves three churches in the area, and alternates among them.

So, still guarding the tortilla, they got into the Rubios' 1968 Chevrolet and drove the seventeen miles to the city of Dexter. There, at the Church of the Immaculate Conception, was the Reverend Joyle Finnigan.

Mrs. Rubio explained about the image of Jesus appearing in the tortilla.

Father Finnigan examined it.

"I think this is just a coincidence," he said.

"It is not a coincidence," Mrs. Rubio said. "I have been rolling burritos for twenty-one years, and this is the first time the face of Jesus ever appeared in a tortilla."

So, reluctantly, Father Finnigan blessed the tortilla. He warned Mrs. Rubio that if she tried to save it, it would undoubtedly get moldy, even if she kept it in the refrigerator.

But Mrs. Rubio had different plans for the tortilla. She drove back to her home, and placed it in a plastic frame, covered with glass. Beneath the tortilla she placed a mass of cotton, giving the appearance that Jesus was floating on a cloud.

She built a small shrine to the tortilla, placing it on a table and erecting a makeshift chapel around it.

"This is a miracle," she announced to her friends. "It is meant to change my life."

She resigned her job as a maid, and said that she would be tending to the tortilla full-time. Her husband kept his job as a farm worker.

Soon the word spread about the tortilla with the face of Jesus. People began to come to Mrs. Rubio's front door. She let them in and led them to the tortilla shrine.

According to witnesses, many of the visitors dropped to their knees as soon as they saw the tortilla. Some prayed aloud. Many cried, the tears streaming down their cheeks.

Local newspapers heard about the tortilla, and sent reporters and photographers to take a look. More and more people came to the Rubio house, and became convinced that it was, indeed, the image of Jesus in the tortilla. (In fairness, it must be mentioned that reporter Ken Walston of the *Albuquerque Journal* said, "It looks more like Leon Spinks to me.")

Mrs. Rubio put a sign on the outside of her green stucco house, inviting anyone who wished to see the tortilla to come in, free of charge. The tortilla shrine rapidly became a phenomenon; Mrs. Rubio purchased guest books, and so far more than eight thousand persons have signed the registers.

"They have come from New Mexico, Texas, Arizona, Colorado, California, New York—everywhere," she said.

The visitors began to light candles in front of the tortilla, and place flowers around it. They placed photographs of members of their families who were ill in front of the tortilla, and left the photos there, hoping for a healing power.

"The tortilla has not become moldy," Mrs. Rubio said. "It is just like on the day I first saw the image of Jesus on it.

"I used to be an impatient woman. I used to have troubles. Since this miracle happened, I am no longer impatient. I do not know why this has happened to me, but God has come into my life through this tortilla.

"I see happiness come into the faces of the people who visit the tortilla. That is enough for me."

So still the visitors come, and every night Mrs. Rubio kneels down and prays in front of the tortilla. Some people have offered to buy it from her, but she has refused.

"It is my own miracle," she said. "I will keep the tortilla forever."

A Man and His Music

ON A TUESDAY evening, at a nightclub called the Blue Max, in Rosemont, Illinois, a comedian named Jerry Dye told his last joke of the night and walked offstage. Simultaneously the house orchestra began to play and the featured singer, Frank Sinatra, Jr., came forward holding a hand microphone.

Sinatra, thirty-seven, wore a neatly pressed tuxedo with a red handkerchief showing from the breast pocket. "Good evening, everyone, and welcome to the show," he said, and then began a number called "Singin' the Blues."

The house was perhaps sixty percent full. Sinatra finished the song and, almost without taking a breath, segued into the next one, "Too Close for Comfort." When he had completed it, he said, "I'll bet it's been a while since you've heard that number."

For the next hour, Sinatra worked his way through a list of middle-of-the-road standards. The members of the Blue Max's orchestra were young men, many in their early twenties; they were paid by the evening to back up whoever was booked into the room. But Sinatra turned to them as if they were the Nelson Riddle Orchestra and said, "Ladies and gentlemen, the wonder of the large band is that it possesses many colors."

During his first break for patter, Sinatra motioned toward the rear of the room and said, "All you nice folks in the back from International Harvester, we thank you for coming tonight," and the International Harvester group applauded themselves. For the first thirty minutes, Sinatra made no references to his father, but then the orchestra hit the opening chords of "That's Life," and he said, "As they say on Madison Avenue, let's put up the flag and see who salutes."

He did a fine job with the song, standing with his legs apart and jabbing at the air with his right arm, and when he had finished it the audience was cheering as they had not cheered his previous efforts. And with the smallest of smiles, Sinatra said, "Every night we do that number, and every night I know wherein your loyalty lies."

He did not perform any more songs associated with his father, although factors he could not control—his face, the timbre of his voice—were a constant reminder to the audience, and would have been even if he had had another name. Certain mannerisms were almost haunting in their familiarity; the way he lit his cigarette so that the action was a part of the song's percussion, the way he credited a songwriter with "A marvelous song—Johnny Mandel." But when a man in the audience, perhaps emboldened by the drinks the waitresses kept delivering, called out for "My Way," the singer said, "No, I only sing one Sinatra song per show."

At the end, he said, "This is the curtain call. Except we don't have a curtain, and you didn't give us a call." He sang two more songs, a ballad and an up-tempo number backed with lots of brass, and then he said, "We are delighted that you are here. This nightclub gets very, very lonely when no one is here." And then he walked off.

I had arranged to meet Sinatra in a hotel coffee shop half an hour after the show. He walked in precisely on time; he had replaced the tuxedo coat with a dark-blue poplin jacket. We shook hands and took a table.

He had told me on the telephone that he was reluctant to get together with me; not because he didn't want to talk, but because he could not figure out why anyone would be interested in anything he had to say. We were handed menus, and he immediately started up on the same theme; he said he was afraid he was wasting my time, because he could think of nothing of importance he might offer on any subject.

"All I've ever been is a traveling singer," he said. "For seventeen years I lived on the road, and that's all I know about."

Up close his face looked even more jarringly like the face on a 1955 Frank Sinatra album cover; the eyes, though, were deep brown. In the front, his dark hair had begun to turn gray. Although the publicity photos I had seen of him made him look like a young boy, the man sitting across from me was fully grown, at the beginning of middle age.

"I only travel fifteen weeks a year or so now," he said. "For one thing, it isn't easy to find clubs that want to feature my kind of music. But the main problem is paying for musicians. I used to have a full band travel with me, but I can't afford it anymore. The airline prices are just too high. So I have a guitar player and a pianist who work for me, and then I hire musicians in each city.

"No one gets rich doing this. You don't make forty thousand dollars a night, like you would if you were a rock group. This week I have to pay four trumpet players, four trombone players, and five saxophone players. I'll be lucky if I walk out of here with a hundred dollars."

I asked him if he ever considered any other way of making money. He shrugged.

"This is what I have always done," he said. "I have to work. I don't own stocks. I have a house with a mortgage.

"I know I don't sing the kind of music that appeals to this generation. A rock concert . . . I do not understand that kind of commerce. I won't call it music. I would have no more chance of succeeding at that than landing the space shuttle. I know that rock bands play to tens of thousands of people every night, but to me the number of people in the audience is immaterial. I've worked clubs where the capacity was sixty; the incentive is not in the number of people you sing to, but singing right for the people who are there."

I asked him if he didn't envy the entertainers who could, indeed, pack a football stadium with fans.

"I travel with two people," Sinatra said. "Jeff Morrison is my conductor and pianist. Dan McIntyre is my guitarist. None of us gets famous. None of us gets rich. I've never sold a million records, never had a hit movie, never had a hit TV show. I've worked in joints all my life.

"What you have to understand is that, in this business, I'm a struggling little guy. I'm one of many singers who are trying and not quite making it. I do not have a recording contract, for example. Would I like to have one? Of course. I'm a singer. Of course I'd like one. But all during my career I've been singing the music of the forties, and they have wanted rock stars. In all these years I have made a total of four albums, and none of them sold.

"I'm going to be forty years old soon, and I'm too damn stubborn to change. All I can do is go out there whenever someone will hire me, and sing, and hope someone in the audience sees me and likes me. If people like me, then perhaps there will be more offers, and if that happens, perhaps the price will rise."

We had been talking for an hour when I finally brought up his father. He had not mentioned it, but I could not avoid it any longer. So I asked him: How did he deal with being Frank Sinatra's son, and with being a singer who had trouble finding work?

"Even if I didn't have the name, it would be a problem," he said.

"People see me, and they say, 'This guy looks like Frank Sinatra, this guy sounds like Frank Sinatra.'

"That will always be with me. So you ask me how I deal with it? I don't dwell on it. What would you do? If I dwell on it, I will be in a straitjacket in an institution. If I dwell on it, it will kill me."

If he were not Frank Sinatra's son, of course, I would not have come to see him. That fact was so obvious that it did not need to be verbalized. He knew it and I knew it, and to say it out loud would have seemed to serve no purpose.

And if I had not thought to come see him, neither would the people in his audiences. For all his life he must have been living with that knowledge, and if he is ever tempted to forget it, there will always be a man like the one in the audience this night, who, at the end of a song, said in an audible voice: "Well, he's not his old man."

Of course he isn't. We are a nation of men who spend most of our lives trying to escape the shadow of our fathers, whether they are famous or obscure. With most of us, it is simply a matter of growing older, of building our own lives and our own identities until, one day, we wake up as our own men.

For some, though, it is destined never to happen, and I sought out Frank Sinatra, Jr. because he seems faced with a curse few of us will ever know. He told me that he did not, in fact, go into the music business at the urging of his father, or in an attempt to imitate: "When I was five years old, my mother arranged for me to take piano lessons. I wanted to go out and play ball with the other boys, but she insisted, and soon I couldn't get Rachmaninoff and Chopin out of my head."

And if there was ever any doubt about how he would spend his life, it disappeared one night when, as a high school boy, he went to see Leopold Stokowski conduct a 124-piece orchestra in New York's Carnegie Hall: "I stared at that old man, and I listened to the music coming from that orchestra, and I sat in my seat and I just trembled."

That will never matter to the men and women who come to see him in a lounge somewhere. They will pay the cover charge and buy the drinks because of the name, and because by some twist of their own fortunes they find themselves not in Las Vegas or Atlantic City, but in Rosemont, Illinois, on a Tuesday night with nothing to do. They will demand something that the singer cannot provide, but he will do his best to come close; because for him, too, it is a Tuesday night in the middle of his life, and he, too, by a configuration of the fates, has found himself in Rosemont.

We were the last people in the coffee shop. Sinatra was in no particular hurry to leave; although it was late, his next shift did not start until nine o'clock the following night, and all that lay ahead was a day in his hotel room.

He said he didn't feel like going to sleep yet; back home in California, he said, he could kill time during the day by auditioning for television shows, but here there was really nothing for him to do in the afternoon. If he went to bed now, that would only mean he would wake up that much earlier. I asked him if he really walked into Los Angeles casting sessions cold, reading from scripts with the other hopeful actors.

"Oh, yes," he said. "I'm not at the point where I won't read for a part. And once in a while I get a small part in a show . . ." He let his voice trail off.

He said again that he didn't feel like going to his room just yet.

So we talked into the night. I asked him about the tuxedo. It seemed, in a way, part of another age; entertainers for the last twenty years or so have been dressing a bit more casually, and especially for members of his generation, the tuxedo seemed an oddity.

"That's the way I was raised," he said. "It's the idea of bringing a little class to the nightclub and showing a little respect for the audience. I know some people might not understand that, but I wouldn't feel comfortable dressing any other way."

He said after his week's engagement at the Blue Max had ended, he would return to his home in Los Angeles and continue looking for work. He does not have a manager; he books his own appearances and arranges his own travel. He has never married, and he said, "I live the kind of life that most single men lead. I do my laundry, and take my dry cleaning in, and go to the market."

The waitress came by and said that she was about to unplug the coffeepot, so if he wanted another cup, now was the time to say so. She left the check and walked away.

Sinatra got up to leave. "The thing that keeps me going is that I like my life," he said. "It's not the greatest, but I can get by doing the thing I like the best, and that's nice. I have my pianist and I have my guitar player, and very shortly, if everything goes okay, I'll have my own drummer again. If it doesn't take much to make you happy, then your chances of being happy are pretty good."

Backing onto the Unemployment Rolls

As SOON AS the new photo-copying machine appeared in the office, Jodie Stutz knew what she had to do. Eventually she would lose her job over it, but she was a woman obsessed.

Miss Stutz, twenty-one, was a secretary for Deere & Co., the giant farm machinery manufacturing firm in Moline, Illinois. All day long she looked at that photocopier, and all day long the same desire danced through her mind.

"I had to make a Xerox copy of my butt," Miss Stutz said.

In her younger days, Miss Stutz had made Xerox copies of her face. She would open up the lid of the machine, smash her face against the glass—always keeping her eyes closed to protect them—and grope for the "Print" button. Then the machine would whir, and the photocopy would come out, all grainy and neat-looking.

But this new machine was so beautiful. She knew it called for something special.

So she waited for closing time. After everyone else had left the office, Miss Stutz recruited another secretary to stand lookout for her. Then she closed herself in the Xerox room. She yanked her pants down, leaped up on the machine, sat on it, and pressed the button.

In a few moments she had the finished photocopy of her posterior.

"It looked great," she said with no false modesty.

She stashed the copy in her purse, and she and her friend left the office without being noticed.

But her vanity got the best of her. Within a few days, she showed the photocopy to some friends in the office, and the word began to spread.

"People were begging me to see it," Miss Stutz said. "That's when my troubles began."

The following events are Miss Stutz's version of what happened next. Deere & Co. officials will not comment on their version.

A few weeks after the furtive evening in the Xerox room, Miss Stutz was summoned to the Deere & Co. personnel office, where a woman named Joyce Kuehl waited for her.

"She said that there were rumors that I had taken a Xerox copy of my rear end, and wanted to know if it was true," Miss Stutz said.

Miss Stutz, who was carrying the photocopy in her purse, said it was completely untrue.

"Hey, I lied," Miss Stutz said.

Next she was called in by Jack Fritts, administrative manager of the advertising office where she worked. He asked her if she had made a photocopy of her posterior.

"Just a rumor," Miss Stutz said.

Fritts reportedly said to her: "You go back to your office and you think about it, and if you decide that the rumor is true, and if we find out it's true, you will be fired."

Miss Stutz was determined to keep lying, but next Fritts and Jim Coogan, Deere's director of advertising, reportedly called in the other secretary who had watched the door during the photocopying session.

"They really gave her the third degree," Miss Stutz said. "They threatened to fire her if she didn't tell the truth, so she started crying and admitted it."

So Coogan and Fritts called Miss Stutz back in.

"They said that making a Xerox copy of my butt was not in the best interests of the company," Miss Stutz said. "I said that I was real sorry, and I would never do anything like that again, but they said I had a choice. Either they would fire me or I could quit. So I didn't want being fired on my record, so I quit."

Miss Stutz said that various rumors—all of them false—had made their way to the management of Deere & Co.:

1. That she had thrown a big party in the Xerox room on the night of the incident.

2. That she had put a routing slip on the photocopy of her posterior, and had sent it to all the Deere & Co. branches and factories in the United States.

3. That she had autographed copies and given them away.

4. That she was completely naked in the Xerox room, taking shots of various parts of her body.

5. That three men had helped her get undressed and then guarded the door for her.

6. That she had sent out copies as an invitation to a birthday party.

Deere officials do not deny Miss Stutz's story, but neither will they confirm it. "On individual personnel, we do not discuss company matters publicly," a company spokesman said.

Miss Stutz is annoyed that she had to resign, and lost a good job. "It was just a silly mistake," she said. "Deere & Co. creates a routine that everyone follows. The corporation breeds mediocrity and dullness. If you don't conform, you are simply eliminated. The company can tolerate sloppy work and lazy employees, but it can't tolerate humanistic mistakes."

Miss Stutz is now working as a waitress in a Mexican restaurant. Her career at Deere & Co. is over, but she has her memories.

"It was such a great picture," she said.

A Matter of Time

P ROBABLY EVERY MAN has fantasized about it. That didn't make it any easier to do. I held the telephone to my ear, but I couldn't make myself punch the buttons.

During Vietnam, when I was breaking in as a newspaper reporter, I would often be ordered to call the families of casualties and get information on the sons they had just learned they'd lost. I found it easy; it was part of being professional. I have had to make calls like that all my working life, and they don't bother me at all. But now my hands were shaking.

I hit the number, area code first. It rang twice, with that peculiar sound long-distance calls give you. She answered.

"Hello?"

My throat was dry.

"Hello?" she said again.

"Lindy?" I said.

In the summer of 1963, when it dawned on me that I was in love, and for the first time, it didn't occur to me that there would ever be any women in my life other than Lindy Lemmon. I was sixteen; she was thirteen. The whole world was Columbus, Ohio, that summer. We would sit all day on the corner of Bexley Park and Gould, hidden by big shrubs, listening to a transistor radio and watching while the DDT truck went by, and we would calmly discuss what things were going to be like when we were married.

"Little Deuce Coupe" would come out of the radio, and we would hold hands, and when she ended it four months later it was the saddest I ever felt in my life. Within two years I was out of high school and out of Columbus, and suddenly there were all these other people in my world, and with everything I learned I felt myself becoming a little less innocent. I wasn't trying to be that way; it just happens and you can't help it, and sometimes, when I was on the road in some strange hotel room, or typing a story on deadline on a borrowed portable Olivetti set up on an airplane tray table, it would strike me that the boy I had been during the summer of '63 would be worth looking for, if I could ever find the time.

That's when I would think of Lindy. If I had become a little too jaded to suit myself when it came to matters in general, I was probably jaded most of all when it came to women. I would think back to the feeling I'd had in the autumn of our breakup—when all my friends were concerned only with how our football team would do in the Central Buckeye League, and I was concerned only with the fact that I would apparently never get over Lindy—and the memory that I could hurt so intensely left me with a sense of wonder.

All of us have doubtless wanted to go back and see the first girl we loved; we think about it, but we don't consider doing it because we're not supposed to do things like that once we're grown-ups. And yet, the more I thought about trying to find the boy I'd been, the more I thought that I would have to find Lindy, too. I was married now—in love with someone else—but that didn't seem to have anything to do with it.

So I did some checking around back in Columbus. Lindy was married, too. Her husband was an executive with a steel company; they had three children and were living in Toledo, Ohio. Once I had the information, I delayed for days before going any further. But when I did I found that their number in Toledo was listed with directory assistance. And I was still shaking when she said "Hello?" for the second time, and I said, "Lindy?" and, across the miles, she said, "Who is this?"

I don't usually drink on airplanes, but during the flight from Chicago to Toledo I kept calling the stewardess back to my seat.

The phone call hadn't been what I had expected. I thought I was going to have to do a lot of explaining about who I was, but the first thing she had said after "Where are you calling from?" was "I saw you on 'Phil Donahue.' " It didn't make me smile; it made me kind of sad, because the boy I was looking for had nothing to do with anything like that.

But now it was a week later, and the plane came through a low cloud bank, and then we were on the ground in Toledo. I could feel my heart. I walked off the plane; no one was at the gate. So I took the escalator down to the baggage-claim area; there were Lindy and her three children.

I was thirty-two. She was twenty-nine. She wore a sweater and a skirt and boots that reached her knees. She had been beautiful when she was thirteen, and had the same face now, but she was undeniably an Ohio housewife waiting in an airport.

We stood there. She spoke first.

"This is Joey, and this is Matthew, and this is Megan," she said.

We rode through Toledo in her station wagon. The back section was folded down; the children were playing there.

"Who's Bob Greene?" asked the boy named Matthew.

"A friend of Mommy's," Lindy said.

We pulled into her driveway. There were five bikes in the garage, and a snowplow. Her husband was at work. Inside, the house held the artifacts of any American family: a Sears food processor and a copy of *Sports Illustrated* with her husband's name on the address label and an Elton John greatest hits album. I had seen these things in so many other places, but this was Lindy's house, and I looked at the album cover and thought about Elton John's having arrived on the scene and flourished and started to fade away, all in the time since I had seen her.

She made grilled cheese sandwiches for the children and me; they drank red-colored pop with it. I knew that I should be thinking important thoughts, but it was happening too fast. It had seemed like such a good idea to come here, but now . . . Lindy was clearly puzzled about what I was doing in her house. When I had asked if I could come she had said yes, but I could tell she was not entirely comfortable with it, and I couldn't blame her. If I couldn't explain to myself exactly why I was here, I certainly couldn't explain it to her.

After lunch she sent the children upstairs, and we put some albums on and sat in the living room. We started to talk; it was all too polite, and I found myself listening to the sound of my own voice in the big room. It sounded as odd as I felt.

She pulled out an old high school yearbook and turned to the back. Someone had signed: TO LINDY—I'LL NEVER FORGET THE TIMES WE HAD. YOU'LL GO FAR. I'LL NEVER FORGET YOU. STEVE.

"I wonder who Steve was," Lindy said.

There was a pounding above us, and for a moment it was like back in Columbus, when we used to think her parents were coming downstairs, but Lindy said, "That's just Megan trying on my shoes."

When I fell silent she asked me if there was something wrong, and I said I'd like to go to my motel.

She dropped me at the Sheraton Westgate, saying she would come back later to have dinner with me. I spent the next few hours in the first-floor barroom of the motel, chuting quarters into the jukebox and talking with one of the waitresses. It was much easier than talking to Lindy; it occurred to me that I had done this so often in so many different cities that it was far more real to me than the idea of Lindy and her family.

As I waited for her, I realized that I had no right to be doing this; I was so used to intruding into people's lives for my professional purposes that I had blithely intruded into Lindy's for my own personal ones. But I wasn't going to find that boy from 1963—at least not here; all I was going to do was confuse Lindy and make her wonder what it was I wanted.

When she arrived we went to the motel dining room. She had white wine with her dinner; I had never thought of Lindy having a drink. I pretended it was a newspaper interview and asked questions by rote. I learned that she had converted to Catholicism, that she taught a Sunday-school class, and that she took aerobic dance lessons. I was already thinking of flight schedules back to Chicago.

After dinner she said she wanted to call her husband because her nine-year-old had been sick. We went up to my room.

I sat on the bed and watched her as she called, and she said: "The medicine for him is on top of the refrigerator. The instructions are with it." She listened for a few moments and then said, "I'll talk to you about it when I get home." I could imagine his questions; I didn't blame him for asking. When she hung up, neither of us had to say anything; we both got up and headed for the door at the same time.

We sat in the car in the parking lot of the Sheraton. She had left the station wagon at home and brought her husband's sedan to the motel; there were sales-promotion pamphlets scattered on the front seat.

It was raining. She had turned the ignition on and switched on the radio. The drops splattered on the front windshield and then dripped slowly to the hood. She was behind the wheel, turned toward me.

"Bobby, you've been so quiet," she said.

I said I knew it; I tried to explain the things I had been thinking in the bar, about intruding on her life and looking for something I had no right to expect to find.

"I thought it was my fault," she said. "I thought you thought I was boring."

I didn't think I was hearing her right.

"Look," Lindy said. "You have this life that's all worldly and full of experiences. And I'm living in Toledo, Ohio, and I don't see how you can expect to just fly in here and for me to fit into that."

There was no way for me to tell her. The best I could come up with was, "Jesus, Lindy, you don't have to be anything. The only reason I'm here is because you're Lindy."

A song from the radio filled the car. We looked at each other; for a moment it seemed as if we might hold hands, but we both had people at home wondering about us, and so we just kept staring.

The minutes passed, and cars pulled in and out of the parking lot, and on the street the stoplights turned from green to yellow to red and back again. There was nothing much to say; we were two grown-ups in search of something we were probably better off not thinking about. The rain kept falling, and we looked out the windshield at the cold Ohio night.

Grif

THE FIRST TIME I ever saw a copy of the *Chicago Sun-Times* was in September of 1965, when I came to Evanston from Ohio to go to college. It couldn't have been more than a few weeks before I tore a Jack Griffin column out of the paper, folded it up, and stuffed it into my wallet for keeping.

Since that day, there has never been a time when I have walked around without a Griffin column. I ripped that first one out of the paper because I was so stunned that a columnist could capture feeling and emotion and life with the precision that Jack did; I forget what the subject of the column was, but I remember thinking that seeing such a marvelous piece of writing in a newspaper was a rare thing indeed, and that I had better hold onto it.

Later, of course, I found out that with Jack, it wasn't so rare at all. He did it all the time. So it began: I would carry a Griffin column around for a couple of months, and then one morning I would pick up the paper and, damn, he'd done it again. So I would replace the yellowing column with the new one. I used to force the columns on people, make them read what Jack had written, not leave them alone until they had shared the same thing that had touched me.

Later, when I was hired by the *Sun-Times*, I looked forward with almost giddy anticipation to meeting Griffin. But when I first came to the city room, and saw him over in the sports department, banging away at his typewriter, I became nervous and couldn't bring myself to do it. So even though we were working in the same room, I remained a fan from afar.

I kept tearing his columns out, though. I remember one, about a man Jack met in the Cleveland airport. The man was waiting for his son's remains to be shipped home from Vietnam. The column was so moving, so alive with emotion without resorting to maudlin sentimentality . . . when I read that one, I made myself approach Griffin to tell him what I thought. He was in the middle of writing the next day's piece. He looked up and said "Oh. Thanks." That was it.

I used to see him in Riccardo's. He would never sit with the rest of the crowd. Instead he would stand way on the other side, over by the wall, by himself. He would drink his beers and look down at the surface of the bar, thinking his thoughts. Most of the time he kept his trench coat on. And he never got rid of that crewcut. I idolized him.

When the editors of the paper first gave me a column, I found out quickly that all of my self-assuredness might be pure sham. I didn't know the city well enough, and for all my desire to make the thing work, I felt lost. There weren't many people who were too anxious to go out of their way to help me, either.

One day—it must have been during the first or second week I was writing the column—Jack appeared at my desk. "Come on, kid," he said. "We're going to take a little drive." I didn't know he knew who I was.

He took me down to a grimy, ancient gymnasium on 63rd Street, under the L tracks, and we walked up a dark flight of wooden stairs. There, alone in the dimly lit room, was Muhammad Ali, then still in exile from boxing because of his anti-Vietnam views, working out on a heavy bag.

"Hey, Champ, come here for a second," Jack said. Ali came over. We spent the afternoon there—Jack and Ali did almost all of the talking, and I just listened—and on the way home, Jack said, "It's your column." I said that he had done all the work, I hadn't even known what questions to ask—and Jack interrupted and said, "Forget it. Write the column."

We stopped for a drink on the way back. It was the first of many times. Griffin up close was the same as Griffin in the newspaper—tough and soft at the same time, full of knowledge about the harshest sides of life, but just as full of hope that the harshness can be beaten by the good. No one could put anything over on Jack. He was always a sucker for a pretty woman, but that was by his own choice.

He began to invite me down to his solitary end of the bar. It was as high an honor as I ever hope to receive. God, he could laugh. When the cancer infested him last year, he stopped coming around. The space at the end of the bar was empty. It was no fun to be there anymore.

Jack died Wednesday night. I'm trying to figure out a way to end this piece, and even as I'm typing, I know that I'll steal my last paragraph from Jack. He wrote it when Ray Brennan died in 1972, and like most things Jack ever did, there is no way to do it better:

I know he wouldn't want it this way, but I can't help it. I'm going to stay out late tonight and cry for my friend.

Kathy's Abortion

O<small>H, JESUS," SHE</small> moaned softly.
She squeezed my hand.

The vacuum machine purred steadily and the fetus that was her unborn child was sucked through a clear plastic hose and into a large glass bottle.

"Oh," she said again, and scratched my forearm.

"We're almost done," the doctor said. "I just have to check and make sure you're all clean and empty."

She squeezed my hand harder.

"I didn't tell anybody about this," she said. This was the afternoon before.

"My girl friend and I were talking, and she started talking about having babies. This person is a person I grew up with; we grew up in the same parish, and we always had the same ideas about everything. She has this idea about abortions, that they're morally wrong.

"And I started feeling guilty about not feeling guilty. Because I really don't. It's just something I have to do."

In the morning she would be having her abortion. Her name is Kathy; she is a twenty-seven-year-old executive with a marketing firm. She is single. She was one of the thousands of women who have legal abortions in Chicago each week. She was different in one way: the public would be going along with her, through the eyes of a newspaperman who would be with her every step of the way.

"I knew I was pregnant all along," Kathy said. "I knew it before I got the test. The nurse told me. She sounded concerned, like she knew I was single. 'You're . . . uh . . . pregnant.' Not like she was talking to a married woman. 'You're pregnant!' Not like that.

"It's not a baby. I just refuse to think of it as a baby. I mean, I don't think, count up the months, and in October you'll have a baby. I know I'm pregnant, that's true. But I don't think there's a baby growing inside of me. I can't be thinking about that. I just want to go there in the morning and get it done."

That night Kathy went to see a play at the Goodman Theatre. The production was *Much Ado About Nothing*.

At 8:03 A.M., Kathy walked through the front door of the Concord Medical Center, 17 West Grand. She was wearing green Levi's, a down jacket, and Adidas running shoes. Her boyfriend, the man who had made her pregnant, had dropped her off outside. The other women who would be having their abortions during Concord's first shift had already started to arrive.

They came in breathlessly, each of them looking around for the desk where they would check in. If you didn't know where you were, you might think they were college women on the first day of registration for classes. They were handed manila folders stuffed with pieces of paper.

Rock music from WBBM-FM came out of a speaker in the ceiling. A man was singing, "Never gonna fall in love again, / No I never want to feel the pain, / Or remember how it used to be. . . ." The music seemed overly loud.

"I was upset outside," Kathy said. "I guess I'm kind of scared." She flipped through the forms. There were nineteen chairs in the waiting room, most of them a bright yellow. Over the receptionist's desk was a sign saying that the Concord Medical Center accepted Master Charge.

Kathy filled out an informational sheet. "Age?" "Twenty-seven." "Religion?" "Catholic."

The love songs continued to come from the ceiling. Kathy scanned a legal consent form: "I hereby authorize Dr. (Name to Be Filled In by Counselor), and such assistants as may be selected by him, to terminate my pregnancy. . . ."

At 8:37 A.M. Kathy's name was called. She was directed to the cashier's office. She gave the cashier a check for $175.

The room where the women wait before going in for their abortions is called the auditorium.

On the canvas chairs, many women from days and weeks past have written with ball-point pen. They have written their last thoughts before the operation. On one chair, there was a heart drawn. Inside the heart were the words, "Connie and James forever."

The writing on the other chairs was much the same. "Rich and Elaine." "Mike and Michelle." "Shelly and Rich." The love songs from the radio played in here, too.

"Now I know you're going to be tense," said Lydia Dershewitz, the counselor assigned to Kathy. "The best thing you can do if you feel yourself tensing up is to just tense everything up as much as you can, and then let it go. The letting go helps."

Mrs. Dershewitz and Kathy were in a small room going through the counseling session, the last thing a woman does before she has her abortion. The counselors are attuned to the women's emotions; if there is any hesitation about having the operation, the counselors are instructed to advise the women to go back home.

"I don't want to have a baby," Kathy said.

From the ceiling, the radio. A commercial jingle for a clothing store: "Look to the Limited. . . ."

Mrs. Dershewitz picked up a plastic model of the female pelvic area and explained to Kathy, step by step, what the operation would be like. Mrs. Dershewitz pulled the plastic model apart, and said, "First the doctor will examine you to see the size and position of your uterus. This takes about thirty seconds. . . ."

Kathy lay on the operating table.

There were three other people in the room: the doctor, the nurse, and the newspaperman. All three were dressed in surgical scrub suits and masks.

Kathy was on her back. Surprisingly, the radio was playing

even in the operating room. As she waited for the abortion to begin, the Bee Gees sang "Stayin' Alive" from the movie *Saturday Night Fever*.

The doctor looked at Kathy's chart so that he could call her by her first name.

"I'm going to examine your uterus now," he said. "This will be a little uncomfortable."

Kathy looked over at me.

"Come here," she said.

I stepped closer to the operating table.

"Hold my hand," she said.

I did.

"I don't even like going to the doctor's office," she said.

The doctor pushed a lever, and the table rose.

"Lift up your hips," he said. "Now this is going to feel a little wet and cold."

He swabbed an orange-colored antiseptic agent known as Betadine between Kathy's legs.

"Now I'm going to insert the speculum," the doctor said.

She gasped and pulled my hand down to her chest. She began scratching my arm.

"Are you all right?" the nurse asked.

"Fine," Kathy said.

The doctor swabbed more of the astringent inside of Kathy. By now she was shaking softly and gripping me with a great deal of strength.

"I'm going to give you a shot now," the doctor said. "It's a pain-numbing agent."

He passed an enormous needle into Kathy, and injected the drug into her cervix. She couldn't see the needle, and didn't seem to feel the shot.

"Now this is going to feel really weird," the doctor said. "These instruments are dilators. They're to stretch the opening of your cervix." The nurse handed him the instruments and he inserted them.

"Okay," the doctor said. "You're halfway home. You're going to feel a cramping or tugging sensation next." As he spoke, the nurse handed him a long, clear plastic tube. The doctor guided the tube into Kathy's womb.

Without notice, the doctor turned on the vacuum aspirator. It began to hum.

"Oh, Jesus," Kathy said, squeezing my hand. She kept talking as the fetus was sucked from her.

It looked like a mixture of blood and mucus. It was pulled through the tube and into a glass bottle sitting on a table. The red fluid kept flowing from Kathy and into the bottle. The entire process took perhaps two and a half minutes.

"We're almost done," the doctor said. "I just have to check and make sure you're all clean and empty in there."

He reached inside Kathy with a curette and scraped some remaining tissue from the lining of her uterus. Then he turned the vacuum machine on again. More material was sucked from her body and into the bottle.

"You're done," the doctor said.

The nurse lifted the bottle and carried it to another table, out of Kathy's line of vision.

Kathy sat up. She was still holding my hand. Perspiration covered her face. The nurse helped her off the operating table and led her toward the recovery room.

The recovery room was long and bright. Kathy lay on a cot. Other women, fresh from their own abortions, lay next to her on other cots. Kathy lay in silence for forty-five minutes.

At 10:15 A.M. Kathy and I walked out of the Concord Medical Center and into the sunlight. The counselor had told her to eat some lunch and then to rest for the remainder of the day.

"I don't want to think about it now," Kathy said. "I was on the bed in the recovery room . . . and all of a sudden I wanted to burst out and cry a whole lot. I looked at the ceiling and . . . I tried to think about Miami. I didn't want to think about what had happened. I looked up at the ceiling and I tried to pretend I was in Miami."

Thirty-five Years

W<small>E WERE ALWAYS</small> going some-
where. That was part of the deal. Growing up meant getting
away. So one of us set off for Chicago, and one of us set off for
Florida, and one of us set off for Colorado.

Debby came home, but Timmy and I never did. He has climbed
mountains in Peru and now he's a bartender in Boulder, waiting
for the next thing. I do whatever it is that I do. We don't get
home very often, and when we do it is just to hit and run. We
are brothers and sisters, and we call each other once in a while.

My parents are still at home, of course. They didn't leave. We
never thought much about that, Debby and Timmy and I; we
didn't consider that maybe they might want to go away, too, that
maybe the wanderlust wasn't ours exclusively. We assumed that
we would always have a hometown, and that meant that our
parents would always be there. Somehow they weren't allowed
to leave. That was how the rules were.

They seemed to understand it. Not once, during all the years
of our wanderings, did our mother and father express any envy
of our freedom, any questioning of our reluctance to stay put.
Timmy would head for South America in search of a mountain,
or I would go to Europe on a business trip—looking at my watch
the whole time—and never once did our parents say that maybe
they would have liked some of that, too.

We were rootless enough. There was nothing to hold us down.
I don't know where we got it; certainly it didn't come from our
parents, who taught us stability. Timmy is just as likely to be in
Maine tomorrow morning as he is in Colorado, if he feels the

whim; I've lived in so many hotel rooms these last ten years that they don't even feel strange anymore.

Why did we become that way? Probably because we knew that home would always be there. That if we needed a place to go, we could head back for that most familiar destination of all, the one we set off from in the first place. Everything else in the hometown might change, but as long as our mother and father were there, we had a place to call our own. That kind of knowledge gives you the courage to move around.

It is an age of divorce and infidelity and the death of the family. Marriages break up more easily than they are formed, and those who do stay married wait a long time before having children, hedging their bets. Staying together is such a burden. Raising a family is such a responsibility. So limiting. No wonder divorce is becoming one of our most sacred institutions.

My parents have stayed married for thirty-five years. While we, their children, have been free to roam and explore every possibility in life, they have lived in the same town this whole time. We children went out to get lost or get away or get famous—whatever we wanted—and they stayed, having given us that freedom. I don't know what it is that we are trying to accomplish in our disordered lives, but they have accomplished what they set out to do. They raised a family.

Thirty-five years and a family raised. The three of us children never once doubted that they were there to turn to if we needed help, and I don't recall that we ever said thanks. I have been the worst offender. I have become so proficient at putting words on paper for consumption by large numbers of people that I have lost the ability to communicate privately with the two people who have meant the most to me. I can't write a letter; I learned long ago that writing a letter to one person is a skill I have given up in exchange for the other.

Worse, I don't even talk to my parents very well. I am much better with strangers. Put me in an airport bar in an unfamiliar city, and I am quite glib. Stop me on the street and I may even be charming. Any number of waitresses will tell you how easy I am to get to know. It is only with the people I love that I become silent.

Perhaps they understand that; I know I don't. I accept it, though, and live with it, just as Debby and Timmy and I live with the knowledge that of all the things we may accomplish in our scattered lives, nothing can possibly be as impressive as the memory of the house we grew up in and what it represented. That is what my parents have accomplished in this life; they have given us that house, and the memories of the years we were a family in it.

So they have been married thirty-five years now. That is a monument of sorts, and Debby and Timmy and I have decided that finally it is their turn. They spent thirty-five years in the same town, making sure that we would always have a home if, in the course of our moving about, we felt we needed it. Now we are trying to assure them of the same thing. We have asked them to go to Europe, as a gift from us. They have never been there. Now they are ready to depart.

I don't know what they'll find there—in France and Italy and England—but I'm pretty sure it won't measure up to what they have known in our hometown. That's the secret we want them to know: No matter how fine a time they may have in the fabled lands where they will travel, it will never measure up to what they have created in the town of our growing up.

Debby and Timmy and I have known that for years. Now our parents will find it out. Thank you if you have read this far, but today's column is not for you. It is for them.

The Four of Us

THE MAN SITTING across the dinner table said, "I can never make you understand. There's only four of us who will ever understand exactly how it was, and that's John, Paul, George, and myself."

The man, whose name is Ringo Starr, said, "You can talk about it and talk about it until the cows come home. I don't know why it happened to us. Well, actually I do know, or I think I know. I think I was born for it to happen to me. How else can you explain it? There were four of us in the band, and then there was a fifth person, and that fifth person was just . . . a kind of magic, you know? Magic.

"And now some sort of myth has developed around us. A lot of the people who talk about us are kids; they weren't even born when we were still together. I don't know. Every time I talk about it . . . I don't know."

His companion asked him: What about all of the money offers for the four of them to do one more show together? There had been an item in the newspaper the other day reporting that one promoter was willing to pay $45 million for the four of them to sing on one stage for just one night.

"I think it was fifty million," Starr said, toying with his lamb chops and potatoes. "But the thing is, we don't want to do it. We don't want to get together. And if we did want to get together, we could do it ourselves; we wouldn't need anybody from the outside offering us any money. I think these promoters keep coming up with these big money offers just to get their names in the paper. It makes them little heroes for a day.

"Why does everyone want us to sing together again? It's like something they can't have, I suppose. We're all in our thirties now. I'm thirty-seven. A lot of people say, 'I never saw them, and I want to see them just once.' Well, I never saw the Beatles, either. I really wish I could have, but unfortunately I was on-stage. I would have loved to have been out in the audience and have seen the Beatles. I would have liked to see what all the excitement was about.

"We would get the same response every night. The people would cheer and applaud and scream whether we were good or we were bad. And then John and Paul and George and I would go backstage and we would tell each other how we thought we'd done. Because we were the only people who could really judge. We were the only people who were taking an honest look at us.

"Maybe in five years no one will want us to join together again, and then we can forget about it. Someday they'll forget about it. I mean, in forty years, when I'm seventy-seven, I hope there still aren't people saying that the Beatles ought to get together for one more show. There really wouldn't be much point in that, would there?"

Starr, who now works on his own, said that he knows he can never accomplish more than he did as a younger man.

"You have to stop talking to yourself about that or it will drive you crazy," he said. "I'll never top what the Beatles did. But there's the satisfaction of working. I try to get better at what I do. I mean, you'll always be famous as a name. I know I'll never be anonymous. When I'm eighty-five, they'll be calling me 'ex-Beatle Ringo Starr.' But just for yourself, you've got to work and try to do better.

"I'm like anybody else. You get up, you go out, you sit in the sun, you go to the office, you watch the TV, you play records—I mean, I live my life. Just like you."

That couldn't be precisely true, his companion said.

"Well, there are differences," Starr said. "I like to make friends, for example, but people tend to come at me too fast. If you come on straight with me, I'll come on straight with you, but people come at me with some preconceived notions about me. I mean, they've heard of me. And you can't just"—he snapped his fingers—"make a new friend like that."

His companion said that millions of people all over the world now play old Beatles albums as part of a true nostalgia, as an attempt to bring back memories.

"Well I do it, too," Starr said. "I play records by the Beatles. Not a lot, but I do it. It brings back a certain period in my life, too, you know."

His companion asked if he considered himself a part of history.

"I am," Starr said. "I can't help it. I'm being pompous answering that way, but I can't choose it. We changed everything, and I know it.

"And it was . . . fantastic. There were some bad times, but it's like the old saying, even the bad times are good. I'm glad I went through it. Am I making any sense? It's like I told you. There are only four of us who will ever understand it. Just the four of us."

Speck

STATEVILLE PRISON, ILLINOIS— "Parents ought to be careful about their kids," said mass murderer Richard Speck. "Because any kid can end up to be like me. I don't know why it happened to me. But any kid can end up just like me."

Thus spoke the man convicted of slashing and choking eight nurses to death in 1966 in one of the most savage crimes of the century. He had just told me that he receives letters in his prison cell every week from women who want to correspond with him, visit him, meet him, and develop romantic relationships with him.

"A lot of them send pictures," Speck said. "A lot of them women are pretty. Some of them women's gotta be nuts. Here's half the country down on a person, they call him all kinds of names—and these women are trying to get to meet him. It sure gets way out. I give their addresses to my cellmates. I don't want nothing to do with them women."

Why do the women want to meet Speck? Perhaps it is a particularly strange permutation of the same reason you are reading this story, and the same reason I was talking to Speck at the Stateville Penitentiary. There is something about a Richard Speck—some abhorrent evil incarnate in the mass murderer— that defies people to accept the fact that a savage killer is also, undeniably, a human being.

For almost two hours I talked with Speck. He spoke with a slow drawl. He looked like a somewhat sinister, pockmarked John Unitas, in a blue prison suit over a purple T-shirt. Prison officials were startled when Speck agreed to talk to me—he loathes the press, and has consistently refused to grant interviews—and the only reason Speck gave me when I asked was, "I read your column, man."

He shocked me by readily admitting that he had indeed killed the nurses—the first time he had confessed his guilt. But almost as surprising, in a more subdued but equally dramatic way, was the manner in which he talked about his life. It was the paradox again—the mass murderer as a human being.

Speck, wearing handcuffs and chains, said he had just come to the main prison building from his cell in a solitary confinement unit, where he was being kept as punishment.

"They got me in solitary because I turned a job down," Speck said. "They wanted me to work in the vegetable room. I wouldn't do it."

"What's wrong with the vegetable room?" I asked.

"A man's got to get up at four-thirty in the morning to work in the vegetable room," Speck said.

"I don't like to get up that early. Chow starts at about fifteen minutes after six, and that's early enough for me. They got me in the labor pool, which means I'm locked in my cell all day after chow. There's three of us to a cell. We watch TV. We got a color TV in our cell.

"I like Clint Eastwood, Charles Bronson. I watched *Magnum Force* the other night. It was all right. Clint Eastwood, he always plays good. I watch '60 Minutes,' the news, keep up on the outside world. And Carol Burnett. I watch her comedy show.

"What's that dude who played in *Shaft*? Richard Roundtree? I like him. Him and Eastwood and Bronson. They're violent players. I'm not a violent man."

"Then why do you like violent movies?" I asked.

"Same reason you pay and watch 'em," Speck said. "What would you rather see, Walt Disney or a Charles Bronson flick? But I do watch 'Wild Kingdom.'

"I read *Newsweek*s, *Time*s, *Hustler*s, *Playboy*s. I was buying hard-core pornography through the mail, but it got too expensive. It wasn't worth it."

I asked Speck if he ever expected to get out of prison.

"Between now and the year 2000, yeah," Speck said. "I do my time day by day. In due time, I'll get out. I want to go into the grocery store business. I want to own one. I used to work at Jerry's Food Market in Dallas, Texas. I put up stock and kept the place clean. I worked from three in the afternoon until seven in the morning."

Speck said that one of his pleasures in prison was "getting high."

"I like hooch [moonshine] and I like speed," Speck said. "I don't like marijuana. I used to stay high on reds [barbiturates], but no more. It's all right to get high on that stuff when you're young, but I'm thirty-six now. That's too old for reds.

"We had some good hooch in our cell. We have a two-hundred-dollar stereo in there, too, and I turned over two gallons of the hooch and it messed the stereo up. I had borrowed eight tapes from one of the brothers, a black dude, and the hooch just ate the tapes up.

"I like that hooch, though. I stay up at night as long as it takes me to fall asleep or pass out from the hooch or from whatever we have at the time."

I asked him if he wasn't afraid of getting in trouble for talking about contraband kept in his cell. Speck laughed.

"How am I gonna get in trouble?" he said. "I'm in here for twelve hundred years."

I told Speck that, in their day, men like John Dillinger had been national celebrities even though they were vicious killers. I asked Speck if he felt the same way.

"You're talking about two different categories of people," Speck said. "Dillinger and them guys, that was the Depression, they were robbing banks because that was their only way to survive. Me, I'm not like Dillinger or anybody else. I'm freakish."

I asked him if he ever thought about Charles Manson, America's other famed mass murderer.

"What do I want to think about that fool for?" Speck said.

"Why do you think he's a fool?" I said.

"He's doing life in prison, I wouldn't call him too damn intelligent," Speck said.

"You're doing life in prison," I said.

"I'm another damn fool," Speck said.

"Nah, I'm not a celebrity," he said. "That's all propaganda. Here. Look at this."

He pushed up his left sleeve—and there, where his notorious "Born to Raise Hell" tattoo had been, were a number of ugly scars.

"I burned that tattoo off with a cigarette," Speck said. "I had that put on me when I was fourteen or fifteen. By the time I was sixteen or seventeen I knew it was nasty and cheap. I wanted to get rid of it. My mother had an appointment for me at Parkland Hospital, the same place where Kennedy ended up dying. I was gonna get the tattoo removed. But I ended up in jail before I could keep the appointment. I wasn't born to raise hell."

"Then what were you born for?" I asked.

"Same thing as you or anybody else," Speck said.

"What's that?" I said.

"You're making a living, ain't you?" Speck said. "You was on one road. I was on another road. What happened to me was nobody's fault but my own."

Speck said that he paints in his cell—oil paintings of animals, still lifes, African scenes. He said that he does not dream while sleeping.

"Ain't nothing to dream of," he said. "Twelve years behind bars, what's there to dream of. Only ones keeping me going is my mother and my five sisters.

"If I could get out of here for one night, I'd get on a plane, go to Texas, and see my mother. The only women I care about is my mother and my five sisters. And if I was out for two nights, I'd go to a nightclub. I always wanted to own a nightclub. Just a regular nightclub, like Jack Ruby's."

He said that he is not considered a celebrity inside the walls of Stateville, "except by the fools.

"Them's your young dudes. The old-timers, they treat me the same as anybody else. We're all in here doing time.

"I don't get no jobs here in prison. The only ones who gets good jobs is stool pigeons, people who'll tell on another inmate to an officer. I'm not a stool pigeon. You could kill a man in front of me, and I didn't see it. My back was turned."

He talked about the letters he received from women. I asked if he perceived himself as a romantic figure.

"Hell, no," Speck said. "Do you think you're a romantic figure?"

"Well . . . yes," I said.

"Well, you're conceited, man," Speck said, and laughed.

"Do you laugh a lot in here?" I said.

"What am I supposed to do, cry for twelve hundred years?" Speck said.

He said that most of his friends in prison had been black— "guys like Jeff Fort and Bull Harris, guys from the Blackstone Rangers. My hero is Clay, the boxer. In music, I like Clyde McPhatter, Bo Diddley, Little Richard, Fats Domino, Chuck Berry. I never did like Elvis. They called him the king of rock and roll, but if Chuck Berry had been white, he'd have been the king of rock and roll."

Speck said that although at the time he killed the nurses "I had no feelings," he is sorry now.

"I had no feelings at all that night," he said. "They said there was blood all over the place. I can't remember. It felt like nothing.

"I'm sorry as hell. For those girls, and for their families, and for me. If I had to do it over again, it would be a simple house burglary."

Speck said that if he ever gets out of prison, he plans to change his name and try to live anonymously.

"I'd like to be just plain Richard Speck, but that's impossible," he said.

"If anybody messes with me though, they'll be a fool. Because if they do, I'll be back in prison."

Why?

"They'll never mess with nobody else."

What's that supposed to mean?

"That speaks for itself."

Speck got up to go back to solitary confinement. He said he had a final thought for the American people.

"Just tell 'em to keep up their hatred for me," Speck said. "I know it keeps up their morale. And I don't know what I'd do without it."

Baseball and the Facts of Life

H E IS NINE years old; his name is Brett. For three years he has been asking his parents if he could play in the Little League. This summer they said yes.

He is small for his age, with curly brown hair and bright blue eyes. The girls think he is cute, but he tells his mother he doesn't care about that. When his mother and father said he could play in the league this year, he just about exploded with joy. In other summers, he watched baseball on television; this year he was going to play.

His parents took him to the first practice, and they could see it in his eyes: he idolized the man who was coaching the team. The other boys had played in years before—Little Leaguers start young—but Brett didn't care. At last he was going to be one of them.

After the first few games, he would come home from practice, and his parents could sense that something was wrong. It is best not to pry into the secrets of little boys, but they were concerned. So one night, after dinner, they walked over to see his team play.

They watched as the game started, and their son did not get in. There were fifteen boys on the team, some of them very good. But most of them were bigger than Brett, and stronger; they were the ones who played the whole game. The coach let Brett in for one inning; when the inning was over, the coach took him out.

At home, after the game, Brett's parents asked him what had been bothering him.

He said that at the beginning of the season, the coach had said that every boy would play. But for Brett, that meant only the bare minimum—one inning each game. The coach was afraid that if Brett stayed in for too long, the team might lose the game. As it was, he was put in right field, the place that boys who are not good enough are traditionally sent.

His mother started going to every game. She would watch as Brett stood on the sidelines, his eyes alive, everything in his face almost begging to get in. And every game she watched as the coach reluctantly let her son play for one inning, and not a moment more.

At home, Brett would put his uniform on four hours before he was supposed to go to the game. He would walk around the house in it, look at himself in the mirror, check the clock every few minutes; the games were scheduled to start at six P.M., but Brett would get there at quarter to five, just to be sure. Every game was going to be the one when he would really get to play.

And his mother kept going to the games. Even from a distance she could see those eyes lighting up every time it seemed he might get to go in. She would see those eyes, and then she would see the coach not even knowing her son was there. The coach looking at the more skillful boys out on the field, and her son looking at the coach; it made her feel sick to see it.

One day, after the game, when no one was looking, she approached the coach. She asked him why.

"I have to keep the best ones in," the coach said. "We're in a league, you know. We're trying to win. I have five boys on the team who only play one inning. Your son is one of them."

At home, Brett would ask his father to practice with him in the driveway. The father is not an athletically inclined man, but of course he said yes; Brett said he was "working on his arm," as if that would help change things at the next game.

And every game, he would get into his uniform early; every game, he would be the first one at the field.

His mother watched one game as he got in. The boys who got to play regularly—the skillful ones—horsed around between innings, did tricks on their bikes and made jokes with each other. Brett, though, looked only at the game. He never even got a drink of water. This night, when he got to bat, he kept in mind the coach's admonitions about not backing away from the ball. The pitch came in hard and close, and it hit him hard enough to make him cry. When the inning was over he stood expectantly on the sidelines, hoping to get back in. But the coach only called to the regulars: "Double the limit at the Dairy Queen if you win." Brett did not play again that night.

One evening it happened: for some reason a lot of the boys had other things to do, and there were only nine present when it was time for the game to begin. His mother was there again, and she saw the coach tell Brett that he was going to get to start the game in right field. She saw him begin to smile, and then to suppress it; he ran out to right field, part of the starting team.

In the middle of the first inning, one of the regulars rode up on his bike. The coach was clearly glad to see him. When Brett trotted off the field, he saw that the other boy had arrived. The coach took Brett out; his evening was over.

The season is almost finished now. Brett does not put his uniform on four hours early anymore; he does not watch the clock. He still goes to the games, but he has learned his lesson. He doesn't talk about baseball around the house.

His parents are trying to find a moral in all of this. They know it happens to many boys in thousands of cities around the country every summer. His parents tell themselves that maybe it will turn out to be a good experience; maybe it will teach their son something about life, and about dreams, and about putting too much faith in those dreams.

That's what they tell themselves, but they don't believe it. All they know is that their son, at the age of nine, has been shown that he isn't good enough. We all learn that sometime in this life; some find it out earlier than others. The other night, Brett told his parents that he wasn't going to play baseball next summer. The eyes weren't as bright; that's what hurt his parents the most. The eyes weren't as bright.

An Unmentionable Occasion

To UNDERSTAND THIS, we must set the scene precisely. We are in the living room of Kristine Costello, in Methuen, Massachusetts, a suburb of Boston. Color photographs of her two children, Lea and Michael, adorn the walls. Fourteen other women, all invited here by Mrs. Costello, sit in chairs, on couches, and on the floor, drinking rosé wine.

With the exception of the reporter, there are no men in the house. Mrs. Costello's husband, Michael, had run a sweeper over the carpeting before the guests arrived, but he understood that once the party began he was expected to depart.

The women here range in age from their twenties to their fifties. Some of them are housewives; some of them hold outside jobs. The suburb is essentially mainstream American middle class, and so, by appearances, are the women.

Up a short step in the dining room, directly next to Mrs. Costello's supper table, is a metal clothing rack. Right now the rack is covered with a white satin drape, but soon, when unveiled, it will reveal the garments that have apparently drawn the women to the party. There will be filmy, see-through negligees; there will be nightgowns with names like French Connection and Flowing Passion, all gauzy and cut low in the chest and high up the legs; there will be crotchless panties; there will be lacy brassieres with the nipples snipped out.

At the moment, though, Tiffany James is addressing the group.

Mrs. James is running the party tonight, and she invites the women to have another glass of wine. She thanks them for coming and assures them that their husbands won't be disappointed when they get home.

"Relax, sit back, and have the time of your life," Mrs. James says. She hands each woman in the room a scorecard and a pencil, and begins to deliver something called the Sensuality Test:

"If you're wearing a bra and panties of the same color, give yourself ten points.

"If you've ever finger-painted with a member of the opposite sex, give yourself ten points.

"If I say 'whipped cream' and anybody blushes, give yourself twenty points."

When the test is over, Mrs. James has everyone in the room read off her score. There is much giggling. She says she is just about ready to show the clothing, but first she wants the women to be even more comfortable. Once more, wine is poured.

"I want us all to know each other," Mrs. James says, "so I'm going to go around the room, and I'd like each of you to say your first name, and then to say something sensuous about yourself that begins with the first letter of your first name. I'll start: My name is Tiffany, and I like touching."

There is a momentary silence. These women would look at home in a Betty Crocker ad or in a corporate secretarial pool. But within thirty seconds, they have begun.

"My name is Carol, and I like caressing."

"My name is Linda, and I like luscious lip service."

"My name is Karen, and I like kinky men."

What we have here is a phenomenon so startling and yet so obvious that, had one pondered the factors that led to it, one could have almost predicted it. This is the natural outgrowth of free and open sexuality reaching into the heartland; it is the place where the sexual revolution and the Tupperware party meet.

Tiffany James, the woman directing tonight's party, is executive vice-president of UndercoverWear Inc.; along with her husband, Walter, she runs the company. Since this party is so close to the firm's headquarters, in Woburn, Massachusetts, she is acting as the party agent. But there are more than eight hundred UndercoverWear agents in thirty-five states; virtuallv every weeknight of the year, there is an UndercoverWear party going on somewhere in the country.

The premise of these parties is a simple one: American housewives have been titillated and aroused by the sexual openness that has spread across the nation. Most of them are not swingers or cheaters; they may feel a few twinges of raciness, but basically they love their husbands, their children, and their homes. They want to sample some of the exotic new pleasures they know are out there, but they do not want to feel dirty about it, and they certainly do not want to feel guilty.

Enter UndercoverWear Inc. By 1977 Walter and Tiffany James had realized that there was money to be made if they could find a way to offer these women tame, unthreatening thrills; to let them feel vaguely naughty without being unfaithful; to give them some quiet sin for a few hours, and then to deliver them safely home to their families again.

So UndercoverWear built up a line of bedroom attire that ranged from the risqué to the lewd. Instead of advertising it in the backs of true-confessions magazines like the old Frederick's of Hollywood merchandise, however, they arranged to bring it right into the women's own living rooms. There was to be none of the furtiveness of ordering from a magazine coupon. The Tupperware imitation was calculated and intentional; Mr. and Mrs. James realized that a great many women would find it more exciting to purchase nighties that bared their breasts than to watch demonstrations of burping bowls. And yet this was all to be done in the name of pleasing their husbands. This was to be done out in the open with friends; this was to be done with a sense of humor; this was to be a party.

"The party plan eliminates any feeling of embarrassment about purchasing these kinds of products," Mrs. James says. "If a woman wants to wear a garter belt and nylons for her husband, she might hesitate before going into a store. The feeling is, "This salesclerk is going to think there's something wrong with me;

I'm not as sweet and demure as I look, and what's she going to think of me?"

At an UndercoverWear party, however, the emphasis is on making the women feel they're all in it together. Although, as Mrs. James says, "It's our firm belief that what happens between a husband and a wife in the bedroom is private," the UndercoverWear parties are designed to assure the women that they are not having their bedroom fantasies alone.

The UndercoverWear theory of success is based on the assumption that these are not women who usually purchase revealing lingerie—"Maybe the husband would buy the wife one black nightie a year, at Christmas," Mrs. James says—and the whole idea of the parties is to persuade the women that what they are doing is socially acceptable. "We want the women to tell themselves: 'Just because I choose to wear something sensuous in my bedroom, that's no negative reflection on me.' Women today have a desire to be feminine and still think they're normal.

"We're not just selling them a piece of lingerie. We're selling them an UndercoverWear night. Not the night of the party, but the night they get to show the garments to their husbands. That's what the agents tell them at the parties: 'When you get your UndercoverWear, schedule your UndercoverWear night.' "

So, as darkness falls, the parties begin. No men are allowed. As each piece of lingerie is removed from the rack for display, the women are encouraged to talk about it. There is more a tingle of teenage romance in the room than a feeling of lust; the women *ooooh* at the items as if what they are looking at are tiny puppies instead of fringe-covered bras. The phrase most commonly spoken in the room is, "Isn't that pretty?"

The UndercoverWear agent realizes, though, that her commission depends on getting the partygoers to order the products, and that the most effective sales pitch is not based on aesthetics. So when a woman across the room asks, "Does that one come with pants, Tiffany?" Mrs. James looks her in the eye and says, "Yes, but we can't guarantee how long they stay on."

There is an odd combination of forces in play as the party progresses into the evening. On the one hand, the women are indulging their fantasies, feverishly marking down the names of the garments they hope to purchase at the end of the night. On the other hand . . . there is no real flavor of wickedness or raw sexuality here. This is definitely not a female version of a stag party. Times may have changed, and the items the women order may be of the variety that must be hidden from the children, but this *does* feel the way a Tupperware party must feel. The attraction for the women seems to be social; the party is like a gathering of sorority sisters, and the merchandise is, in a way, incidental. Sexy clothing may be the excuse that has brought them here, but simply being together away from men is clearly as important to them as the nightgowns they are buying.

"It's nice to be in someone else's home shopping," says Chris Canto, a social worker, who will purchase $50 worth of merchandise at the end of the evening. "I don't think there's anything dirty in the show; it's all very pretty." And Kristine Costello, in whose home the party is taking place—and who will receive free merchandise for being the hostess—says, "I like shopping at home with my friends. It's like a night out with the girls."

The reasons the women give for being in the room are traditional and almost wholesome. "I'm not one to order from a catalog," says one. "You can't really be sure of the quality and sizes in a catalog." And the youngest woman at the party—Carol Medeiros, eighteen, a salesclerk who plans to be married within the next year and who will spend $150 tonight—says she is planning to save the garments for her marriage. "They're for my hope chest," she says.

It is as if the whole world has changed, yet nothing has changed at all. Twenty years ago many of the fashions being sold here would have been too revealing to be featured in a girlie magazine; but here the women are, writing down their choices, talking quietly with one another, making new friends even as they select Fringe Benefits or Jungle Fever.

Perhaps it is best that the men are not allowed to see this; it would deflate the very fantasies that the UndercoverWear phenomenon is designed to inspire. In the male imagination, the idea of a party like this probably conjures up the dark emotional muskiness of a gang bang. But that's not it; if the truth be told, this is one part orgy, nine parts sewing circle, and the amazing thing about the women here is that they seem able to juggle both elements yet somehow keep them separate.

And now Tiffany James has finished the presentation. The last nightgown and pair of panties have been displayed; now the women are descending on the metal rack, grabbing Softly Sensuous and Double Trouble and the rest.

It is time to try them on. The women take their favorites and head for Mr. and Mrs. Costello's bedroom, for the children's rooms, for the bathrooms. Three or four of them go into each room at the same time, taking their own clothes off, putting the UndercoverWear fashions on.

In a matter of minutes, they are back in the living room. The effect is stunning. Earlier they had been in housedresses or slacks and sweaters. Now they are standing around together like so many hookers, all cleavage and belly and leg, telling one another how cute they look and how pleased their husbands will be. The voices are a jumble:

"Tiffany, does this one have bottoms?"

"Tiffany, does this one come with snaps?"

Tiffany James is busy accepting orders, telling each buyer that the items will be delivered in approximately three weeks. Some of the women are standing in front of a mirror staring at themselves. "Well, Eddie," says one, "you'd better be prepared."

"That looks so pretty on you," Mrs. James says to one customer, even as she is moving to the next and asking, "Did you want to try on Little Bo Peep?" It is 9:45 on a Wednesday evening in northern Massachusetts. In an hour these women will be back at home, ready to tuck the children in and turn on the coffeepot for the morning and drift to sleep. Perchance to dream.

Partying with the Prince

I WENT TO a party with Prince Charles Tuesday night. It was pretty much fun.

His Royal Highness did fling gin and tonic in my eye at one point, but other than that he was a perfect gentleman, and it was well worth taking the time to pal around with him.

I almost blew the whole thing before it even started. A couple of weeks ago, one of my bosses said to me, "How would you like to go to a party with the Prince of Wales?"

I thought that Wales was a fairly insignificant country, and a scribe can't be accepting every invitation that comes his way, so I said, "Well, I just did a story about a race car driver from Wales who got his money stolen at O'Hare, so I think I've done enough Wales stories for one year."

Then, some time later, I was relating this set of events to a friend, and he said, "You idiot, the Prince of Wales is Prince Charles! The next King of England!"

"Are you sure?" I said. "I think Prince Charles is the Prince of England."

"He is the Prince of Wales," my friend said. "And this is probably the only chance you will ever have in your life to meet the next King of England."

I'll admit that I was impressed. I have never known a member of royalty, although I did once meet Fats Domino.

I informed my original source that I would, indeed, like to go to the party. I called out for my secretary to pencil Prince Charles in on my calendar. Then, remembering that I did not have a secretary, much less a calendar, I wrote the date and time down on the surface of my desk.

Soon after, I received a letter from the British consulate general. The man who wrote the letter had dropped his customary English reserve. He even stooped to using an exclamation point:

> I think that you already know that this reception is NOT a press conference and that there should be no attempt to interview His Royal Highness in the course of any conversation, nor should any remarks made at the reception be regarded as for publication. Needless to say, no cameras, microphones, tape recorders, notebooks, or any professional paraphernalia!

Needless to say, indeed. I don't even go to bed without a pen and paper. I was properly chastised. However, no Bic, no Bic. So there was nothing for me to do but run a washrag over my sport coat, dust off my shoes, and head for the Drake Hotel.

I presented my letter of invitation and was directed to a dining room, where drinks were being served for the prince, the British ambassador, the consul general, and a number of us media studs.

Waiters fed us some food. Prince Charles was a little late in showing up at the party, but then his plane had just arrived at O'Hare an hour earlier, and you know how long it can take waiting around that lower level for your bags to come moving by on the conveyors.

When the prince did come into the room, he looked swell. Apparently he is one of those fellows who can wear a suit right off the rack, for his clothes did not look as if they needed any alterations at all. He made his way around the room, saying howdy to each guest in turn, and when he came to me I calmly uttered the line I had been rehearsing all afternoon:

"Charmed, I'm sure."

I would like to tell you what His Royal Highness had to say to me. I truly would. What the hell, you're family. But the constrictions placed upon me by the letter from the consulate general prohibit me from revealing the details. Let me just assure you that the information passed on to me by Prince Charles was quite explosive, to say the least.

Upon rereading the letter, however, I find that while it does forbid me from telling you what the prince said, there are no restrictions about telling you how he said it. His voice, in other words.

It is rather deep. More like John's than like Ringo's.

After Prince Charles had finished introducing himself to all us revelers, he called for a drink and began to make idle conversation with small groups. It was at this point that he threw the gin in my face. He was talking about the Concorde, and how it made too much noise when it was taking off over his castle. He gestured wildly with his left hand, which happened to have been resting on top of his drink. The gin and tonic flew directly into my right eye. I think I'm allowed to report that.

Oh, I'm going to break protocol. It can't hurt if I tell you one little thing that he said to me, and besides, how often am I going to be in this position, anyway?

The next King of England said, "Are they paying you money to be here?"

He carried himself quite well, and in fact had the second most regal bearing of anyone in the whole room. The person with the first most regal bearing was Maxwell McCrohon, managing editor of the *Chicago Tribune*, but then Charles is only twenty-eight. He has time.

Actually, Prince Charles seemed relieved that everyone in Chicago was being so nice to him. He may have been thinking back to his ancestor, the late King George V. Early in this century the old-time mayor of Chicago, William Hale (Big Bill) Thompson, said he would "punch King George in the snoot" if the king ever came to Chicago.

No one punched Prince Charles in the snoot. The party continued. It was quite uproarious, but all good times must come to an end, and before long it was time to go home. I waved goodbye to His Royal Highness. I am not allowed to tell you what he said in return.

Reflections in a Wary Eye

WAITING TO SEE Nixon, I killed time in the cafeteria. I watched a woman eat an egg-and-muffin sandwich and wash it down with a root beer. It was eight o'clock in the morning, in a federal office building in lower Manhattan.

I was early. Nixon's letter had said to come at nine, but I wasn't going to risk being late for this one. I made notes, as if this would be a regular interview, but that wasn't my reason for being there at all. I didn't care if I never wrote about it.

Spending time with Richard Nixon . . . for people of my generation, the people who had been in college during his election and his years as President, the very idea was like a tingling promise. We were the people who had professed to hate him most passionately. Despising Nixon, for a time, was a required course. And yet in the years since he had left office, it had become clear that he was the one political figure of our age who was bigger than life. There was no player in the national drama who came close to Nixon; the *idea* of Nixon was somehow central to the experience of being an American in the second half of this century.

I wanted to meet him the way an eight-year-old wants to go to Disney World. I couldn't imagine anything more tantalizing. In a can't-buy-a-thrill age, the notion of sitting alone with Nixon—just listening to him talk—had an appeal that, for me, went way beyond the idea of journalism. We had exchanged letters. I tried to express some of those sentiments to him, in more formal language. I couldn't believe it when his second letter said he would "welcome a visit."

His office phone number was unlisted; I had been given a floor number and told to look for a certain number on a door. At quarter to nine, I rode the elevator up. There were Spanish-speaking people looking for an immigration-processing office. Thirty feet away, I found the door. There were no words on it. I tried the knob; it was locked.

A woman let me in. There, on the walls, were huge color blowups of the Nixon presidency: Nixon riding in a motorcade, smiling and waving; Nixon with his arm around a young Chinese boy; Nixon with Brezhnev. A lone secret service agent, wearing a brown suit and reading a copy of *National Geographic*, sat visibly bored in a chair facing the door I had just come through. The telephones did not ring.

It looked like the office of a middle-level civil service functionary. The secretary and the secret service man spoke neither to each other nor to me. I figured Nixon would make me cool my heels for a while, let the anticipation build. But at nine o'clock straight up, the secretary said, "Would you like to come with me?"

We walked through a door, and there, sitting next to an illuminated globe at the end of a long room, was Richard Nixon, sixty-seven.

"Mr. President, you have a visitor," the secretary said.

When he rose and said, "So . . . did you just fly in?" the first thought to come to my mind was: Dan Aykroyd.

I couldn't shake it. It occurred to me that in these years since he left office, he has been invisible so much of the time that we have come to know him mainly as caricature. Often it was as if he really *were* just an idea, not even alive. And yet here he was, grayer than I had expected, wearing a blue suit and hunched over ever so slightly. On his desk was a small pile of letters; behind the desk were an American flag and a flag bearing the seal of the President of the United States.

We sat facing each other in armchairs near the globe. He was talking, but I was just staring at him. He was the one who seemed nervous; he was making small talk, trying to be friendly, filling the air with words so there wouldn't be the chance of even the most momentary uncomfortable silence. He was asking questions about where I had stayed the night before and how much it had cost, and when I finally made myself pay attention to his words, he seemed to be saying something about some friends of his who had gone out for a milkshake in New York.

". . . And they said they had gone to Rumpelmayer's," Nixon said. "And they asked me how much I thought a milkshake cost. I thought to myself: McDonald's. Eighty cents? Ninety cents?"

He looked at me as if he expected me to say something. When I didn't, he said:

"Do you know how much that milkshake cost?"

"No, sir," I said, "I don't."

"That milkshake cost three dollars and forty cents," Nixon said.

We began to chat. I had promised myself that I would ask him only the things I was truly curious about. That wasn't Watergate, and that wasn't politics; I figured that if this would be the one time in my life I was alone with Nixon, I'd rather just try to get him to talk about himself.

So fairly quickly we came around to the subject of his stiff and bloodless public image. He said he was well aware of it; he realized that it hurt him in the eyes of some, but that he could never change. "I wear a coat and tie all the time," he said. "It isn't a case of trying to be formal, but I'm more comfortable that way. I've done it all my life. I don't mind people around here in the office, particularly younger people—they usually take their coats off. But I just never have. It's just the way I am. I work in a coat and tie; believe it or not, it's hard for people to realize, but when I'm writing a speech or working on a book or dictating or so forth, I'm always wearing a coat and tie. Even when I'm alone."

I was calling him "Mr. President." I wasn't sure why; before I had arrived I had thought about how I would address him, and I had decided on "Mr. Nixon." But now I wasn't doing it. It didn't seem to be because of his own formality, or even out of intimidation; rather, in a strange kind of way, I sensed I might bruise his feelings by demonstrating that I could skip the title he obviously loved so much. So "Mr. President" it was, but it felt so awkward on my tongue that I decided to ask him about it.

When he had been in office, had he allowed even his closest aides to relax a little and call him anything less austere?

"Never. And none did."

When I said that his best personal friends must have had the luxury of calling him Dick or Richard, he shook his head. He told me that even Bebe Rebozo had followed this protocol.

"So when you were out on a fishing boat," I said, "and you were trying to relax, and Rebozo wanted to offer you a beer— he said, 'Would you like a beer, Mr. President?' "

"Yep," Nixon said. "That's right. That's the way."

I had told him in my first letter that I had been among his legions of young critics. He seemed to be intrigued by this, welcoming questions that sprang from that experience, and when I saw that he was warming to them, I asked how it had affected him when he heard the two famous phrases: "Tricky Dick" and "Would you buy a used car from this man?" I said that when people of my generation and political persuasion had tossed off those words, it had never occurred to us that there was really anyone on the receiving end. Nixon had always seemed so much bigger than we were, so far removed, that at the time it had not seemed possible that he could have his feelings hurt.

"If I had feelings, I probably wouldn't have even survived," he said. "I remember very clearly something. I was speaking down in Williamsburg, Virginia, and this was right after I had become President. And I think we had made the first announcement about our first withdrawal of twenty-five thousand. And this very pretty girl, she was I guess sixteen, seventeen, came up and spit full in my face and said, 'You murderer.'

"I borrowed a handkerchief from a secret service man and wiped it off, and then I went in and made my speech. It was tough."

In a way, telling that story seemed to bring him to life. It struck me that to anyone else, the key part of the tale would have been the girl's spitting. But Nixon's voice rose and the set of his jaw became firm precisely when he said, "It was tough"; that's what he wanted me to understand—that no matter how badly people treated him, he could not be touched.

Our conversation was running well past the hour I had hoped for. I had always heard that Nixon hated anything close to psychological questioning, and as we talked about personal matters, I was watching closely to see if he would recoil. But for some reason he didn't; rather, he seemed to be almost relishing the course the discussion was taking. Twice his secretary buzzed him to give him the opportunity to end the appointment; twice he told her that it was all right, he wanted to keep going. I found myself wondering: Is it possible that he's lonely up here? Is it possible that he really needs the company?

I couldn't think of any other explanation for what was happening. Maybe it was as simple as the fact that when you're the most famous national catchphrase of them all, people stop treating you as if you're flesh and bones. The more I made it clear that I liked hearing these stories, the looser Nixon got; he seemed delighted to have an audience that was treating him neither as a criminal nor as a face from a history book. It occurred to me that maybe, in light of the way it had all turned out for him, he didn't get the chance to do this very much.

He began to ramble a bit, telling brief stories, throwing off quick opinions—about thirteen-year-old girls he had seen smoking marijuana on the street near his home, about Lyndon Johnson's inviting him to the presidential bedroom and greeting him from beneath the covers, about his fears concerning young people's watching television instead of reading books. He was smiling more, and looking me in the eye, and asking me questions. I told him I was noticing this; I asked him why, he thought, this side of him seemed so foreign to people.

"I never wanted to be buddy-buddy," he said. "Not only with the press. Even with close friends. I don't believe in letting your hair down, confiding this and that and the other thing—saying, 'Gee, I couldn't sleep because I was worrying. . . .'

"I believe you should keep your troubles to yourself. That's just the way I am. Some people think it's good therapy to sit with a close friend and, you know, just spill your guts. Not me. No way."

I said that on the surface such an attitude might promise a person self-protection, but that in the end it would probably result in his being so isolated and so remote that no one truly knew him.

"Yeah," Nixon said. "It's true. And it's not necessary for them to know."

We had been talking for nearly two hours. Nixon appeared to be growing tired. His sentences were drifting off; he was looking out the window more often. With no warning, he put his hands on his knees and said, "Well, anyway, I have to knock this off."

We stood up. I was feeling curiously emotional. Nixon did not seem to have the old vigor that had inspired such passions in the land. At one point he had said to me, "Frankly, the sense of your mortality grows as you get older. I mean, after all, you read the obituary page, and you read of people sixty-nine, seventy, sixty-five . . . all of my generation. They cut off. They die. Heart attacks, cancer, what have you."

I suddenly felt a little like a kid who had grown up and moved away and was having a meeting with a father he'd never gotten along with, but who he now finally realized would not be around forever. I tried to say something; Nixon seemed to sense the direction in which I was heading, and moved to cut me off. If I was going to get sentimental, he wanted to avoid it, and so before I could even start he was steering us back to harmless small talk. He asked me if I had seen the World Series game the night before.

"George Brett's hemorrhoids," Nixon said. "They put that in the paper. Damn. They shouldn't do that. That's private. Who the hell wants to read about hemorrhoids?"

All the while he was moving me toward the door. I started to thank him for seeing me, but he wasn't listening.

"Carter had them," Nixon said. "Remember, he had them early on? It's probably the tension that creates them."

And then he was opening the door and shaking my hand, and I was walking out.

He called out to me, and I turned around. He was framed in the doorway.

"How old are you?" Nixon asked.

"Thirty-three," I said.

Nixon smiled. "Thirty-three," he said. "Let's see. I was thirty-three years old when I was first elected to the House. It's a good time to be alive."

He nodded almost imperceptibly. Then the door closed. I had a real desire to say something to someone, but the secretary was typing a letter, and the secret service agent was still reading his magazine, and there was nobody else around.

Business Lunch

I AM NEVER going to make it in the world of big-time business and grown-up behavior. It's not that I can't balance a checkbook (which I can't) or that I'm not sure how to read the stock tables (which I'm not). Those are obstacles which, I have found, can be overcome.

My shortcoming is far worse, and it dooms me to failure in the world of commerce forever.

I do not know how to have lunch.

Oh, I know how to eat a sandwich or go to McDonald's. I know how to put food down my gullet in the middle of the day. If I can do it by myself, I'm fine.

What I can't do is have a business lunch. "Let's have lunch" has become the most common phrase in white-collar workaday America, and I don't know how to do it. I have tried and I am terrible at it.

Most people, it seems, are perfectly capable of making a lunch date with a business associate, breaking bread, having pleasant conversation, and then going back to work.

I can't do it. Dozens of times every week a telephone caller or letter writer will suggest, "Let's have lunch and discuss it," and I will panic and tell a lie. I will say that I already have a luncheon engagement that day. Which is not true. I never have a luncheon engagement.

But to lie is better than to have to go through with it. Others may sparkle and charm at lunch. I sit at the table and twitch. I look at my watch. I stare dumbly over my companion's shoulder. I yawn. I take my handkerchief out and make a ball of it. I kick the floor. People ask me, "Are you feeling well?"

I do not mean to be doing these things. It is just that I feel very awkward and uncomfortable having lunch with a person who has anything in mind but eating. I realize that I am alone in this, but I feel that the place to conduct business is the office. Business at lunch makes me nervous. Business should not be discussed over food. It makes the food bad and the business bad.

I am not just talking about my specific business, which is writing newspaper columns. I gave up on luncheon interviews long ago, when I kept dropping my notepaper in the gravy and losing my pen in the lettuce. Every time my interview subject would say something worth writing down, I would have a fork in one hand and a knife in the other. It became disconcerting for everyone, with me throwing the silverware to the table and grabbing for my writing utensils. And every time I thought of the perfect question, it would be garbled through a mouthful of cheeseburger.

But even when people understand that no interview is going to be conducted, they still want to have lunch. To "try out an idea," or "tell you about something you might want to consider," or "discuss an interesting opportunity with you." When I tell them to tell me right now, on the phone, they are shocked. To most people involved in business in this country, if it doesn't happen at lunch it doesn't happen.

I guess the reason I am so bad at having a business lunch is that I am never sure which part is the business and which part is the lunch. We sit down at the table and the other person starts making small talk and I just slump there and don't say anything. I know that this person does not really want to talk about the Cubs or what he saw on TV last night. He is just filling the air until the business part. Which is a perfectly fine concept, except that something inside me tells me that I'm not allowed to talk until the official part starts. I mean, somebody's writing this off, and I don't want to cheat.

I also get the impression that we're supposed to be laughing all the time. Not hilarious laughter, but the laughter of good fellowship, to let each other know that although this is business, it is also still lunch. I am not a very good laugher, and often I sound to myself as if I am gagging when I try to make an appropriate response to my luncheon partner's good-natured storytelling. All around the dining room there is pleasant laughter filling the air, and then there is me, smiling broadly and making a heaving sound.

When someone I can't say no to suggests having lunch, it ruins my day. There are so many decisions involved in having lunch, and from the time I get up until the time it is over, my day is totally devoted to the lunch. Where should we go? Should he suggest a place or should I? Is the place too impressive or too shabby? When should I get there? Should I risk being too early and have to stand around, or take a chance on getting there too late and making him impatient? When the waiter asks if we would like a drink, should I have one and seem like a daytime drunk, or say no and seem like a prissy great aunt? And if I say yes and he says no, what will he think? Or if I say no and he says yes? It goes on and on, until the time the check comes and we both hesitate, then both grab for it, then both pull back, then both reach again.

What it does is make me exhausted. I get up from the lunch and go back to the office and collapse on the typewriter. I feel as if I have just been to dancing school.

So what I do, when the rest of the world is at lunch, is to sit at my desk. It does no good. I call people, and their secretaries tell me they are out to lunch. I wait for the phone to ring, but it never does, because everyone is out to lunch. I look for someone in the next office to talk to, but there is no one, because they are out to lunch.

I have two pieces of white bread and a glass of ice water. I put it on my expense account as steak Diane for two. Then I stare at the wall and wait for everyone to come back. It's pretty interesting. We should talk about it. Let's have breakfast sometime.

The Country's Going Through a Rough Spell

I'M IN LOVE with a wonderful girl. She's thirteen years old, she lives in El Paso, Texas, and her name is Paige Pipkin. In an age of glamour girls and disco queens and Playmates of the Month, Miss Pipkin has the rarest of qualities. She can spell.

Last week Miss Pipkin correctly spelled the word *sarcophagus* and thus won the 54th National Spelling Bee in Washington, D.C. She triumphed over a young man who misspelled the word *philippic*, and thus she finished first in the competition, which is sponsored each year by the Scripps-Howard Newspapers.

The idea of a National Spelling Bee seems somehow out of date, but I think it's great. If you deal with the written word and you receive a lot of mail, then you know that people simply can't spell anymore. It is a skill that is becoming extinct in America—people apparently feel that they don't need to know how to do it, or that it is too hard to bother with.

When I go through the mail each day, I am constantly dismayed by this trend. It is getting to the point where a letter with no misspelled words is the exception. The problem goes across the board—letters from students, letters from businessmen, letters from people in public life. Even the most prosperous executives have secretaries who can't spell. And—worst of all—I sometimes get letters from teachers, and even their letters are full of misspellings.

This may seem like a minor thing, but I don't think it is. If I know that a person can't spell, then I have trouble trusting anything else about him. If he can't even get the spelling of a word right, then why should I put any faith in his version of events, or his opinions? Obviously he is sloppy in his thinking if he can't even take the trouble to make certain of the spelling of the words he uses.

I fear I am in a minority here. I don't know if there have been any official studies done on the problem, but just from personal observation I know that, in the last decade, the ability of people to spell has diminished rapidly. And yet you hardly ever hear it discussed.

I identify with Alexander Portnoy, the fictional protagonist of Philip Roth's *Portnoy's Complaint*, on this issue. In the book, Portnoy meets a beautiful, loving, affectionate woman and immediately falls for her. But he soon makes a terrible discovery about her. He finds notes she has left for the cleaning lady, and sees that each note contains five or six misspellings. It dismays him. He wants to love her, but he knows that this awful flaw rules such a thing out. He could never truly be in love with a woman who can't even spell.

Say what you will about my writing. You may think it's lousy, it may annoy you, it may even make you sick. But believe me on one thing. I am a hell of a speller. Ask any copy editor I've ever worked with. They will tell you. In the ten years I have been writing a newspaper column, I have misspelled no more than three words. And that's an outside estimate; to be truthful, I don't think I have misspelled any.

It's not such a great feat—all you have to do is look up the words you aren't sure of. Today, for example, before I turn this column in to the copy desk, I will look up *protagonist*, which was used two paragraphs above this one. A simple enough step.

But most people aren't willing to take it. That's the worst thing about the new inability of Americans to spell. If it just had to do with misspelled words, it would be one thing. But it is symbolic of an overall lack of discipline, a readiness not to care, a willingness to be second-rate. I know it may seem like a small thing to you, but it's really not. All the talk lately about the U.S. auto industry suffering because workmanship allegedly is inferior to workmanship in Japan—that's precisely the sort of thing that starts with a nation of people who can't even spell correctly.

And it's destined to get worse. In the television age, all print skills are going to suffer, and spelling is going to be the first one to go. People are going to decide that knowing how to spell is an archaic discipline, and they are going to decide they can get along without it. And the worst thing is, they'll be able to—if enough people just can't spell, then businesses, by default, are going to have to employ them anyway, and try to look past this fault.

Which takes us back to Paige Pipkin, the thirteen-year-old spelling champ from El Paso. For some reason, she has grown up believing that she must have enough pride in herself to be a perfect speller. It is difficult to imagine that she will ever fail in any important area of her life; you know instinctively that she is the kind of young woman who will succeed, because she cares about doing things right.

So congratulations to Miss Pipkin for winning the National Spelling Bee. If there were any justice in this world, they would have crowned her Miss America.

We Came for the Killing

POINT OF THE MOUNTAIN, UTAH— We came for the killing. There was no other reason for us to be waiting outside the fence at the Utah State Prison, so early in the morning, with chill darkness still shrouding the hillsides.

We came for the killing. That is not what we told ourselves, of course; we are in the news business, and it was easy to say that we were only here because our jobs demanded it. Leave that for the Ethics of Journalism textbooks. The fact is, we came for the killing, and we could hardly wait for the killing to begin.

We came for the killing because we, just like our fellow citizens, are caught up in the bizarre morbidity and eerie attraction of death rites, and the thought of a firing squad bringing the death penalty back to our lives was a magnet we could not resist.

We came for the killing, and because we carry press cards, we were allowed on the killing site. And you, fellow citizen—you would have been on the killing site, too, given the opportunity. And if you say that this is not true, if you say that you want no part of the sickness that drew us toward the house of death— well, if not you, then your neighbor. We got the message a long time ago. You want to hear about the death rites, and you want to hear it all. You have read every word of the firing squad stories, and you will read every word of this. There is no escaping it.

It is the strangest of paradoxes. Here, in this early week of 1977, two stories dominate the news, and the national consciousness is homed in on them both. Let us take the second one first: the inauguration of a President who spoke during his campaign of love, and goodness, and the spirit of life. It worked, his words of love and life; we elected him, and now he will be our leader.

But that is the second story of the week. The first one, the story at the Utah State Prison, the Gary Gilmore story, may tell us more about America than the happy story in Washington. The story in Utah was about hatred and evil and the tingly drama of violent death, and if the relative fevers of American interest in the two stories were somehow to be measured, which do you think would win out? In your heart of hearts, which story would you rather hear a teller of stories unfold?

We told you everything we could about the house of death in Utah. We told you what the condemned man ate for breakfast. We told you what color were his clothes. We told you how the shed for the riflemen was constructed. We told you about how the man's body shook and trembled as the bullets bored into his chest. We told you how the blood poured from beneath his shirt, and how it covered his pants. We told you where the blood remained, a sign of the killing ritual even after the killing was done, and the dead man driven away.

We told you everything, but we didn't tell you everything. We told you what you expected to hear; we told you everything we knew about the killing and the killed.

But there is something we left out, something we didn't tell you. We didn't tell you about ourselves. We didn't tell you what we did up on Point of the Mountain. We, your representatives in the free press, your guardians of the First Amendment—we didn't tell you about us.

We didn't tell you how we rushed to the death shed the moment we knew we could get away with it. We didn't tell you how we crawled around the sandbags in front of the dead man's chair, the sandbags still fresh with his blood. We didn't tell you how we hurried into the firing squad's canvas booth, and how we squinted out of the vertical slits where the rifles had been, squinted out at the chair and made ourselves a gift of the same view the executioners had viewed.

We didn't tell you how we touched everything, touched every possible surface in the death shed. We didn't tell you of the looks on the faces of the prison guards, who watched in amazement as we went about our doings with such eagerness, such lust. We didn't tell you what we did to the death chair itself—the chair with the bullet holes in its leather back. We didn't tell you that, did we? Didn't tell you how we inserted our fingers into the holes, and rubbed our fingers around, feeling for ourselves how deep and wide those death holes were. Feeling it all.

Why didn't we tell you that? Why didn't we tell you about ourselves? Probably because we understand the basic truth of it all. We understand that we are you, and you are us, and there are some things that we don't want to admit out loud about ourselves. Don't even want to think about. If we were monstrous, we were monstrous in a small way; probably better if we just forget about it, we and you both.

And besides, the killing at Point of the Mountain was only the beginning. There will be others; there will be more. And we will be there, too, and you will be right along with us. Oh yes you will. We will always come for the killing.

Fade to Silence

H E WAS A big man on the radio then. Cruising in our cars, we would hear him every night. He was the first person to play the Beatles for us. We knew his name.

He had a professional voice, I think. It was hard to tell. This was the era of the AM shouters, and he was one of them. We never heard him talk in a regular voice, except once.

We were driving around. It was the night of the day Kennedy got killed. There wasn't much traffic. Most people were home watching TV. A lot of the radio stations were giving news, or playing symphony music without ads. Not his. His station kept playing rock and roll.

Someone got the idea to go down and see him. We didn't think it was odd that we had never thought of it before. The station was right off the main street, the call letters shining in vertical neon on the side road. On the way to the station we listened to him shout. Downtown was empty.

We drove up to the front door of the station. It was locked. The building was dark, except for one window on the second floor. He was talking on our radio. Then he read an ad. A song came on, and we got out of the car.

We tossed pebbles at the lighted window. A man appeared. Then he went away. The car door was open in the November night. His voice came back on again. He talked some more. We threw some more pebbles. On the air he said something about somebody being at the window. We looked at one another. We were kind of thrilled.

When the next song came on, he walked to the upstairs window again. He looked down at us, and then he yanked it open. He asked us what we wanted. He didn't sound friendly. He didn't sound like him. He wasn't shouting.

We didn't say anything for a moment. Then one of us said that we had just wanted to come down and see him. He acted as if he were surprised; he asked us if we were kidding. We yelled up that we weren't. The song was ending. He said to wait a minute.

He was gone and his voice was back on the radio. He said that he had some visitors. He read another commercial. We talked to each other. We said that he didn't look like his voice. He was short and he wasn't young. Some of us said that was wrong; we said it just seemed that way, looking at him up through the window.

When the song came on he was back again. Now his voice was welcoming. He had a piece of paper. He asked us our names, and he asked us where we went to school. We were wearing our letter jackets, stomping our feet against the sidewalk to keep warm. We asked him if we could come in. He said no. He said he could get fired.

We stayed outside for about an hour. He talked to us between each song. He seemed happy to have the company. I think it was our idea to leave.

The rest of the night he talked about us about once every half hour. It was unusual. We were cruising the same streets, listening to the same station, and there were our names. We thought the whole world must have been listening; we felt very famous. Five minutes before each hour there would be news from Dallas. They had a man in custody.

The next weekend there was a dance. We heard that he was going to be the emcee. We paid our fifty cents to get in. He was at a microphone. He was shouting. We waited on the floor next to the stage. When there was a break we motioned for him. He came over. We told him who we were. He remembered us.

He went back to the microphone and said our names. After that we would listen to see where he would be appearing each weekend, and then we would go to the dance. He seemed to like us. He seemed to like the idea of having someone to talk to. Once one of us asked him how much money he made. He said fifty dollars a week. But he said the big money was in the weekend dance appearances.

It didn't occur to us that there were thousands of him, in every city and small town in the country. Voices in the night, narrating the lives of the people growing up in the miles of the station's reception. To us he was a star; he was like the famous singers whose records he played. It didn't make much sense that he would want to have us around, but clearly he did. The more we saw of him, the less of a star he became. We must have followed him around to weekend dances for about six months before we stopped. I don't remember why.

We all went away to college, and when we came back he was not on the radio anymore. He was still in town, though. The last time I saw him he was selling men's shoes in a department store about three blocks from the radio station. I saw him, kneeling on the floor, putting someone's socked foot onto one of those hard metal measuring devices. I was sure it was him. I was going to go over and say hello, but then I didn't. Sometimes it's better not to say anything at all.

Boy at His Best

Today, MAGAZINE READING is a part of your life that you take for granted—one of the predictable pleasures of your adult years. Chances are, though, that you were already a magazine reader back when you were nine and ten and eleven. You probably don't remember it right off-hand, but every month there was a magazine you waited for the mailman to deliver.

That was an important event in your life. And if you think about it, maybe it will be the advertisements that bring the name of the magazine back to you: the coupon allowing you to become a salesman for the American Youth Sales Club's all-occasion greeting cards (if you sold enough, you could win a Daisy air rifle). The picture of second baseman Johnny Temple urging you to buy a MacGregor baseball mitt.

And the stories: "We Canoed the Arctic Ocean." "Batboy for the Braves." "Here's How They Make Rope." "Lucky 13" ("In one terrific week we met President Eisenhower, breakfasted with Congressmen, and toured Washington and New York. We knew for sure we were the Lucky 13 Explorer Scouts").

The magazine, of course, was *Boys' Life*. At its peak, it had 2.65 million subscribers and a phenomenal hand-to-hand pass-on rate. *Boys' Life* was what American boyhood was all about; you read it because you were a young male, and it entertained you and made you feel as if you were part of something bigger than yourself.

You probably haven't seen *Boys' Life* in years; for all you know, it doesn't even exist anymore. It would seem difficult to believe that today such a publication could still be sold to American males who are approaching the brink of adulthood. You've seen so many twelve-year-olds leafing through *High Times* and *Hustler* on the newsstands; come to think of it, you've never seen *Boys' Life* for sale anywhere.

And you may wonder: Is the magazine still alive? Or did it die with so many of the now-moldering dreams and delusions about boyhood in America?

On the third floor of a modern glass-and-brick building in a secluded industrial park outside Dallas, in Irving, Texas, the editorial office of *Boys' Life* sits quiet as a computer-operations room. The floors are thickly carpeted; the staff of twenty-three work in sound-absorbent red-and-white cubicles.

Boys' Life is owned and published by the Boy Scouts of America; although its motto is "For All Boys," about eighty-five percent of its readers come from Boy Scout and Cub Scout troops. Fifty-two percent of all Scouts subscribe to *Boys' Life*. A subscription is not included in the membership fee, but troop leaders sell it to Scouts or their parents. Over the years there have been several attempts to offer *Boys' Life* on the nation's newsstands, but all have failed. Circulation is down to 1.5 million these days, and the magazine has been reduced in size, too, from the one in the memories of generations of American men. Gone are the old *Life*-size pages, replaced now by ones the size of *Time*'s—a change necessitated by escalating production and postal costs.

Pinned to the wall of the executive editor's cubicle is a list of proposed stories for an upcoming issue. The rundown could have been written in 1953: "How to Hit a Softball." "Repair a Dripping Faucet." "Pets: Rabies Is a Killer."

Recent editions are stacked on a table. The graphics are sharp, the color photographs of excellent quality. The articles are about junior golf champions and learning how to water-ski and building plastic models. The Think & Grin joke pages, featuring contributions from readers, are filled with little-boy humor. From Alan Smith, of Bedford, Texas: "*Smart:* 'What do you call an elephant that lives in Los Angeles?' *Alec:* 'An L. A. Phant.' "

There is little laughter in the *Boys' Life* office, though; it is spacious and sterile, and the editors, writers, and graphic designers toil away in their own work spaces. Chatter is at a minimum; as the staffers pass one another they will say hello, but mainly they stay at their desks and efficiently put together their monthly message to the boys of America.

Robert E. Hood, fifty-five, the editor of *Boys' Life*, joined the magazine in 1953. Since then, he has worked nowhere else; he has watched America change and has seen the number of names on his subscription list slip by more than one million.

"I've done what I can to keep up with the times," Hood says. "The look of the magazine has changed. Because of television, we had to go to big color pictures, since boys were used to the TV screen. And boys' attention spans have shortened. We used to publish articles that ran up to thirty-five hundred words. Now, though, if we go over fifteen hundred words, they won't stay with it."

Hood knows, however, that the reason for the magazine's decreasing readership has nothing to do with any editorial failings on his part. American boys in the 1980s are not the same as American boys in 1955, and yet Hood feels his responsibility is to put out a magazine that reflects the values of a quarter-century ago.

"You have to come back to the word *wholesome*," he says. "The parent is buying the magazine for the boy, and the parent has a certain idea of what he wants the boy to be like, even if he isn't really like that.

"So what do we write about? There is a heavy slant toward sports, adventure, hobbies, and Scouting. And the kid will still save his magazine, will still keep it in his room the same way boys did back in the Fifties.

"Remember," Hood says, "*Boys' Life* is probably the one piece of mail that boy will receive all month. It's very important to him."

When *Boys' Life* was founded in 1911, there were four other magazines aimed at the same young-male market, all of them successful: *St. Nicholas, Youth's Companion, American Boy*, and *Open Road*.

"Now we're the only one left," Hood says. "And if it wasn't for the Boy Scouts of America, *we* wouldn't survive."

His point is an obvious one. *Boys' Life* subscriptions are sold for $4.20 a year through Scout troops. And since the magazine is not considered an attractive sales medium by many national advertisers, it relies on those subscriptions for its continued existence. "Think about it," Hood says. "They can't advertise tobacco in our magazine. They can't advertise alcohol. They can't advertise cosmetics, the way they can in a magazine like *Seventeen*. They can't even advertise clothes very well. We never could attract the clothing business. Boys are just not fashion plates."

Indeed, Hood is convinced that in many such ways, American boys today are not all that different from the boys of twenty-five and fifty years ago. "If you're asking me whether the basic nature of the boy has changed, I'd have to say that the answer is no," he says. "They are still interested in collecting stamps, the same way they were in 1955. Why? I don't know, but it's consistent. Why do they continue to read that corny joke page, Think & Grin? I don't know, but they do. What is the most popular feature in the magazine? A True Story of Scouts in Action, just as it has always been."

Hood is not certain, but he feels that the remaining *Boys' Life* readers are the American boys who are managing to resist the salacious temptations of the present-day United States, and who desperately want something to cling to. "I can't promise you that none of our readers are also flipping through *Playboy* and smoking pot," he says. "But I know those things aren't as prevalent as among boys who don't read *Boys' Life*.

"The subject of sex I haven't dealt with at all. It's too big to handle. With our readers, we'd get hit with all kinds of hell if we started writing about sex or sex education. The repercussions from the churches and the parents . . . look, the editor of this magazine has an implied contract with the mother or the father of the boy who reads it. And to publish certain kinds of stories in the magazine would be to violate that contract, no matter how the boys would respond to them."

The staff members of *Boys' Life* agree. They feel that regardless of the negative influences in American society, there is a part of a boy that remains unchanged—a "pocket of innocence," as one editor puts it.

Dick Pryce, a fifty-five-year-old senior writer for the magazine, thinks that the mothers and fathers who subscribe to *Boys' Life* for their sons are yearning for an America that reminds them of the days when they were growing up.

"Many, many parents out there want that kind of life for their boys," Pryce says. "They want a childhood that is good and non-sexual and non-drug-related, and we've got it in this magazine. We provide it for them."

So *Boys' Life* publishes stories about magic tricks and camping trips and circus clowns. Its letters to the editor are addressed to a mythical burro named Pedro; its regular columns are about bicycling and fishing and nature and coin collecting. Its editors look around them and wonder about the magazine's—and their own—future.

Are the men and women who put out *Boys' Life* shouting optimistic messages into an empty canyon? It is not that easy simply to dismiss the magazine and its editorial philosophy as anachronisms; for one thing, the Reagan years promise to be a period during which Americans grasp for earlier values, and for another, *Boys' Life*'s circulation figures, while drastically reduced from what they were twenty years ago, are nevertheless far from unimpressive.

So even if the magazine is doomed to slide even further from its status as an American institution, a visitor to its offices can't help but be affected by the people who put it together. To use a corny phrase, they are doing good work; they may be unsure how much of an audience remains for their philosophy, but the very fact that they are attempting to provide a clean, upbeat, general-interest magazine for young boys—during a time when such a thing seems unwanted and out of date—should count for something.

It is also heartening to see what the magazine seems to have done for its staff members. They may be living in a time warp, but working at *Boys' Life* has kept the children in them alive, too. That's probably inevitable when your morning mail brings you a letter from a ten-year-old boy in Tacoma, Washington, who just wants to let you know that his favorite fish is the trout.

"There is no such thing as a mature man," one editor said to me, and the sentiment was offered without a trace of cynicism. His voice sounded almost hopeful as he said it.

Robert Hood gazes out his window. The Texas plains beyond are like a moonscape; Dallas is somewhat off in the distance, but from the offices of *Boys' Life* the rest of America seems very far away.

"The whole world is changing," he says. "A generation ago, when a boy was growing up, Mommy was home in the daytime, so she could be a den mother. But today? Mommy works. She's never home. So the Scouts can't get leaders."

He flips through some galley proofs for an upcoming edition. The proofs are piled neatly on his desk, and he seems preoccupied as he glances at them.

"Sometimes I'll get together with friends at night," Hood says. "And often there will be people there who I don't know, and I'll be introduced, and they'll ask me what I do. And I'll tell them that I'm the editor of *Boys' Life*. And they'll be amazed. They'll wonder how it can survive. They'll ask me, 'How can you continue to do this in the teeth of what goes on in the world these days?'"

Hood looks out his window once more.

"I ask myself the same questions," he says. "Are we coddling these boys? Are we spinning cotton webs of fantasy with an idealistic view of a life that just doesn't exist anymore?

"I don't know. I wish I knew what the answer was, but I just don't know."

Retirement Dinner

THE EVENT WAS a retirement dinner for a man who had spent forty years with the same company. A private dining room had been rented for the evening, and the man's colleagues from his office were in attendance. Speeches and toasts were planned, and a gift was to be presented. It was probably like a thousand other retirement dinners that were being held around the country that night, but this one felt a little different because the man who was retiring was my father.

I flew in for the dinner, but I was really not a part of it; a man's work is quite separate from his family, and the people in the room were as foreign to me as I was to them. To me most of them were names, overheard at the dinner table all my life as my father sat down to his meal after a day (one day in forty years) at the office; to them I was the kid in the framed photograph on my father's desk.

Names from a lifetime at the same job; it occurred to me, looking at the men and women in the room, that my father had worked for that same company since the time that Franklin Delano Roosevelt was president. Now my father was sixty-five, and the rules said that he must retire; looking at the faces of the men and women, I tried to recall the images of each of them that I had built up over the years at our family dinners.

My father was seated at a different table from me on this night; he appeared to be vaguely uncomfortable, and I could understand why. My mother was in the room, and my sister and brother; it was virtually the first time in my father's life that there had been any mix at all between his family and his work. The people at his office knew he had a family, and we at home knew he had a job, but that is as close as it ever came. And now we were all together.

A man's work, if he is any good at it, is as important to him as his family. That is a fact that the family must, of necessity, ignore, and if the man were ever confronted with it he would have to deny it. Such a delicate balance; the attention that must be paid to each detail of the job, and then the attention that must be paid to each detail of the family, with never the luxury of an overlap.

The speeches began, and, as I had expected, much of their content meant nothing to me. They were filled with references and in-jokes about things with which I was not familiar; I saw my father laughing and nodding his head in recognition as every speaker took his turn, and often the people in the room would roar with glee at something that drew a complete blank with me. And again it occurred to me: a man spends a life with you, but it is really only half a life; the other half belongs to a world you know nothing about.

The speeches were specific and not general; the men and women spoke of little matters that had happened over the course of the years, and each remembrance was like a small gift to my father, sitting and listening. None of us really change the world in our lifetimes, but we touch the people around us in ways that may last, and that is the real purpose of a retirement dinner like this one—to tell a man that those memories will remain, even though the rules say that he has to go away.

I found myself thinking about that—about how my father was going to feel the next morning, knowing that for the first time in his adult life he would not be driving to the building where the rest of these people would be reporting for work. The separation pains have to be just as strong as to the loss of a family member, and yet in the world of the American work force, a man is supposed to accept it and even embrace it. I tried not to think about it too hard.

When it was my father's turn to speak, his tone of voice had a different sound to me than the one I knew from around the house of my growing up; at first I thought that it came from the emotion of the evening, but then it struck me that this probably was not true; the voice I was hearing probably was the one he always used at the office, the one I had never heard.

During my father's speech a waiter came into the room with a message for another man from the company; the man went to a phone just outside the room. From my table, I could hear him talking. There was a problem at the plant, something about a malfunction in some water pipes. The man gave some hurried instructions into the phone, saying which levers to shut off and which plumbing company to call for night emergency service.

It was a call my father might have had to deal with on other nights, but on this night the unspoken rule was that he was no longer part of all that. The man put down the phone and came back into the dining room, and my father was still standing up, talking about things unfamiliar to me.

I thought about how little I really know about him. And I realized that it was not just me; we are a whole nation of sons who think they know their fathers, but who come to understand on a night like this that they are really only half of their fathers' lives. Work is a mysterious thing; many of us claim to hate it, but it takes a grip on us that is so fierce that it captures emotions and loyalties we never knew were there. The gift was presented, and then, his forty years of work at an end, my father went back to his home, and I went back to mine.

Voices in the Night

O N THE NIGHT she finally knew she was in trouble, Alix Lacy was near the end of her shift. It was almost two A.M.; she had been on the air for four hours. As usual, she was alone in the studios of KBCO-FM, in Boulder,

Colorado. She worked without an engineer; there was no one else in the building.

The light on her telephone was blinking again; like the phones in most sound studios, hers was wired to flash a light rather than to ring. She knew it was him. By this time, she thought she could feel it when he called.

She spoke into the microphone. In her soft, unthreatening voice—perfect for Boulder—she announced the next record. For all the listeners who were waiting, she put an album on one of the two studio turntables. The music played, and the telephone light kept blinking, and with the microphone turned off she started to sob.

It is a phenomenon of American late-night radio: the female voice wafting over the airwaves, comforting and stirring at the same time, offering a promise of companionship for listeners who are lonelier than they might want to admit. For women disc jockeys with the right kind of voice, the night shift offers professional opportunity; men want to hear women play them music when it is dark outside, and station managers all across the United States are aware of this.

Alix Lacy is one of the women who sought a career doing this kind of work. Lacy, twenty-seven, worked the ten P.M.–two A.M. shift at KBCO. Her voice was not overtly sexual; in the words of one of her bosses, she came across on the air "like the typical Boulder lady—beautiful, yet simple and wholesome."

Ray Skibitsky, who is the KBCO station manager, said, "I think some listeners have a fantasy in the back of their minds that the female late-night disc jockey is sitting there talking to them, and them alone."

There are no surveys that measure that type of attitude. But one thing Skibitsky and Dennis Constantine, KBCO's program director, were sure of: when they walked the streets of their town and stopped in at bars and restaurants, people would find out what they did for a living, and one of the first questions was always, "What does Alix Lacy look like?"

When the calls started, Alix Lacy barely noticed them. As a matter of routine, she gave out the station's telephone number during her show. The purpose was to allow listeners to call with requests.

At some point—she does not remember precisely when—she realized that someone was calling and hanging up on her, and that a pattern was beginning to emerge. Right when she would start her shift, the phone would blink, she would answer it—and the caller would hang up. This would occur several times. Nothing would happen until the middle of her shift. Then the caller would do it again; a flurry of calls. Things would get quiet. Then, near the end of the shift, another flurry. She would answer; the caller would hang up.

The KBCO studio is in an office complex that is deserted at night. Alix Lacy worked alone in a room on the second floor, up a flight of stairs. The only entrance or exit for her was the glass door at the top of the stairs. As the hang-up calls continued, night after night, she found herself, for the first time, thinking about that.

One night, after her shift, she left a note on the bulletin board: HEY, EVERYBODY, IS ANYONE ELSE GETTING HANG-UP CALLS A LOT? She asked the other on-air performers to initial the note if they were receiving similar harassment. No one else was.

The caller never said anything. Lacy told herself that "he'll burn out pretty soon. At least he'll say something." She realized she had already decided the caller was a man.

Station employees went on vacation, and Lacy was shifted to fill in for some of them. One week she was on the air from six A.M. until ten A.M. Just after six, the phone flashed. She answered it. The caller hung up. Then again in the middle of the shift. Then just before ten. Another week she was assigned to the two P.M.–six P.M. shift. The caller did it again.

She felt something funny happening inside of her. The caller was beginning to become a person to her—a man—and she was frightened of him. She asked her superiors to authorize a phone trace on the calls, which they did; but the telephone company said that, because of technical limitations, they were unable to isolate the calls.

Against her will, she began to feel her stomach knot every time she arrived at the studio for her show. The caller had never threatened her, had never said a word. Yet he was reaching her.

She began to refuse to answer the phone during the first hour of her shift. She would see the phone blink, and she would know it was the caller, and she would not pick it up. She would talk on the air and play the records, and all the time she would be looking at the light on the phone. Finally, she would make herself pick it up. Then the caller would hang up. Sometimes the caller would let the phone ring for an hour and a half before she picked it up; when he heard her voice, he would replace the receiver.

There were other callers, too, of course; KBCO listeners who wanted her to play records for them. When she looked at the lights blinking, she thought she could tell which callers were normal, and which was the one. "I kind of know what his calls feel like," she said. She realized that such a thing sounded absurd. "I know that something like this can run away with you, but once it's happening, knowing that doesn't help." She had become obsessed with the blinking light: "Every time it blinks, it's like a knife going into me again and again."

Her bosses knew that something was wrong. "I listened to her tapes, and it was clear that she was distracted," said Dennis Constantine. "It's fairly easy to tell when a disc jockey isn't paying attention to what she is doing."

To Alix Lacy's great consternation, the presence of the caller was taking over the hours she spent at the studio. "I feel as if he is trying to touch me," she said. "He's not touching me by saying anything; he's touching me by getting me to react to his consistency." Ray Skibitsky told her that by refusing to answer the phone when she thought it was the caller, she was only encouraging him; she was verifying to him that he was getting to her. She knew this was true; still, when she felt it was the caller on the other end, she could not pick up the receiver. She could only stare at the light and try to get through her show.

Her conviction grew stronger. She was fearful that the caller was going to come to the studio with a gun, shoot his way through the door, and come up the stairs to where she sat before the microphone. One afternoon she called Peter Rodman, a KBCO host and Boulder journalist. She told him about her fear about the gun; Rodman said, "Alix, the door is glass. If anyone wants to do anything, all he has to do is kick the door in. Why are you thinking about a gun?" Rodman's talk persuaded her to ask the station management to have a man answer her phone for one night; maybe if the caller heard a man's voice, he would stop.

Ray Skibitsky agreed to do it. He came to work with Lacy one evening; when the phone began to blink, he picked it up. Whoever was on the other end hung up. He sat with Lacy throughout her shift. Near the end, the caller hesitated before hanging up. The caller let out an exasperated sigh. It was definitely the sigh of a male. Then the line went dead.

The next two nights, he did not call. Alix Lacy was ecstatic. She thought she had been silly in the extreme for worrying about it. At the end of the week she worked an earlier shift than usual and her voice on KBCO was replaced that night by fellow disc jockey Rick Lofgren. Lofgren worked his shift. When he finished and walked out to his car in the parking lot, one tire had been slashed and all the air let out of another.

Both Lacy and her bosses knew they had a problem. It was not so much a horror story as something even more disturbing: the idea that someone with access to a medium of mass communication could become mentally trapped by one person in the audience with a will to disrupt her life. When Lacy had gone into radio work, she had liked the idea that, sitting behind a microphone in an isolated room, she could reach thousands upon thousands of strangers. Now one of the strangers was reaching her.

"I sensed there was a guy out there doing this," Ray Skibitsky said. "But what was there to do? He obviously gets his gratification and his kicks by doing this to her. But there have been no overt threats. When you look at it objectively, it's just an annoyance. If she could just ignore it, she would see that. But she can't."

When Lacy arrived at work one day, there was a letter addressed to her from Bob Greenlee, the owner of the station.

"I am not unaware of your concern over the belief you are being harassed by a telephone caller," the letter began.

Ray mentioned that he came in this week to answer the phones while you were here and he too senses that there may be someone on the phone who, for whatever reason, gets off on having you answer the phone and then hang up.

As you know, we have little control over sick minds who would do this to someone. Try as we might, it is impossible for us to do anything to trace or catch up with the person calling you. And even though you are upset by having to put up with this situation, I believe it is a continuing disruption of your work at this station and must now step into the matter. I have authorized Dennis Constantine to find a person to answer the phone for you during your shift for the next week. If, at the end of that time, you cannot pull yourself together and live in peace with yourself, the situation is not correctable by any further actions from us. I will need to address the matter of finding another person to do your work. . . . You are an excellent employee, we all like you very much, and hope you can find the inner strength it will require to get over the fear you have.

Alix Lacy decided to take a vacation. As of this writing, that is where she was.

She was sick at heart. She knew that when she returned to work, the caller would be waiting for her; and she knew she could not continue to live her life thinking about him. To her, the only logical solution seemed to be to leave Boulder, or to get out of radio work. It almost made her shake to think about it; the best thing about the vacation was that she did not have to see the phone blink at her every night. She had talked to Constantine and Skibitsky about a possible leave of absence, but she knew that was only delaying her final decision.

She had gotten some jobs around Boulder playing records at parties; it was a big step down from talking to the listeners of KBCO, but at least she could see her audience. She was also studying jazz piano; something was telling her that she had to come up with an alternative way to make a living.

"My voice . . ." she said. "I've always had a voice that people commented on. I just think it's a pleasant and conversational voice. I've never felt it necessary to project my sexuality through my voice. The last thing I ever wanted to do was provoke someone with it.

"I know that if I don't quit, I'm going to get fired. It's funny, isn't it. . . . I know how foolish all of this sounds, and I know that everyone thinks I should just ignore it. I feel like a fool for letting it get to me."

But it has. All over America, there are voices being sent out into the night; all the voices entering all the bedrooms and automobiles and bars. Implicit in the voices is a sense of power; the power to reach people, to touch their minds and change them, if only in small ways. Seldom do you hear about someone touching the voices back.

"There is this movie, *Forbidden Planet*," Lacy said. "It's about this invisible monster that attacks a spaceship. They try to find the monster, but it turns out that there's really nothing there. See, the monster was the subconscious mind of the scientist himself. I've been thinking about that a lot. Why am I creating this invisible monster in my life? And then I realize how far it's gone. I'm even questioning myself."

One thing bothers Lacy most of all, she said. It is a belief she holds—a belief that goes beyond all the rationalizing and all the intellectual understanding of what has happened.

"I'm not afraid, but I know I will meet him someday," she said, "I know how that sounds, but I've thought about it and I know it's true and there's nothing I can do about it. He's created this thing between us, and he's out there, and someday we'll meet."

What a Man, Part One

ALL LITTLE BOYS have idols when they are growing up: John Wayne, Roy Rogers, Mickey Mantle.

I was no different. I had a boyhood hero. But he wasn't a movie star, a cowboy, or a baseball player.

My hero was Ellsworth (Sonny) "What a Man" Wisecarver.

Ellsworth (Sonny) "What a Man" Wisecarver became a headline figure in the news during the 1940s when—starting at the age of fourteen—he eloped with two married women. Both women already had children. The newspapers tagged Wisecarver with the nickname "What a Man," and called him the "Boy Lothario." For a while every move he made was a national event.

The Sonny Wisecarver story began in 1944 when Sonny, fourteen, eloped with Mrs. Elaine Monfredi, twenty-one, of Compton, California, the mother of two.

The couple met as Sonny walked by Mrs. Monfredi's house after school one day.

"He whistled at me as I opened the door to look in the mailbox," Mrs. Monfredi recalled.

After that day, Sonny and Mrs. Monfredi saw each other after school and holidays. Her husband was a metal worker in a war plant.

In May of 1944, Sonny and Mrs. Monfredi eloped to Colorado and were married.

"Sonny is an ideal husband," Mrs. Monfredi said then. "He doesn't believe in hitting women."

Sonny said:

"Elaine's the kind of wife I want because she likes to have a good time without getting drunk."

Mrs. Monfredi's husband, James, when informed of the incident said, "She can choose between me and this boy. She can stay away or come back."

However, Sonny's mother, Mrs. Mildred Wisecarver, called the police and reported that Sonny had run off with Mrs. Monfredi. The mother said that "Sonny is a good boy but large for his age."

The couple was apprehended in Denver, and Mrs. Monfredi was charged with child stealing. The marriage was annulled.

But a year later—in November of 1945—Sonny eloped again, this time with Mrs. Eleanor Deveny, twenty-five, of Los Angeles, whose husband was serving in the Army in Japan. Mrs. Deveny had two children whom she left behind. Sonny was now sixteen years old.

"I thought I could be as happy with my husband as anyone could be," said Mrs. Deveny. "Then I met Sonny. It was love at first sight. I couldn't resist him. He's a perfect lover. I love him more than I do my own husband. He's the kind of guy every girl dreams about but very seldom finds."

It was at this point that the press gave Wisecarver the name Ellsworth (Sonny) "What a Man" Wisecarver—although some papers referred to the boy as "Woo Woo" Wisecarver. In headlines, where there was not room for the full name, Wisecarver was usually referred to simply as the "Boy Lothario."

Mrs. Deveny said that she had met Sonny when she had gone to visit an ailing friend at a house where Sonny was boarding. Sonny and Mrs. Deveny said that they were going out for a sandwich, and then fled the state together.

"I knew how old he was," Mrs. Deveny said, "but it didn't make any difference. He's more of a man at sixteen than a lot of men are at thirty-five."

She said that she was not concerned about her husband in the Army.

"I don't know if my husband knows, but I still love Sonny," she said. She cashed one of her husband's Army paychecks and gave the money to Sonny.

Police apprehended the two before they could get married, and Sonny was taken to an Oroville, California, jail cell.

Mrs. Deveny said that she would like to join Sonny in his cell. "If Sonny still wants me, I'd like to divorce my husband," she said.

Sonny, however, told jail guards that he "didn't give a hoot" if he ever saw Mrs. Deveny again.

Judge A. A. Scott of the California Superior Court—who had presided over the Sonny Wisecarver case at the time of his first elopement at fourteen—said, "He's done this before and he'll do it again."

Sonny's mother said that the first time her son had run away with a married woman she had thought that he had been seduced, but now she was convinced that Sonny was the aggressor in his romantic adventures.

The judge asked Sonny's mother to sign a complaint against Mrs. Deveny for contributing to the delinquency of a minor.

In court, Sonny's mother said, "I can't go through life signing complaints against girls who run away with my son."

"Don't do it, Mother," Sonny whispered.

But she signed the complaint anyway. Sonny was charged with "leading or in danger of leading an idle, dissolute, lewd, or immoral life," and of being "persistently and habitually beyond the control of his parents." He was sentenced to a term in a youth detention camp.

The judge said, "If Ellsworth gets into any more of these jams, he will be the most sought-after man in the United States, especially if these floozies keep making lurid statements to the press."

"Why can't I live my own life, without people always telling me what to do?" Sonny said.

He went to the youth detention camp, but escaped in 1948 because he wasn't allowed to smoke.

When news of his escape was reported, the Los Angeles Police Department was besieged with telephone calls from women wanting to know if Sonny was still at large.

He found work as a busboy and a baby-sitter, and sold magazines door-to-door in the Northwest, using the name "Johnny Donovan." At one point he tried to join the Army, but was rejected because of his juvenile delinquency record.

Meanwhile, Mrs. Deveny's husband, Corporal John Deveny, read the news about his wife and Sonny in the Japan edition of *Stars and Stripes*, the Armed Forces newspaper. He said he was "shocked." He came back to the United States and said, "It's a husband's duty to stand by his wife. I'm going to stand by her."

Mrs. Deveny said that she would probably resume her marriage, "because John has been sport enough to forgive me."

In 1947, at the age of seventeen, Sonny Wisecarver married Betty Zoe Roeber, also seventeen, of Las Vegas, Nevada. Miss Roeber had been an usherette in a Las Vegas movie theater, and had met Sonny while showing him to a seat.

"I've been through a lot, and I don't want my wife to suffer any embarrassment from my past," Sonny said. "If folks will only forget the mistakes I made as a kid, now that I'm really and honestly married, I'll prove that all this talk about me is untrue. I just want to live a normal married life with Betty."

The two set up housekeeping in a trailer home. But a year later, Betty left Sonny, saying that he "couldn't make a home for me."

Ellsworth (Sonny) "What a Man" Wisecarver hopped a freight train for Salt Lake City to look for a job.

What a Man, Part Two

ELLSWORTH (SONNY) "What a Man" Wisecarver, the fourteen-year-old Boy Lothario of the 1940s who became a national headline figure by eloping with two married women, today is a bus driver in Las Vegas, and describes himself as "just an average forty-eight-year-old man with a little potbelly."

Wisecarver—who as a teenager became a heartthrob for the women of America because of his reputed prowess as a lover— says that women do not even give him a second glance today.

"That whole thing was just a crock," Wisecarver says. "Just a crock."

Wisecarver—who says that he always detested the "What a Man" and "Woo Woo" nicknames given to him by the press— said that when he began eloping with married women at the age of fourteen, he was merely a victim of circumstances.

"Opportunity just presents itself, and you answer it," he said. "It was World War Two. All the husbands were gone. The women wanted attention. I gave it to them. Wouldn't you take advantage of the same circumstances?"

He said that his enormous fame in the Forties was more a

result of the newspapers' needing bright feature stories to write than of any real power over women held by him.

"The papers were full of stories about the war," Wisecarver said. "They needed to write something different. So the newspaper writers heard about me, and they wrote a lot of crap."

Of the two married women he eloped with—Mrs. Elaine Monfredi, twenty-one, whom he wed when he was fourteen, and Mrs. Eleanor Deveny, twenty-five, whom he ran away with when he was sixteen—Wisecarver said:

"I never hear from them anymore. I don't know what happened to either of them."

Wisecarver's name dropped out of the news in the late 1940s, after he, at age seventeen, had married a seventeen-year-old usherette in Las Vegas. The papers reported the marriage, and then a year and a half later, reported that the girl had left Sonny, and that Sonny had hopped a freight train heading for Salt Lake City.

"We got back together after that, but by that time the newspapers had forgotten about me," Wisecarver said. "Our marriage lasted for twenty-three years. Then we were divorced."

Wisecarver is married again. He and his wife, Elaine, thirty, have a nineteen-month-old son, Michael.

"I drive a tour bus for Transportation Unlimited here in Las Vegas," Wisecarver said. "I met my present wife on the job. She was a hostess on the bus company's nightclub tour. She used to ride with me."

Asked to explain his reputation as a young Romeo, Wisecarver said:

"I have no idea. All it was was luck, that's all. Women ride my bus every day now and don't even give me a second glance.

"I think the women fell for Sonny because he is a very nice person," his wife said. "Other than being a very nice person, I don't think there's anything. I mean, I don't think he has any special magnetism or anything like that. Women do like a very nice person with an honest and open personality. That's an admirable quality in any person."

Wisecarver is devoted to his seventy-seven-year-old mother—who, during the days when he was eloping with older married women, pleaded in tears to a judge, "I can't go through life signing complaints against girls who run away with my son."

"My mother still lives in California," Wisecarver said. "She's forgiven me. She loves me. That's a woman's place in life, isn't it?"

Reminded that a judge once warned, "If Ellsworth gets into any more of these jams, he will be the most sought-after man in America," Wisecarver said:

"It never happened. I wear a bus driver's uniform with the company emblem, but my name's not on display in the bus, so no one ever notices me. I drive tours to Hoover Dam, to Death Valley, to the Grand Canyon, sometimes to Disneyland.

"I'm just an average run-of-the-mill bus driver who goes home to his family. We live in Las Vegas, but we never go to the Strip. This town is only a swinging town for the little old ladies with nickels. An old people's Disneyland is all it is. People who live here don't go out. I try to raise my little boy, make my house payments, and just get by."

Asked why he decided to run away with married women when he was such a young boy, Wisecarver said:

"Oh, every boy does that."

Asked if he had a good time back when he was the Boy Lothario, he said:

"I suppose I had a good time. Wouldn't you?"

And then Ellsworth (Sonny) "What a Man" Wisecarver laughed out loud.

Classroom Lesson

Phoenix, Arizona—It was a drizzly Monday morning, and Don Stanley, thirty-five, was teaching his class of twenty-seven fifth-graders in Room 30 of the Hopi Elementary School on Lafayette Boulevard.

The day was not extraordinary; just another March morning in Arizona. I was sitting in the back of the classroom, at a desk designed for the ten-year-olds who filled Room 30. Just watching; a normal day in a normal American school.

Stanley, wearing casual slacks and a sweater, was running the boys and girls through math exercises. He would call them to the blackboard one by one; he would set up a multiplication problem, and then have the children work out the solution.

"Why did you place the decimal point there?" Stanley would ask, and a little girl would reply, "Because it belongs there."

Most adults—if they aren't teachers or school administrators—never see the inside of an elementary school classroom while it is in session. We are used to getting our news of schools from the papers: teachers' strikes, and vandalism, and problems with reading scores. Life in an elementary school becomes blurred together with other topical things that pass in and out of our consciousness.

Which is why this morning spent in Room 30 was proving so interesting to me. There would be no news made here today; no conflict, no passion, no violence. And yet what was going on was so important; here in Room 30, as in hundreds of thousands of other classrooms around the United States, these children were being formed into what they will be when they suddenly turn into the next generation of fully grown American citizens.

I watched Don Stanley with the children. Teachers are paid absurdly low salaries, compared with what people in business and industry receive as compensation. But as I watched Stanley going from desk to desk, I was reminded that his job—and the jobs of other elementary school teachers around the nation—are so much more important than the things the rest of us do in the name of commerce.

He stopped to help a girl with a word she was stumbling over in a textbook. He explained to a boy why the multiplication sum he had just completed was wrong. He bent over a desk to answer a question another girl had for him.

It must be easy not to care. For a teacher, usually there is no one looking over your shoulder, and especially in an elementary school, the people you're in contact with every day are too young to really know whether you're doing a good job or a bad one.

If you're not putting out, they won't know; they have no frame of reference.

And that is the awesome thing about the American educational system. As easy as it is to say that children's characters are shaped at home and not at school, that's probably incorrect. Certainly children spend so many hours at school that the classroom experience becomes the central one in their lives. A bad home environment can damage a child forever, but an indifferent school environment can bring results that are every bit as ominous.

What can a child pick up if the classroom environment is good? That it's important to be curious. That making an effort to be correct is better than being sloppy and letting yourself be wrong. That progress is one of life's most important elements, and that if you let yourself stay in the same place you were yesterday, your vistas will never change.

Those attitudes are almost as important as the specific information a teacher imparts. When you're ten years old, if your teacher lets you know that he or she cares that you're learning, cares that your reading is becoming more sophisticated, cares that you are trying to master complicated mathematical concepts—if those things happen—then you're going to be a ten-year-old who stands a much better chance of being a successful and happy twenty-five-year-old and thirty-year-old and forty-year-old.

That's what I was thinking about in Room 30—how parents blithely turn their boys and girls over to strangers who will have such a monumental effect on their lives. Even the most concerned parent can have very little control over what goes on in his child's classroom—and yet that is where much of what the man or woman that child grows up to be is determined.

It's such a moving responsibility that teachers have—and it's made all the more so when you realize that they are among the least-honored groups of Americans. We expect them to be there, and we give our children to them, and then we go about our own daily lives—seldom thinking about what they mean in regard to what the people of this country, and ultimately the country itself, will become.

So I sat in Room 30 of the Hopi Elementary School. Don

Stanley announced that it was "free reading time," and the boys and girls reached into their desks to pull out the books they wanted to spend time with.

They sat silently in their chairs and opened the books to the pages where they'd stopped last time around. Don Stanley stood at the front of the class, next to the blackboard, and he looked out at the twenty-seven children. I think there was pride in his eyes. That's what I think.

We Interrupt
This Program . . .

IF YOU ARE too young to remember it, or too old to have been a part of it, there is no explaining. Cruising the streets of the hometown in 1964, accompanied by the voices of the Beatles coming from the car radio, it was a time when anything seemed possible. This was during the days when a new Beatles record would be released every six weeks or so; each one was like a gift, a new chorus for the sound track of our lives.

We were all indestructible. I remember speeding down a highway through a snowstorm with some friends, late at night; the car skidded and swerved, and suddenly we were crashing through a guardrail and the car was tumbling down a gulley. When it came to a rest, we looked around at one another; there we were, in our high school letter jackets, unhurt, and the radio was still blaring and there were the Beatles singing "I Want to Hold Your Hand." And we stood in the snow, laughing; young and new and invincible, laughing.

They made us happy. That's a simple thought, and it's hard to conceive of in these times when everyone is so sophisticated about the machinations of the music industry. But we didn't know about the music industry then. We weren't even buying albums yet. Those voices coming from the car radio, though, didn't need any translating. They were narrating the happiest times of our lives.

If you ever drove by a lake on a warm summer night, with the sounds of "Things We Said Today" filling the car; if you ever parked with your high school date as "Please, Please Me" came out of the radio; if you ever headed home from your part-time job to the strains of "A Hard Day's Night"; then all the words that are being written and spoken about John Lennon's death are superfluous. You don't need to hear. You know.

That's what struck me Monday night. The television was on, and the newsmen were trying to explain the murder in stiff and mundane words. A few feet away, in the kitchen, a radio was playing; the station had already started to broadcast Lennon's songs, and so as the TV newsmen announced the details of the shooting, there was John Lennon's voice, singing "A Day in the Life" and "I Am the Walrus."

And the Beatles music coming from the kitchen made the words on the news seem . . . stupid. Made them seem stupid in the way that Beatles music always made more traditional forms of communication seem naive and incomplete and uncomprehending. Part of that had to be illusion, of course, but magic is always largely illusion.

The impressive thing is that the magic never went away. Within an hour of the news of Lennon's death, my phone at home started ringing; I was hearing from friends I hadn't spoken to in years. And when I started to make my own calls, I discovered that everyone was having the same thing happen: All over the country, men and women were reaching out to hear familiar voices, to touch friends in the aftermath of the news.

Maybe the men and women hadn't given more than a passing thought to Lennon in years. That's not what mattered. The important thing is that, grown-ups now, living in condominiums and town houses, raising families, surviving busted marriages, seeking corporate successes, realizing career failures, they were finding themselves drawn together again by the idea of the Beatles.

We are a generation that has never been very enthusiastic about the idea of growing up, anyway; we hang onto the memory of our younger years with a ferocity that surprises people older than us, and puzzles people younger than us. And it is hard to explain; certainly the experiences we had during the years in which we came to maturity are no more or less deserving of preservation than similar time periods lived through by those who came before us.

One of the manifestations of this attitude has been a recurrent cry that the Beatles reunite, as if by appearing onstage together again, they could somehow give us back the time that we have lost forever. The Beatles themselves—especially John Lennon— realized the folly of this; perhaps one of the most valuable things they did was to refuse to be a part of that. For by attempting to recapture something that belonged to the past, they would have run the very real risk of ruining even the memory.

No, it is good that when we think of the Beatles now, it will be in terms not of some multimillion-dollar reunion concert in the Eighties, but of four young men who were as fresh, as cocky, as exuberant, and as innocent to life's darker moments as we were when we and they were fortunate enough to share the planet.

Our thoughts should not be of a December night in 1980, when voices on the news told us of a shooting in New York. We have been through similar nights before, when the voices were telling us of the loss of other men who were important to us, and our memories are filled to overflowing with the details of such tragedies.

Besides, those are the thoughts of grown-ups, and there are enough of those to last us a lifetime. Better to think of summer nights with "Sgt. Pepper" coming out of the car radio, and life stretching out ahead like the most perfect and level two-lane highway ever built.

Those nights are what John Lennon and his friends gave us. It was something very simple, and yet something that no politician, no author, no artist was ever quite able to do. The Beatles made us happy. God, it was something.

Captain of His Ship

Sometimes, when you're not looking for anything, something comes up and strikes you as clear as daybreak. I had been traveling by bus through corn-and-soybean country for several days; my reasons were personal ones, and I had found what I was looking for, and now I was on my way back to Chicago.

I seldom ride interstate buses, but these few days had been enough to convince me that there is little romance to them. As a traveler who usually finds himself in airports, I had become numbed by this week's endless hours in dank, musty buses, heading slowly between places that no other form of public transportation serves.

My fellow passengers were not inflation-fighters; they were on the buses because buses are the lowest common denominator of American transportation. There is nothing cheaper; the low price was the only reason that the people were aboard. They were the bottom social stratum of the country's travelers; they needed to get someplace, and the bus was all they could afford.

Now I was on the last leg of my journey; the Trailways bus I was on had started the trip in St. Louis, and was on a nine-hour run through Missouri and Illinois. Several hours into the ride, I began to notice something.

It was the driver. He was a young man with a mustache and sideburns; I would have to guess he was in his early thirties. What struck me was the manner of crispness and precision he brought to his job. He was dressed neatly, and he addressed his passengers politely, and at the rest stops he timed his schedule exactly with his wristwatch.

When a passenger approached him with a question along the

way, the driver did not act as if he were annoyed; he took time to answer in a friendly, informed way. It was, frankly, a lousy route; instead of heading directly to Chicago, the schedule called for him to stop at any number of tiny towns along the way: Clinton, Fullerton, Farmer City, Gibson.

Usually there was no bus station in these cities; the driver would pull the coach into a gas station parking lot, or stop in front of a restaurant. One person might get off, or two might get on. It hardly seemed worth his time to be making the detours to serve so few passengers.

And yet he carried out his job with class. He welcomed each passenger to the bus; hurried out the door to assist with baggage; made a fresh count of travelers for his logbook at every stop. I got the impression that he was memorizing all of our faces; we might be with him only for one gray autumn day, but we were his passengers and he seemed to be making an effort to take a personal interest in that.

He was just a long-haul bus driver heading up some forgotten route in the middle of the country, but for his attitude, this might have been a Boeing 747 on its way to Paris. I found myself wondering what struck me so oddly about this man, and in a second the realization came. This attitude of his—this pride in the work he was doing—was the very thing we have for so long been told has vanished from the American work force.

Had the driver taken a lazy and slovenly approach, no one would have ever known; the passengers on an interstate bus aren't the kind of people who have the pull to make trouble. They have no alternative; if they don't like the bus, there's no cheaper way for them to go. Certainly there was no prestige built into the driver's work. Trailways isn't even the big name in long-haul buses; Greyhound is.

But on this ride, it was as if the idea of not doing his job well had never crossed the driver's mind. And a funny thing was happening; because the driver found dignity in his own work, he instilled his load of passengers with a small feeling of dignity, too. Oh, they knew they were riding on an uncomfortable bus with men and women who probably couldn't afford any other means of transportation; but because the driver had pride, the passengers seemed to feel a little better, too.

At one toll booth the driver paid the attendant, then leaned out the window to say something. I listened. The driver had seen a car stalled on the side of the highway several miles back, and was advising the toll-booth man to telephone the state police to inform them that there was a traveler in trouble. I hadn't noticed the stalled car, but the driver had, and he obviously considered this part of his job.

When we pulled into the station in Chicago's Loop, the driver stood at the bottom of the steps leading out of the bus, helping each passenger depart, saying goodbye to each of us. He stayed there until the bus was empty.

It was something to see. Most of the passengers had no one to greet them; they wandered out of the station one by one. In a bus station there is none of that sense of drama you're always getting at a big airport; here the feeling was not of an adventure beginning, but of dreary, uneventful life continuing.

And yet, because of his attitude—the way he feels about his work—the driver had, for a few hours, made things different. When I arrived home, I realized something inexcusable: for all the driver's impressiveness, I hadn't even bothered to learn his name. So I called the Trailways dispatcher and found out. It is Ted Litt.

Paper Boy

WHEN I WAS twelve, maybe thirteen, I would ride the bus downtown with my best friend, Jack Roth, and we would kill the day just walking around the stores. When darkness came we would wait for the bus to take us home. Standing on Broad Street just east of High, we would look over at the big building across the street from the State-house. It was the building that was the home of the *Columbus Dispatch*. Atop the building was a red neon sign that spelled the paper's name out in Old English script, and beneath the logo was the slogan: OHIO'S GREATEST HOME NEWSPAPER.

We would stand there, Saturday dusk after Saturday dusk, and we would stare up at the sign, blazing red in the sky, and it would seem that there was nothing more powerful in all this world than the *Columbus Dispatch*.

I've been thinking about that lately because, with the seemingly endless stories of great newspapers wheezing and dying, I figure it is unlikely that young boys and girls stand on corners in awe of newspaper buildings anymore.

Which is probably not all that unhealthy; there was a time when newspapers were thought of as so all-potent that nothing on earth could stand in their way. They were burly and arrogant and at times despotic; they ruled their cities, and to cross the publisher or editor of the town's leading newspaper was akin to political suicide. Newspapers were in fact what governments were supposed to be in theory: the rulers of their constituents, the monarchs of their municipalities.

So it is probably good, in a way, that such a thing is disappearing. But I find it mostly melancholy; I am a newspaperman, I have been a newspaperman since I was sixteen years old, and I sense the passing of an era. Newspapers will surely survive, in one form or another. But many newspapers will die—many already have—and even the ones that live are unlikely to cause young boys to stand on the street corner in reverie.

When the *Washington Star* was going down, Mary McGrory, the paper's superlative columnist, complained that people often stopped her as she went about her rounds and said, "And how is the *Star* doing?" It made her feel awful; the question was asked as one might ask about a relative with a terrible and incurable disease. More than anything else, that question made her understand how things were changing. In a past that seems shockingly recent, such a question might have sounded absurd. Newspapers occasionally died before, yes; but never did they seem so generically weak, so fragile; never did they seem worthy of the public's worried concern.

Newspapers have been hated, and they have survived that; newspapers have been idealized, and they have survived that. But never before have newspapers been patronized, and even pitied. It is happening now, in each town where a great newspaper faces death. Speeches are made on city-council floors, and statements are read by concerned mayors, and eulogies are delivered by television anchormen to audiences the newspapers would love to have. It used to be the newspapers that told the councilmen and the mayors and the television reporters what the agenda was. Everything seems to be turning around.

There is a temptation to go overboard in telling what it feels like to walk into a newspaper's city room. The fact of the matter is, there is no way to go overboard. When I first entered a city room it was the most intoxicating feeling I had ever experienced, and that feeling stays with me to this day.

Much of the sensory onslaught has changed in this electronic age; but twenty years ago, to hear the clatter of a floorful of typewriters, and smell the musk from the pastepots, and hear the reporters yelling "Boy!" as they summoned the copykids to pick up their stories—to wander into that atmosphere for the first time was to know, instantly, what you wanted to do for the rest of your life.

Forget literature; immortality lay in a front-page by-line about a four-car fatal on I-70. In the city room, suddenly nothing seemed smalltown anymore; if you went out and saw something, and then came back and wrote it up, everyone you knew—all of your neighbors, all of your family, all of your friends—would know about it in the morning, too. If you hadn't seen it, no one would know it had happened; because you were there, everyone would know.

There was no feeling in the world like finishing your last paragraph on deadline and seeing the sheet of yellow paper move from city editor to copy editor to slot man to pneumatic tube—and then, forty-five minutes later, while the rest of the city slept, to see the first papers come up with that story on Page One, and your name riding atop it.

It was a guarantee of eternal adolescence; the world was rein-
vented each day, each morning you were going to see something
you had never seen before . . . and then you were going to get
paid to tell people about it. And the people were out there; that
was a given, they needed you, they had always needed their
newspaper, they were waiting for that paper boy to show up
with their daily news. You sat in the city room and you could
almost sense those people waiting for that thump on the front
stoop, the sound that announced that you and your newspaper
had arrived again.

There was no real hint that the audience was not always going
to be there. Television was a presence, true, but it seemed not
to threaten the local morning and afternoon papers. In the city
room, you sensed that over at the TV stations they were waiting
for that thump at their front door, too, to learn what the news
really was. All through the decade of the 1960s, that was the
case; television was everywhere, but it was taking its cues from
the papers.

It was during the 1970s that this changed. Working in the city
room, you did not notice it right away. You were too busy fash-
ioning the day's facts into newspaper stories; that consumed so
much of your time that it did not occur to you that, just maybe,
people weren't reading the front page the same way they used
to. They didn't particularly like to read, and now they didn't
have to. Television had become the front page, and if you were
candid with yourself, you had to admit that television was pretty
good at it. This skill you were so proud of—this boiling of ac-
cidents and local disasters into swallowable stories—was easily
transferable to the television screen. And those people who were
waiting for that thump at the front door . . . now they were
waiting for the anchormen whose names they knew instantly. A
by-line suddenly seemed like something out of the Gay Nineties.

If you were lucky, your publishers and editors were anticipating what was going on, and were changing your newspaper
into something it had never been before. They were conceding
the front page to television, and concentrating on special sections
and features and columns. If you were unlucky, your publishers
and editors were pretending that nothing had changed, and the

product you were putting out every day was being delivered to an audience that, maybe without even knowing it, felt that it was somehow quaint in the 1980s. The delivery process itself—the printing of thousands of papers, each to be hand-delivered or peddled individually—seemed ominous in an age of electronic efficiency and economic peril. In any event, the newspaper you dreamed of as a kid—the newspaper that was your town's major way of finding out what happened yesterday—was gone forever. You could pretend it was still the same, but there were days when you noticed that even you didn't read most of the front-page stories past the first two paragraphs. And you were a newspaperman.

When newspaper reporters gather these days, it is this kind of thing they talk about. They have all had the experience: they have run around on a story all day, hurried back to the office, gone over their notes, crafted the information into a smooth and concise report. And they have gone to bed knowing that, by the time the readers reach out the front door for their papers in the morning, all of the information will seem very old. The readers will have heard all about it on the late-night TV news before going to sleep. As often as not, the newspaper reporters will have watched the same broadcasts.

The common response among most of us is to try to do what we do better or in a different way than the television reporters. Give the story a different twist, or a literary flair that can't be carried off on TV. Sometimes this works; many newspapers prosper. But they aren't what they were before. They aren't their communities' principal source for news—and that is what made us go into newspaper work in the first place. If someone had told us that we were going to be working for a sort of daily magazine published on newsprint, we probably would have said no thanks.

I have hedged my bets. I work for this magazine, and I also work for "ABC News Nightline," a television program whose technological reach astounds me each time I come in touch with it.

But I am different from the other people who work for *Esquire*, and I am different from the other people who work for ABC.

I am different because I am a newspaperman; not a former newspaperman, but a newspaperman who walks into a city room every morning of his life. My home base is the *Chicago Tribune*, and I am a little embarrassed to admit that the feeling I get in that city room is the same I got so many years ago, when I was first allowed to feel whatever it is in the air of a newspaper office.

In many ways I am afraid to leave it; all the signs tell all of us that newspaper work is like manufacturing buggies in the days when automobiles first took to the streets, but when you are in love with something, you cannot walk away. My magazine colleagues deal with proofs for glossy pages as part of their daily routine; my television colleagues watch the news being fed to New York from satellite points around the world. I wait for the first edition to come up, just as I did when I was sixteen years old.

Some people dream of writing great works of literature; some people dream of stirring people's imaginations with the beauty and flow of their prose.

For some of us, though, for some reason, the goal was considerably less grand. All we wanted to do was go out every day and see something new, and then write what we saw into stories that people would read in their newspapers the next morning. Everything else was extra.

And the funny thing is, the dream goes on. In today's mail I received a letter from a young man with whose work I am familiar. He has a job in a fairly secure part of the publishing industry. In his letter, though, he told me that he wanted desperately to be a newspaperman. He named the paper to which he is applying; it is a newspaper that—if I know anything about this business—will be dead within two years.

But I wrote him the letter of recommendation; I said that he is a fine young talent, and that he will do good work if only he is given a chance. He is not an obtuse person; he must realize that there is no certain future in what he is pursuing. But something inside him makes him want to do it, and I did not feel like talking him out of it. I just wrote the letter and mailed it off, and I hope he gets the job.

So it is not the best feeling when we see what is happening in the newspaper community. We are supposed to be fairly glib when it comes to any other subject—newspapermen, it is said, can write about cats or kings—but we stumble around when we try to explain what all of this is doing to us.

For me it's fairly simple. I have my limitations, but I have the ability to do something that I doubt Saul Bellow or John Updike can do. Sitting on the rewrite bank, I can give you fifteen inches about a four-alarm fire on a twenty-minute deadline. It may not count for anything, but I can do it.

Michael Testifies

IT BEGINS WITH a boy running downstairs to buy ice cream on a muggy August night. This is how it ends:

Early afternoon Monday. Michael McCullough, sixteen, is wheeled into a second-floor dayroom on Ward B-23, Oak Forest Hospital. The orderlies are quick as they steer Michael's bed; within seconds, the boy is attached to a blue-and-white Bennett Respiration Unit, Model A-1. A long white tube is stretched from the machine over toward Michael's neck. A green nozzle is inserted into Michael's trachea. The machine, replacing a portable device Michael has worn in the hallway, is switched on; the noise begins. A steady pounding, once every four seconds. The oxygen, stored in a large green tank behind the respirator, is being pumped into Michael's system. It is the only way he can breathe.

The judge, Wayne W. Olson of the Cook County Circuit Court, looks briefly at Michael. Michael cannot look back; his head rests on a white pillow, and his eyes are directed toward the ceiling. He is paralyzed from the neck down.

"All right," Judge Olson says. "Please bring the jury in."

The jurors, who have come by bus from Chicago's Criminal Courts building, begin to file in and to find their places in plastic chairs that have been set up in the hospital room. When they have settled, a gavel sounds; court is in session. There is silence in the room, save for the ceaseless, once-every-four-second thump of the machine that is keeping Michael McCullough alive.

He is not expected to live very much longer. Dr. Joseph Woo, who has treated Michael at the hospital, has told Judge Olson that the chances are "very slim" that Michael will ever move his limbs again; that the prognosis for Michael's life expectancy is "very poor"; that in all likelihood Michael will "very slowly waste away."

But on Monday, Michael is not wasting away. On Monday, even though he cannot speak and he cannot move, Michael is trying to find justice for the horrible thing that happened to him last summer. Which is why the extraordinary courtroom session is being held inside the walls of Oak Forest Hospital.

Briefly, this is the background:

Michael, who lived in one of the high-rise Robert Taylor Homes public housing buildings at 4946 South State, was watching television around 8:30 P.M. last August 17. He told his mother that he wanted to go downstairs and buy some ice cream from the Good Humor man. He decided not to take the elevator; instead, he began to run down one of the building's staircases.

When he got to the ninth floor, he was stopped by two young men. They tried to rob Michael. He resisted. One of the boys pulled a gun and shot Michael in the face. The bullet lodged in one of his vertebrae, paralyzing him below the neck. Since that evening, Michael has not been able to move, has not been able to breathe without the respirator, has not been able to speak a word above the level of a hissing, barely audible whisper.

But on Monday Michael was going to talk.

The two young men accused of shooting Michael—David Bracey, eighteen, and Tony Gathings, also known as Tony Jackson, seventeen—both of whom live in Michael's building, sit at a makeshift defense table in the hospital room. They stare at Michael curiously, as if they are watching a TV program. Their faces show no other expression. Michael's face is propped at an angle where he cannot look back at them.

Judge Olson swears in Dr. Patricia Scherer, an associate professor at Northwestern University who specializes in speech disorders. Judge Olson explains that Dr. Scherer will act as Michael's interpreter. Dr. Scherer walks over to Michael's bed, and leans close to his face. A team of doctors and nurses stands nearby, ready to come to Michael's assistance if he needs them.

George Pappas, an assistant state's attorney who is prosecuting the two young men charged with the attempted murder of Michael, stands across the room and says in a very loud voice, "Michael, I want you to tell the ladies and gentlemen of the jury and everyone here your first and last name."

Michael moves his lips. No words come out.

Dr. Scherer, hovering over him, watches. She turns to the jury and says, "Michael McCullough."

"Michael, how old are you?" Pappas asks.

The lips move again. Dr. Scherer watches again.

"Sixteen," Dr. Scherer says.

Pappas asks, "Is your address 4947 South State?"

Michael's lips move rapidly. Dr. Scherer looks at the motion, and then responds:

"He says no. He says that he lives at 4946 South State."

Pappas and his co-prosecutor, George Lynch, exchange short smiles. Michael has just let the jury know that his mind is still sharp enough to allow him to be a credible witness. Now Pappas begins to get into the meat of the testimony.

Pappas leads into the night of the shooting. He establishes that Michael was on his way to the Good Humor man.

"After you left your apartment on the twelfth floor, how did you begin to go downstairs?" Pappas asks.

Michael's lips move.

"I walked," Dr. Scherer answers for him.

Pappas: "What happened on the ninth-floor landing?"

Michael: "Two boys stopped me."

Pappas: "Two boys you knew from before?"

Michael: "Yes."

Pappas: "Can you identify those two boys?"

Michael: "David Bracey and Tony Jackson."

Pappas: "What did they say to you?"

Michael: "I don't remember exactly."

Pappas: "Well, what happened next?"
Michael: "David Bracey grabbed me around the neck."
Pappas: "Where was David Bracey standing?"
Michael: "Behind me."
Pappas: "And where was Tony Jackson standing?"
Michael: "In front of me."

It is becoming very difficult for Michael to do even this much moving of his mouth. The discomfort shows in his eyes. The doctors and nurses bend over him to see if he wants to stop. But he is not finished with what he has to say. The two defendants stare over at the hospital bed.

"What happened next?" Pappas asks.

"Tony Jackson tried to get in my pockets," Michael's lips say.
Pappas: "And what were you doing?"
Michael: "Holding my pockets."
Pappas: "Did you see a gun?"
Michael: "Yes."
Pappas: "Who had the gun?"
Michael: "Tony Jackson."
Pappas: "What did he do with the gun?"
Michael: "He shot me."

The respirator thumps away. There is no other sound. Pappas hesitates before asking his next question, then manages to continue.

"Before he shot you, did he say anything?" Pappas asks.

Michael's mouth begins to move uncontrollably, wildly. Dr. Scherer attempts to comfort him.

"Just relax, Michael," she says.

Pappas repeats his question. Dr. Scherer moves her face closer to Michael's.

"He says that Tony said, 'I ought to shoot you,' " Dr. Scherer says.
Pappas: "After that did he pull the trigger?"
Michael: "It was already cocked."
Pappas: "Where did he shoot you?"
Michael: "In the jaw."
Pappas: "What happened next?"
Michael: "I fell to the ground."
Pappas: "What did Tony Jackson and David Bracey do then?"

Michael: "They ran."

Pappas: "No further questions."

Outside the windows of the hospital room, the February wind blows the empty limbs of trees. A brightly painted red fire escape and a green delivery truck are the only flashes of color in the area.

Sherwood L. Levin, the attorney for the two defendants, begins to question Michael in detail, making him go over the story one more time, in greater length. Michael is exhausted; at one point he has to stop and rest for fifteen minutes, but he goes on. He does not waver in his testimony.

Levin says, "To the best of your knowledge, Michael, did you know that the gun was loaded?"

The respirator pounds away. Michael moves his lips.

"I was shot," Dr. Scherer says for him.

More pounding. More moving of Michael's lips.

"It must have been loaded," Dr. Scherer says for him.

Michael's mother, Bernice, watches her son, motionless beneath his white hospital sheet. She has other children; she knows that Michael probably will not live; she also knows that, because of Michael's testimony, her other children may be threatened, may be in danger. She has said that Michael is the quietest of her children, and that he has few friends; before the shooting, his greatest joys had been to play solitary games of basketball, and to watch television alone. This is a proud moment for her, watching her paralyzed son stand up for himself.

There is more cross-examination, more questions from both sides.

"He is very tired," Dr. Scherer pleads.

But Michael goes on.

Defense attorney Levin asks Michael if David Bracey has come to see him in the hospital.

"Yes," Michael's lips say.

But prosecutor Pappas has another question.

Pappas: "Did David say that you should testify that you shot yourself?"

Michael: "Yes."

The two defendants glare at Michael, whose eyes cannot focus back at them. He has not testified the way they wanted; his

testimony has been that the two boys tried to murder him. There
are no further questions.

Judge Olson dismisses the jury. They leave by way of Michael's
bed, looking at him as they pass. The defendants walk by, also,
but Michael will not look back. The day's testimony is ended;
the jury is expected to retire for a decision later in the week.

Soon Michael is alone in the room with his doctors and nurses.
His lips have stopped moving. He is so tired. But his eyes shine.
The nurses nod at him in approval. His day in court is over.
The respirator drones on. When he had set out to get the ice
cream last August, he had been carrying two dollars in his
pocket. . . .

Putt-Putt à Go-Go

IT WAS A nasty day in the city.
The headlines told of murders and warfare. The people on the
street were full of meanness and sarcasm. Even the traffic lights
seemed to be staring insolently. I needed solace.

Some guys turn to rotgut whiskey. Some guys turn to cheap
women. Some guys will even have a cigarette.

Me, I'm different.

I go to Putt-Putt.

I pulled up to the Putt-Putt on Devon Avenue in Elk Grove
Village, Illinois.

I sauntered in. The fellow at the desk knew not to fool with
me. He handed me a putter and a blue ball.

"Red," I said, not looking at him.

He quickly replaced the blue one with a red one.

I hit the course. The Elk Grove Village Putt-Putt is a triplex;
you get your choice of Course No. 1, Course No. 2, or Course

No. 3. My luck was still rotten. It was a Wednesday night, and Course No. 1 was being used for the weekly tournament. I always like to try Course No. 1 when I hit a new Putt-Putt. But tonight I didn't feel like company.

So Course No. 2 it was. No sooner had I teed up than the strains of "Hurt So Good" were replaced on the Putt-Putt loudspeaker by the voice of the course manager:

"Ladies and gentlemen, the discount bonus has been won on Course No. 2 by Carol, with a red golf ball. We will now be switching back to the blue or the green. First person scoring a hole in one after the conclusion of this announcement with a blue or green golf ball, please bring the golf ball to the clubhouse and claim your discount prize."

That did it for me. My red ball was out of the running for a while. No free game in the offing. I didn't care. I stroked it toward the cup. Naturally it missed.

I could tell you about Putt-Putt. I could tell you that there are more than one thousand Putt-Putt courses around the world. I could tell you that Putt-Putt is to miniature golf what Wheaties is to the generic grain cereal at your local discount grocery store: the genuine article. I could tell you that Putt-Putt courses are generally found in smaller towns and medium-sized cities; there are no Putt-Putts in New York or Los Angeles or Chicago. I could tell you that there are no windmills or trick holes on a Putt-Putt course; the game is all skill.

I could tell you that Putt-Putt was founded in Fayetteville, North Carolina, by a fellow named Don Clayton in 1954. I could tell you that one of the main reasons he built his first course was as therapy to prevent a nervous breakdown. I could tell you that there is a Professional Putters Association that sponsors a full-scale national tour, with prize money all the way. I could tell you that in cities like Albany, Georgia, and El Paso, Texas, and Grand Rapids, Michigan, the professional Putt-Putt tournaments are seen weekly during the summer on a syndicated television show.

I could tell you a lot, as a matter of fact. But I didn't come to the Elk Grove Village Putt-Putt for you. I came for me.

You can spot the hotshots a mile away. I spotted one.

He had that glazed look in his eye: the look that says he plays six or seven hundred rounds of Putt-Putt every summer. I tossed my ball in front of his and introduced myself. He said that his name was Steve Baumgartner.

"Sounds familiar," I said.

He nodded in the direction of one of the Court No. 2 light poles. His name was posted near the top. He held the course record. Twenty-five.

"Ever played this course before?" he said.

"Not this one," I said.

He offered to show me around. Putt-Putts always look simple; the holes are short, and they're each par two. The bumpers are orange, and the carpets are green. But each hole has its own personality, and if you don't know the breaks, you aren't going to get your aces.

"This one breaks very lightly to the right," Baumgartner said as he knocked the ball toward the first hole. It did. He put it in the cup.

We began to walk the course. Putt-Putt isn't as time-consuming as, say, medical school. Twenty minutes is a long time for a round.

"You can play this hole thirty times and never get the ball to roll the same," Baumgartner said as we walked to the tee mat on the fifth hole. "The secret is to play the ball off the back wall."

He said he was twenty years old; he spent virtually every night from spring to autumn at the Elk Grove Village Putt-Putt.

"I came here for the grand opening seven years ago," he said. "I saw the spotlights and my ma drove me over. I shot about a forty—a couple over par—and that hooked me right away."

He was a gangly fellow with the beginnings of a moustache. He said it was hard to explain to other people his addiction.

"They say, 'What's Putt-Putt?' " he said. "Even the ones who know it's miniature golf think of those courses with the elephants and the windmills. They don't realize how special Putt-Putt is.

"When you're playing well, there's nothing else in the world. You want to play fast. You want to play the course in ten minutes.

You know what all the course records are, and breaking them is all that matters to you."

"Crimson and Clover" was on the loudspeaker. I asked him if the constant music broke his concentration.

"No, not at all," he said. "When you're putting well, the music seems to be turned off. There are no other sounds than the ball banking toward the hole. Here on sixteen, you never want to bank the ball with the break." Three seconds later it was in the cup.

On Devon Avenue the trucks and cars roared by just feet from the Putt-Putt course. Next door was VFW Post No. 9284. The VFW signboard said that Friday was fish-fry night; Saturday was prime-rib night; Wednesday and Sunday were bingo nights. Bingo didn't interest me. I wanted to talk about Putt-Putt.

I walked to the clubhouse. The owner of the course, Shirley Swiglo, was passing out scorecards and pencils to customers. I motioned with my head for her to join me at the picnic bench by the Coke machine when she had a chance.

She looked like she expected trouble from me. She seemed relieved when she saw that I only wanted to know about her Putt-Putt course.

"We open every year in mid-April, and we stay open as long as the weather lets us," she said. "Sometimes we're still open in mid-November, but usually it's mid-October.

"We're open seven days a week. We open the gates at ten in the morning, and we stay open at night until the last person is off the course. As long as they want to play, we'll stay here. The latest that's ever been is three-twenty in the morning. Some nurses from the Alexian Brothers hospital came over after the night shift. They said they would rather play Putt-Putt than drink after work, so we accommodated them."

Mrs. Swiglo's husband, Bob, joined us at the picnic bench. As gentle as she was, he was that tough. He said he had to be that way. When you own a Putt-Putt, it's an invitation for the wrong elements to try to take over.

"Why do you think we keep the lights turned on so brightly out on the courses?" he said.

I said I didn't know.

"You turn the lights down, you get your undesirables," he said. "It's a fact. Bright lights is family-oriented. Dim lights isn't."

"If people are proud to be seen," Shirley Swiglo said, "they have no reason to object to bright lights."

"There's no loitering here," Bob Swiglo said. "No hanging around. I won't have it. In seven seasons, we've only had to call the police three times."

I asked him about those three occasions.

"The first time was for a hopped-up kid. Marijuana. The second was when a ten-speed bike was stolen; the owner forgot to lock it, out in the parking lot. The third was when our neighbors over there were having a cocktail party, and they started hitting golf balls at us from their back yard."

He said that the marijuana problem posed the greatest potential threat to the tranquility of the Putt-Putt.

"I know when they're hopped up," he said. "You can see it in their eyes. I tell them, 'Sorry, boys. You can do it. But you can't do it at the Putt-Putt.' "

As much as I liked talking to the Swiglos, I hadn't come to Elk Grove Village to jawbone. I had come to putt.

I went out onto Course No. 3. Playing directly ahead of me was a twenty-four-year-old truck driver named Jim Daniels. His putting partner was Cathy Benjamin, eighteen, a cook at the local Burger King. They invited me to play along. They told me this was their first date.

Jim stroked the ball toward the hole.

"Nope," he said as the ball missed.

"No can do," Cathy said.

He said he had asked her out planning to go to the movies: "I was going to go to *Conan* or *Foxfire*." But they had mutually decided that Putt-Putt was a better idea.

"You can talk while you play, and get to know each other," Cathy said.

"The sport is important too, but not that important," Jim said. "If you cheat, the only person you're cheating is yourself."

They were having a good time. Too good a time for me; I was itchy to hit the ball and keep moving. I played through, but in a couple of holes I ran into a foursome. The players were

Tom Polak, a thirty-six-year-old program analyst for United Airlines; his daughter Lisa, twelve; his other daughter, Lauri, eight; and Lisa's friend Julie DePrado, twelve.

"The wife brings them here more often than I do," Polak said to me. "But I have the night off, and they wanted to play."

Lauri tugged at his pants.

"Oh, Lauri, we're in trouble on this hole again," he said.

They were obviously playing best-ball; the father and the eight-year-old against the two twelve-year-olds. Lauri putted and missed.

"Bravo! Bravo!" Lisa yelled.

I moved on.

At the clubhouse, Shirley Swiglo was giving an orange ball—the symbol of a hole in one, the replacement ball a winner is given along with his discount coupon prize—to a girl who had just claimed an ace. After the girl walked away, I asked Shirley how she could be so sure that all the holes in one really were holes in one.

"I have to be honest with you," Mrs. Swiglo said. "Some of the kids cheat. But when we catch them, we just tell them to go back out on the course and try again. We don't actually call them cheaters. They get the message. And we make a friend."

On the wall were dozens of snapshots of birthday-party groups that had come to the Putt-Putt. Bob Swiglo was inspecting the snapshots, and making sure that nothing unruly was taking place on the Putt-Putt premises.

By this time about a hundred people were on the three Putt-Putt courses. A crescent moon hovered above. I sat back down at the picnic bench. My new *Esquire* had just arrived; it was the issue celebrating the glories of New York City.

I read silently from a story on New York night life:

At night, Manhattan island is speckled with the light of a thousand campfires. From downtown to up, from East Side to West, illuminated signs and soft-glowing rooms mark the spots. Elaine's. Studio 54. P.J. Clarke's. The Red Parrot. Rúelles. The Odeon. Le Cirque. One Fifth. Café Central. Joe Allen. Raoul's. Central Falls. Bathed in the glow are the people of New York who like, who crave, the social whoopde-do. No other place in America has, in variety or number, so many incandescent gatherings.

I wasn't so sure. It seemed to me that if they built a Putt-Putt in Times Square, New York might instantly be rid of about half its problems. But I wasn't here to solve New York's troubles. I was here to play Putt-Putt. I was going to stay late. Who knew? I might even finish my night with some Alexian Brothers nurses. Stranger things had happened.

Ira

IRA IS TWENTY-NINE and lives with his parents. He has never spoken a word.

When he was born on September 12, 1953, he seemed to be a normal baby. After a few months, though, his mother and father began to worry. Ira seemed unable to hold up his head properly.

His parents took Ira to a number of doctors. When the baby was eighteen months old, the diagnosis seemed certain. Ira was suffering from severe brain damage. The physicians warned that he would probably never be able to function as anything but an infant.

The parents are middle-class Jewish people; they live on Chicago's Far North Side. They made a determination early on: They would not put Ira in an institution. He would live with them. If he remained a baby forever, so be it. He was theirs.

And now he is twenty-nine. When friends call his parents' home, they hear an almost constant low, rumbling sound in the background. The sound is made by Ira. Because of the problem in his mind, he cannot help himself from making the noise. It fills the house all day, every day.

He must be watched constantly; he is in danger of hurting himself by damaging his head with his fists. His mother, who is fifty-two, bathes him and helps him go to the bathroom. His father shaves him.

Ira seldom goes outside. In addition to the brain damage, he developed curvature of the spine when he was a teenager, and because of this, he is forced into a stooped posture. He feels pain when he walks. Sometimes his mother will take him into the back yard, but that is about all.

He has never been to a barber shop, never been to a dentist. Friends of his parents who work in those fields visit the house. Other old friends, though, don't visit the way they used to. When Ira was small, they seemed to be able to deal with his handicaps better than they do now.

"It's hard to blame those people," Ira's mother says. "When their children were growing up, they could identify with what we were going through with Ira. Because Ira was a child just like their boys and girls. But their children went to school, and graduated, and went to college, and got married. Ira remained a child. And they don't know how to respond to that."

Ira's parents do not know how much he is aware of them. He is their son, though, and they do what they can to make his life more serene. They play music for him—classical works and operas. The music seems to soothe Ira. He will kneel by the record player, and he will appear to be content.

At night Ira will become restless. His mother has not slept through until the morning since Ira was born. She will hear him in his room, and she will go to him and turn him over and cover him with blankets. She will stay with him until he has fallen back asleep.

She does not think about what might have been. "I made the decision a long time ago," she says. "He is with us, and that's the way it will be. Certainly our life is not like most people's. We can't really go out, and it's awkward to invite people in.

"But that's all right. Ira has given my life a purpose. He has taught me about love. By trying to give him a good life, I feel there's a reason for me to be on Earth. When you think about it, what am I giving up? I don't go to the movies, and I don't go out to see people as much as I might. But isn't all of that sort of minor, compared with providing a life for my son?"

Once each year, on a Jewish holiday, Ira's parents take him to their synagogue. It is a holiday filled with songs, so they do not have to worry about his noises bothering the other worshipers. The mother and the father sit on either side of Ira, each of them holding one of his hands, so he does not start hurting himself.

The rest of the time, though, they are at home together. Once in a while his mother will wonder about whether he truly knows who she is. Twenty-nine years have passed without any definite sign. "I do think he knows that he is loved," she says. "I can't guarantee much beyond that. There's no definite way that he responds to me. It's just a sense I have, that he knows.

"Sometimes he will look at me straight in the face. He will look me in the eye, and I will think that it's a sign of recognition. Maybe I'm fooling myself, though."

She has one great fear. She has lived all these years with him in the house. She wonders what would happen to Ira if she and her husband were to die before Ira did.

"My hope for him is that his parents will be alive all of his lifetime to take care of him," she says. "I don't know what else to do but to hope, because if I think too much about it, it makes me too uncomfortable."

She is resolved to the life she has chosen. Her days begin and end with Ira. She has learned to limit the things she yearns for.

But she does allow herself to have one dream.

"I know it will never happen," she says. "But I would give almost anything to hear him talk before I'm gone.

"Not a sentence or anything. I know that will never happen. But if he would say a word one day . . . I know it sounds selfish. I think about what it would be like if I was sitting with him one day and he looked at me and said 'Mama.' "

O'Hare Ballet

IT IS ALMOST midnight. Here it comes again, off in the distance. A small light; if you hadn't been doing this for hours already, you would think it was a star. But the light grows; it enlarges and comes closer, and then it picks up speed and in the final seconds you can see the silver metal hurtling toward the ground, and then it hits and rolls, and back where it started, almost precisely in the same place, another light has appeared and started to grow, started to come toward you.

You are sitting in the window, as you have been all evening. You have touched a button, and all the curtains all around the suite have pulled back. Beneath you and directly in front of you is O'Hare International Airport. This suite is meant for serious business, but that is not your purpose; you are at play here, and you are hypnotized.

The complex is called the Mayor's Suite; built by the management of the O'Hare Hilton—the hotel that is located directly on the grounds of O'Hare—the suite is designed to be offered for use to the mayor of Chicago during an emergency or weather crisis at the airport. It wraps around one entire end of the top floor of the hotel; there are speaker-equipped telephones and telescopes mounted next to the floor-to-ceiling windows, and every amenity that could be needed in a command post.

You are staying in the suite tonight; not to judge its efficiency as an emergency center, but to watch O'Hare from this vantage point, and to think about this miraculous combination of steel and glass and concrete out on the midwestern plains. O'Hare has become such an integral part of modern American culture that it is taken pretty much for granted; unless there is a crash or a hijacking, it is seldom in the news.

But O'Hare, perhaps more than any similar piece of real estate in the United States, has an importance that was unknown in earlier decades, and will probably only be fully appreciated in decades to come. We know that we are the "mobile society"; the phrase has become a cliché, so much so that we accept it and do not think about it. O'Hare is the epicenter of that mobile society—perhaps the greatest single symbol of American life today.

If you think of O'Hare as a city in itself, it is the largest municipality in the world—50 million people a year pass through its concourses. It is the world's busiest airport; if you are an American and you do any traveling at all, you are likely to spend time in O'Hare. Because of its position between the coasts, it is the one point where travelers venturing from one spot to another inevitably end up.

And yet it is easy not to think about it, other than to know it is there to use. Which is why, sitting in the window on this autumn night, you have been so transfixed by what you are seeing. The Mayor's Suite gives you a view of O'Hare you have never been privy to before—stretching out below you are all of the individual terminals, all of the massive jets. When you hurry to O'Hare on business you think only of Flight 224 or Gate G-7; tonight you are in no rush, and all the flights, all the gates lie beneath you, with those jets moving in and away with a rapidity and tempo that is dizzying. It never stops, not for a minute, and the geometric beauty of it is such that you sometimes have to remind yourself that it is not a liquid piece of art you are watching, it is basic transportation, human beings meeting schedules to move from one American city to another.

Those dots of light off in the distance are the baubles that draw your eye the most. Hours ago, at smaller airports all across the land, men and women and children said goodbye to their loved ones, and climbed on board the jets that—right now—are approaching O'Hare. Important trips to every one of those families, nagging worries in the minds of every one of those husbands and wives and mothers and fathers, waiting at home for a telephone call to say that, yes, we have arrived safely.

You sit in the window, though, and all of those lives are a series of the bright dots, each forming in the same piece of the blackness out there, each moving toward you at the exact rate of one every thirty seconds. Turn your head to the right, and you can see the men up in the control tower, bringing those dots in. It is a hard bit of magic to put on paper; but there are two color television sets in the Mayor's Suite, and not once in all these hours have you been tempted to turn one of them on. You have taken advantage of the stereo, though; music is coursing through each of the speakers mounted in the walls of the Mayor's Suite, and all of those dots—all of those planes filled with human hope and trust—are dancing for you to that music as they move in toward you, and their appointment with the ground.

And down to your left, the other facet of O'Hare: illuminated silver cylinders thundering down a runway and up into the air, these leaving O'Hare, these, too, at the rate of one every thirty seconds. Lining up and waiting and then disappearing into that same blackness.

The pioneer days seem longer ago than you can imagine—the days of spending months crossing from one end of America to the other. Perhaps some of those early Americans passed over this very piece of midwestern ground on their way west, not knowing what time would bring about.

You fall asleep in the window; when dawn opens your eyes, the music is still playing. Now, in the early light, the jets are breathing puffs of exhaust into the cold morning air, pulling away from their gates one by one, lining up still to greet the sky. And off in the distance here they come, screaming silver players in a drama that never ends.

Railroad Man

H E WAS A railroad man, and
there was no grandeur at the end of the line.

He was a railroad man for forty-two years, but that ended last week. His name is Charles Ford. Back in 1936, when he was a youngster of twenty-three, being a waiter on the railroad was one of the best jobs a black man could hope for.

"If you worked for the railroad, you were decent," he will remember now. "It was good for the neighborhood to have a railroad man. Stores would give you credit."

So he went to a training school for railroad waiters, run by the Pennsylvania Railroad. The waiters would learn their trade in abandoned dining cars. The railroads ruled the nation then, and for Charles Ford it was a prestigious life he was setting out on. He graduated from the training school and got his first job. The pay was $47.50 a month.

He was good at his job. He liked to serve people. It was almost an outmoded calling in the twentieth century, but it is what he did. He yearned to work for the railroad he thought was best, the Atchison, Topeka and Santa Fe, and before long he did. He was hired to be a waiter on the Super Chief, the queen of the Santa Fe line, the luxury train that traveled between Chicago and Los Angeles.

"Oh, it was a beautiful job," he will remember now. "You had to know you were sharp. You had to know what you were doing."

He waited tables on that train, and his superiors recognized his skill. He was promoted from waiter to valet, and then to bartender. He wore a white jacket and white bow tie, hand-tied, and he was proud about what he did.

Maybe he was invisible to most of his passengers; he was just the man with the friendly and helpful face, the man who mixed the drinks and passed the hors d'oeuvres and made the passengers feel special as they rode the train in pampered comfort. Soon he was promoted again, this time to serve in the first-class section of the train; it was the epitome of accomplishment for a man like Charles Ford.

Yes, he may have been just the man behind the bar to his passengers, but he remembered them. There was Walt Disney, traveling to Hollywood and telling the bartender about someone called Mickey Mouse; there was Elizabeth Taylor, sitting up at the bar most of the night after she had left Nicky Hilton; there was a skinny young woman named Diana Ross and her two partners, the Supremes, heading off for Hollywood to seek their fortune. Sometimes Charles Ford would serve drinks in the Turquoise Room, the elegant private dining room of the Super Chief; always he would try to make the trip memorable for those on board.

That railroad run became his life. He had a family, but he missed birthday parties, graduations, funerals, Christmases, anniversaries, because he was on his run. Air travel became dominant in the United States, and the railroads diminished in their importance, but Charles Ford stayed on the job.

Then Amtrak was born; the railroads were nationalized, and his beloved Super Chief was no more. He had been a waiter and bartender on the railroad for so long that his seniority outdistanced almost everyone else's, and he accepted a job with Amtrak; he put in for runs from Chicago to New York and back, so he could be with his family on weekends.

It was not the same, of course. With the government running the railroad, there was not the same pride and special feeling he had known as a young man.

"The other men who worked on Amtrak, they would look up to those of us who had been on the Santa Fe," he will remember now. "They wanted to do things the way we had done it on the Santa Fe."

And all of a sudden it was 1978; Charles Ford would be sixty-five. It was time to retire.

For a railroad man like Charles Ford—a waiter, a bartender—there is no glory at the end. No gold watch. No banquet. No word of thanks. When a railroad man's final run ends, he leaves the station. Someone else bids for his run, and the man with the next highest seniority gets it, and everyone moves up a notch in the pecking order. For a faithful worker, there is not much of a "Well done" given.

The scenario for a man like Charles Ford is to come into the station, turn in his money, sign his report, pick up his bag, and say, "So long"—to men who do not even look up from their paperwork to know, care, or acknowledge the final farewell to the work of a lifetime. And it is no surprise—many of the men in the station were not even born when the Charles Fords of this world started working on the railroads.

In August a private club made up of retired railroad waiters, bartenders, cooks, and Pullman porters gave a dinner in recognition of retirees. Charles Ford bought a new suit and new shoes for the occasion; he took his family to the dinner. But somehow his name was forgotten, it was left off the list; when the names of the railroad men were read, Charles Ford was not mentioned. It would only have been thirty seconds of recognition, but he missed it.

So last week Charles Ford turned sixty-five, and he rode his last run from New York into Chicago's Union Station.

On the train, he changed from his bartender's uniform to his street clothes. He turned in his equipment and his receipts. He walked into the station. He stopped at the bar and had a drink. Then, his life as a railroad man over, Charles Ford went home.

1964

T HERE'S AN OLD question: If you found your home on fire, what's the one item you would carry out to safety?

I wouldn't have to think twice. At the bottom of my shirt drawer—buried safely beneath the shirts that don't get worn in either summer or winter—is a spiral-bound book with a cover of imitation black leather. Embossed on the cover, in faded gold ink, is "1964."

Down near the bottom, the cover informs me that the notebook was a gift from "Archer, Meek, Weiler Agency, Inc.—All forms of Insurance—175 So. High St.," in Columbus, Ohio. And inside the book is the most precious commodity I own. It is the year I turned seventeen years old, recorded day by day, in pencil and in ball-point pen. It is the thing we all wish for and are seldom granted: time preserved.

I suppose there are millions of teenage girls who keep diaries, but I would guess that the number of boys who do it is tiny. I know it is a secret that I kept to myself. What happened was, at a convention of high school journalism students from around the state of Ohio, a teacher advised us that the best way to discipline oneself as a conscientious reporter was to keep a daily journal—to make oneself record the minutiae of each day, whether one felt like writing or not. So, for the year 1964, I did it.

I wrote late at night, just before bed. That year, cruising the streets with my friends, questions would often come up about when a specific major event—meeting certain girls, getting into a fight—took place. My friends would mention a day, and I would know they were wrong; I had it recorded in the Archer, Meek, Weiler diary. But I never said anything. To admit that I was keeping a diary would be—to use the only appropriate term of the era—queer.

I did it for just that one year. And now, when memories of time escaped are the most valuable currency I can imagine, I have 1964 available to me any time I want it. And I am finding that I want it quite often.

The notations are nothing if not cryptic. Day by day, in a style reminiscent of the late Walter Winchell, they recorded concerns long forgotten but at the moment of writing so current they needed no elaboration:

Did OK in Algy—Got unknown in Chemo—I wish Dianne
would ask me to Sadie Hawkins—Pariser said I could have
his STP date—Senior—but Marje said Roth should take it—
I might get some Dayton girl—We're doubling with Gary
Robbins—I hope this girl (if she comes) is cool—Reserve
match after school—Got 80 and C+ in French—damn!—I
tried so hard—that's getting me down—got poorboy and
Towncraft shirt after dinner—played ball at White's house—
she's cool—like to get her—did a lot of Chemo—hope I go
up!—Didn't think too much about L.

And that was what Tuesday, April 21, 1964, was like in my
life. The value of the book is that, unlike most men of my generation, it makes it impossible for me to bathe my teenage years
in a warm, unfocused glow of nostalgia. For some reason, those
of us now in our thirties take great pleasure in looking back on
those years as if they were some pleasant, seamless movie backed
by a sound track of Top 40 songs. I have no such luxury; I know
specifically what it was like. So my friends from those years like
to joke about the time we went through the guardrail. They tell
the story as if it were a prank. Here is what the diary says for
the day of February 15:

I'm awful lucky to be around to write this tonight—Today
Chuck, Dan, Gi, Jack, + me went to Dayton—Chuck, Jack,
+ me didn't have permission—messed around in Dayton—
got chased by a guy in a 409—scared—saw Bart, Gary Sny-
der, Joyce Burick—Jack kissed Joyce—on the way home, all
went well until about 10 miles out of Columbus—we hit an
ice patch, swerved four times—each time we slid farther—
finally Gi yelled "Here we go"—we crashed into the guardrail, flew over an embankment—hit 3 times—I was sure I
was going to die—but everyone was all right—2 ambulances
came, towtruck, cops—We were so scared—Gi drove home—
parents don't know yet—We went to Candy's and Robyne's
at night.

There it is. Early in the evening we almost died. By the end
of the night we were trying to romance Candy and Robyne. We

were invincible; life was going to go on forever. Death, when it did show up, was a passing notation. November 27:

> Up at noon—Took mom to beauty parlor—went downtown with Jack at 3—got "Gone, Gone, Gone"—cool girl waited on Jack—Uncle Abe died—went with Katz, Dan, Chuck at night—talked about stealing liquor—went to Jackson's party—took ¹/₂ pint of vodka—Gingold party in Eastmoor—went to Dan Goldberg's—I took ⁷/₈ bottle of 151 proof rum—didn't like doing it, but had to prove I had balls.

"Uncle Abe died." A man's full life had ended; in my priorities, it fit in between buying an Everly Brothers record from a good-looking salesclerk and stealing a bottle of liquor from the parents of a friend. It's not the way one would choose to remember the time, but apparently that was the reality.

The combination of naiveté and sophistication is startling. We were all virgins at the beginning of 1964; on the night the first of us made love to a girl, the rest of us—unbeknown to him—locked ourselves in a bathroom next to the bedroom where it was going on. From June 6, 1964:

> Scott got Carla—screwed her—Cruised with Dan in morning—went to Excelsior Club with Jack, Dan, Scott—played ball, got friendly with Sue Young—she's a good girl—can't decide whether I'd like to go with her or not—went to dinner with Scott—after dinner went to the apartment—fixed stuff up, locked ourselves in bathroom—they came in—started to talk—quiet for about 20 minutes—then he said "I can't get this damn package open"—but he did—and he got her good—she was breathing real hard and crying a lot—we told him later—had some beer—talked to Bill Shenk for a real long time—Boy, I have to get a screw—It sounded like hell, but it's just something I have to do—that's my goal for this summer—got home after 2.

And yet, later that summer, when—in a gift from the fates I am still thankful for—I had a brief affair with a twenty-seven-year-old married woman, the notations in the diary do not read like the thoughts of an inexperienced high school boy who is

being seduced by a bored housewife. If I were to re-create it
only from memory, I would tell it as if it were something out of
Summer of '42, with the woman plotting to take me to bed even
as I dreamed of fishing trips and bike rides. But reading the
diary now, it is apparent that I was the instigator.

From the moment my friends and I met the girls for whom
this woman was acting as a summer-outing chaperone, the diary
makes it clear that I was falling for her. And not doing it silently;
trying to make her notice me, to make her think of me not as
some seventeen-year-old kid hanging around with his buddies,
but as a person so special that she had to let me into her life. At
one point she urged me to take out one of the teenage girls she
was in charge of; she said that the girl liked me, so, almost on
command, I spent a few hours with the girl. But afterwards, I
was back again, too shy to ask the woman myself, but putting
myself in place, waiting for her to ask me.

In the diary, it is in shorthand:

> . . . she kept touching me—talk got to love—I said I'd get
> her later—she said "talker"—I said "wait and see"—she said
> "I've been waiting all week"—she put her arm over me—I
> was going nuts—she said "What are you thinking about?"—
> then she put her hand on my chest—She said "It's about
> your heart"—we started. . . .

And later:

> . . . all night long I kept touching her. . . .

I feel funny committing this to print now; but there seems no
other way to convey how much this book labeled "1964" means
to a man now thirty-four. It was half my life ago, and yet because
of the book I am there again. When you are seventeen you are
too new at things to edit yourself; you put it down as it happened,
and let it go at that. Some nights I feel the book is burning itself
up in that dresser drawer.

My guess is that a grown man could not keep a journal like
the one kept by a seventeen-year-old boy. By the time we are
adults, we censor ourselves even in our thought processes. In

the diary, if something bad happened in my life, I could write, "And the all-time loser loses again," and I would mean it. The next day I would write of cruising with my friends, and there would not be a hint of despair.

And the longing . . . that spring I was named an editor of my high school newspaper. At the same time, I was a returning letterman on the varsity tennis team. To be an athlete at my high school was far greater in prestige than to be on the paper, but I knew I wanted to be a writer, and it was important for me to do the job. So I skipped practices so that I could get my page in the paper prepared for the printers. Slowly and steadily I began to drop in position on the tennis team; by May it was apparent that I was not going to earn a letter again that year.

It doesn't sound so bad now; as a matter of fact, in light of the way things turned out, I seem to have made a fairly wise decision. But the diary tells me what the specter of failure meant to me:

> . . . Coach Weis said that I'm down to fifth doubles—I pray so much that I can get back to my old position—I need that letter—without it, I'm just nothing again—Please, God, help me. . . .

"Without it, I'm just nothing again." How many of us have felt that way in the business world, or in our personal lives? But it is an emotion that you can never express when you're supposed to be mature and responsible. You swallow hard and put on a good face for the world and let your insides churn. And you lie; you tell everyone how well things are going, while all the while something inside you is crying, "Please, God, help me. . . ."

Maybe that is the thing the book marked "1964" gives me above all else. Reading the book now, I see—raging and uncontrolled—the emotions that, as a man who is a reporter, I try to chronicle in others every day. They are buried so deep in most of us that they will never surface; but when you are seventeen, writing for an audience that, at the time, you are sure will never be anyone but yourself, they lie there at the level of your skin. You will never see them more clearly.

When I take the 1964 diary out, it is usually to look up a specific incident. What prompted it this last time was a phone call I got from my brother. He just had his tenth high school reunion. At the party, a woman told him that, back when she was a little girl, she had once had a tantrum and had tried to beat me up.

I knew it was in the diary. And I found it. June 19, 1964:

. . . Went to Sue Dworkin's—Crummy—watched *King Creole* with Bill and Kenny at Gi's—then back to Dworkin's—this little kid beat the hell out of me—went to White Castle with Ed and Ken. . . .

As usual, once I had the diary in my hands, I couldn't put it back. I turned to January 1, and closed the door, and for the next few hours, I was seventeen again.

There is a place in the diary—August 9—where I write about the first words by me ever to appear in a newspaper. I was working as a copyboy on the night shift at the *Columbus Citizen-Journal.* I was doing the fire runs—the little agate lists of emergency calls—and I saw something unusual, about a man who had been hospitalized by a golf ball with a liquid center that exploded.

. . . I phoned the man's house and talked to his wife—Got the story and wrote it up—Keesee changed it slightly and said good—at first I was scared he'd throw it away—Stine headed it "Golf Ball Fights Back"—I saw it on the galley— it was a thrill to see it in print—My first printed work. . . .

There are days when 1964 seems a thousand years away. But it is always right there when I need it; why I should need it is another question, but I can't seem to find the answer to that one anywhere in the diary.

Normal

THIS IS REALLY getting perverted. When the letters began to arrive, I ignored them.

That wasn't hard to do. A lot of mail comes into this office, much of it nuts. If you want to read about degradation, evil, degeneracy, larceny, and madness, it's all there. For some reason a cross-section of the worst aspects of humanity shows up in each of my mail deliveries.

So I was a little surprised to read the message contained in the first letter:

Hi! I'm writing to you neither to complain nor to be very interesting or important, but because you ought to get some mail from some normal people. I assert that I am normal.

The writer was a woman from the south suburbs. She wrote:

Before backing my claim to normalcy, please let me state that today is every bit as sunny and lovely as yesterday! I am normal because I like America, good steaks, soda pop, my nice husband, our little rented house, multivariate calculus and "Tucson," a fur-bearing dog.

I had to admit, the letter was different from what I am used to. The woman wasn't asking me to intercede in a child-custody case; she wasn't telling me how her husband was beating her or how she had been abused as a child; she wasn't complaining that a lawyer or a doctor was defrauding her; she wasn't, in short, writing about any of the things that the people who write me usually concentrate on.

"As a normal person I feel that I have a certain obligation to correspond with you," she wrote. "So this is my first in a series of letters."

Like I say, I ignored it. But soon there was another message from her:

Did you watch the Indy 500 race on the TV? What a great race! The cars were incredible and the drivers superb! I am happy that Gordon Johncock won the race because he is an Indy veteran, he had won an unhappy victory in 1973 and because he was Mario Andretti's team partner. My husband and I drove to Indianapolis to see the final day of time trials and so had the opportunity to watch Andretti practice. His car was excellent, he suffered a great loss when his car was ruined before the race ever began.

I went about my business. The news of the world was the usual: murders, wars, meanness. And there was a letter from the woman:

We enjoyed a pleasant Memorial Day holiday. We began the morning by driving our bicycles down to Crown Point for the annual Dunes Century bike ride. We followed the arrows that are painted on the street to the "Y," and golly, I guess the ride was on Sunday, so we drove the bikes back home. Boy, those hills outside of "Crowntown" went smooth that morning!

After work I hit the places I usually hit. I heard the usual ration of complaints and groaning. When I got to work the next day, I realized that I was subconsciously anticipating the morning's first mail delivery. When it arrived I quickly flipped through all the envelopes. I figured out that I was hunting for something from my "normal" correspondent.

She didn't disappoint me:

My dad came over with his electric lawn mower. Remember how it rained last week? This is the time of year that grass sends up its stalks of seed. My husband scythed down the lawn with the ol' push-mower. I got to mow most of the lawn, instead of my dad doing it, because he would have, but he did do the dog yard and he followed me, holding the cord and pointing to spots.

A man called up yelling about some dispute he was having with a government agency; a woman told me that she had hired a private eye to follow her cheating husband around, and would I expose the husband in print? I waited for the next letter.

Here is what the "normal" woman said:

My mom had a barbecue with salads (green, Jello-O and potato), steaks charred on the gas grill, baked beans, the choice of two homemade salad dressings, garlic bread, hot dogs and hamburgers, cottage cheese and tomato slices and then watermelon and chocolate cake. My sister and her new husband brought the center irises from their lovely garden, and his grandparents brought two of the salads. Afterwards we went home. My husband drank some beer and we watched television.

I went out to do an interview that night; some public relations people from California were trying to sell me on their client. They were quite persuasive, but I found myself wondering if I would hear from the "normal" woman again.

The next day I did.

My mother and I went to my sister's new husband's grandparents' house to pick peonies. My mother loves peonies! After we had lunch, we took a walk.

As I mentioned, this is getting perverted. But I can't help it; with all the terrible news the world has to offer, I find myself looking forward to hearing the details of this "normal" woman's life. For example—you might not know it, but she and her husband are thinking about renting another house:

It's an old-fashioned house. It's a block away from the commuter bus stop. It has a washer and dryer in the basement, a large kitchen, porches, an attic, a yard for Tucson the fur-bearing dog, and a garden. And what a garden it is! The owner keeps the garden as a relaxing hobby. He's a barber.

He's also quite friendly, a silver-haired man. He doesn't sell the vegetables, so we can eat all we want.

I don't know where this is leading. All I know is that when I arrive at work each day, I have my choice of the two Chicago newspapers, the *New York Times*, the *Wall Street Journal*, and a stack of mail. I can read any of it. But these days, all I want to do is read about the "normal" woman and what she's up to. Perverted. But nice.

Handled with Care

THE DAY THE lady took her clothes off on Michigan Avenue, people were leaving downtown as usual. The workday had come to an end; men and women were heading for bus and train stations, in a hurry to get home.

She walked south on Michigan; she was wearing a white robe, as if she had been to the beach. She was blond and in her thirties.

As she passed the Radisson Hotel, Roosevelt Williams, a doorman, was opening the door of a cab for one of the hotel's guests. The woman did not really pause while she walked; she merely shrugged the robe off, and it fell to the sidewalk.

She was wearing what appeared to be the bottom of a blue bikini bathing suit, although one woman who was directly next to her said it was just underwear. She wore nothing else.

Williams at first did not believe what he was seeing. If you hang around long enough, you will see everything: robberies, muggings, street fights, murders. But a naked woman on North Michigan Avenue? Williams had not seen that before and neither, apparently, had the other people on the street.

It was strange; her white robe lay on the sidewalk, and by all accounts she was smiling. But no one spoke to her. A report in the newspaper the next day quoted someone: "The cars were stopping, the people on the buses were staring, people were shouting, and people were taking pictures." But that is not what other people who were there that afternoon said.

The atmosphere was not carnival-like, they said. Rather, they said, it was as if something very sad was taking place. It took only a moment for people to realize that this was not some stunt designed to promote a product or a movie. Without anyone telling them, they understood that the woman was troubled, and that what she was doing had nothing to do with sexual titillation; it was more of a cry for help.

The cry for help came in a way that such cries often come. The woman was violating one of the basic premises of the social fabric. She was doing something that is not done. She was not shooting anyone, or breaking a window, or shouting in anger. Rather, in a way that everyone understood, she was signaling that things were not right.

The line is so thin between matters being manageable and being out of hand. One day a person may be barely all right; the next the same person may have crossed over. Here is something from the author John Barth:

She paused amid the kitchen to drink a glass of water; at that instant, losing a grip of 50 years, the next-room-ceiling plaster crashed. Or he merely sat in an empty study, in March-day glare, listening to the universe rustle in his head, when suddenly a five-foot shelf let go. For ages the fault creeps secret through the rock; in a second, ledge and railings, tourists and turbines all thunder over Niagara. Which snowflake triggers the avalanche? A house explodes; a star. In your spouse, so apparently resigned, murder twitches like a fetus. At some trifling new assessment, all the colonies rebel.

The woman continued to walk past Tribune Tower. People who saw her said that the look on her face was almost peaceful. She did not seem to think she was doing anything unusual; she was described as appearing "blissful." Whatever the reaction on the street was, she seemed calm, as if she believed herself to be in control.

She walked over the Michigan Avenue bridge. Again, people who were there report that no one harassed her; no one jeered at her or attempted to touch her. At some point on the bridge, she removed her bikini bottom. Now she was completely un-dressed, and still she walked.

"It was as if people knew not to bother her," said one woman who was there. "To tell it, it sounds like something very lewd and sensational was going on. But it wasn't like that at all. It was as if people knew that something very . . . fragile . . . was taking place. I was impressed with the maturity with which people were handling it. No one spoke to her, but you could tell that they wished someone would help her."

Back in front of the Radisson, a police officer had picked up the woman's robe. He was on his portable radio, advising his colleagues that the woman was walking over the bridge.

When the police caught up with the woman, she was just stand-ing there, naked in downtown Chicago, still smiling. The first thing the police did was hand her some covering and ask her to put it on; the show was over.

People who were there said that there was no reaction from the people who were watching. They said that the juvenile be-havior you might expect in such a situation just didn't happen. After all, when a man walks out on a ledge in a suicide attempt, there are always people down below who call for him to jump. But this day, by all accounts, nothing like that took place. No one called for her to stay undressed; no one cursed the police officers for stopping her.

"It was as if everyone was relieved," said a woman who saw it. "They were embarrassed by it; it made them feel bad. They were glad that someone had stopped her. And she was still smiling. She seemed to be off somewhere."

The police charged her with no crime; they took her to Read Mental Health Center, where she was reported to have signed herself in voluntarily. Within minutes things were back to as they always are on Michigan Avenue; there was no reminder of the naked lady who had reminded people how fragile is the everyday world in which we live.

One in 100 Million

SOON IT WILL be summer.
Baseball games will dominate the television screen, and millions
of men and women will be sunning themselves at poolside, pranc-
ing around tennis courts, slamming golf balls into the distance.

And I will still be trying to explain why I did not go to the
Super Bowl.

I arrived in Detroit on Monday of Super Bowl week. I had
every intention of going to the game the following Sunday. I
did what any tourist could be expected to do: I checked into the
Westin Hotel, nodded hello to the robot standing sentry in the
lobby, went to the magazine rack and picked up copies of *Industry
Week* and *Easyriders* to read in my room, and accepted with grat-
itude one of the John Weitz designer briefcases that were being
given free by the National Football League to all reporters covering the game.

I went to the Silverdome in Pontiac. Both teams were scheduled for workouts, and reporters were being allowed to visit.

Since I do not regularly cover sports, my attitude toward
professional athletes has always been the same as that of most
media consumers: these are huge, wealthy men. But as I walked
among the San Francisco 49ers, all I could think about was that
these people were *babies*. I mean, we are used to seeing them in
uniform, with those bar-fronted helmets covering their faces;
and anyone you see on television becomes sort of ageless, anyway.

Here, though, in the flesh, it was striking to notice just how
young they were. If they weren't playing in the NFL, they would

have looked at home pumping gas in a service station. They were clearly awed by all the attention they were receiving on this morning. It was close to zero outside, but inside the Silverdome it was seventy and some of the star players had up to two hundred reporters swarming around them.

I approached Milt McColl, a twenty-two-year-old rookie line-backer. On Sunday, he would be playing in front of 100 million people. He was wearing his jersey with the number 53 on the front. He was looking over at the mobs surrounding Joe Montana, the famous quarterback, and Bill Walsh, the famous coach.

"I hope they can get out of there safely," he said.

Like a few of the other nonstars, McColl was in the awkward position of waiting around on the forty-yard line to see if anyone wanted to talk to him. No one seemed interested. Another 49er in the same situation was Rick Gervais, a twenty-two-year-old safety. As I watched him glancing at the reporters who kept passing him by, I felt that the dynamic reminded me of something. I walked up to say hello, and right away he got it exactly.

"This is sort of like my first high school dance," he said.

I asked him which was more fun.

He glanced up at the girdered dome of the stadium. "Oh, probably my first high school dance," he said.

There was a party for visiting press at the Henry Ford Museum in Dearborn. Much laughter and music filled the room; people were drinking and a band was playing, and the atmosphere was clearly one of fellowship and good fun.

I stood in a group that surrounded an automobile that was part of the museum's exhibit. The men and women in the group were telling each other dirty jokes. By this time the Up With People singers were performing, and an old Beach Boys number was being amplified on the public-address system.

I kept looking at the car. It seemed familiar. Someone spilled a drink, and a waiter went to fetch a fresh one, and then a woman came around carrying a tray of champagne. I couldn't quit staring at the car. It was an old black Lincoln, a kind I have never owned, but still, I was having the distinct feeling that I knew it.

So I broke off from the group. With their voices behind me and the music in the air, I looked at the plaque that was mounted on the wall above the car. The plaque informed me that it was the car in which John F. Kennedy was riding on the day he was assassinated.

In the Super Bowl press room, a sportswriter was morosely drinking a beer. He had just received a message from his editor. The editor was dissatisfied with the writer's coverage of pre-game week. The editor had said that the reports were "not trivial enough."

I rode out to the Silverdome again. It was a weird sight, just off the highway in an isolated part of southern Michigan. For miles it seemed like there was nothing but freeway and franchise fast-food restaurants, and then, rising off the ice and snow, there it was.

It was completely wired by now. CBS trucks were parked in the lot outside the stadium, and there was nowhere you could walk without being physically reminded of the fact that on Sunday half of America would be looking at this structure. In person, the Silverdome seemed more a mirage than a real place; it didn't truly have to exist—its actual presence here in Michigan seemed almost unnecessary. CBS had paid $6 million for the right to telecast pictures of it during Sunday's broadcast; but the eighty thousand or so people who would be here in the seats were so insignificant next to the hundred million who would watch the television show. The morning after the game, the network images of the Silverdome would have disappeared. It would seem odd to find the structure itself still here.

Everyone involved in the Super Bowl knew that they were basically taking part in a television program. Which was only right; the young men on the playing field were children of the television age. Ricky Patton, the 49ers' running back, had the given name of Ricky Riccardo Patton. When his mother had been pregnant with him, she had been a fan of I Love Lucy.

The parties at night began to seem bizarre. At one, a striking blond woman in a low-cut black dress was stationed at the front door to welcome guests. An ABC camera crew turned its lights on her to get a shot, and the effect was to make the dress disappear. She stood there smiling, and in the lights you could see her entire body. She wore no underwear.

About an hour later she circulated from group to group. A reporter who had had too much to drink looked at her and said, "You really have nice tits."

She smiled at him and said, "Thank you."

Later I talked to her; her name was Barbara Nichols, she was thirty-one, she was a model, and she was volunteering her time to the Michigan Host Committee. I asked her if she had been offended by what the man had said.

"No," she said. "It happens wherever I go. I have the best body in the city, and men are always saying things like that. It's no different than if he had told me I had nice legs."

I asked her if she had trouble dealing with moments like that.

"You just learn that men are little boys," she said. "The funny thing is, though, that little boys are beginning to act the same way. I was modeling at a show at Cobo Hall, and this twelve- or thirteen-year-old boy kept hanging around and looking at me. About the fifth time he came up, I said, 'You're so cute, I'd like to have you for my son.' And he said, 'Are you kidding? I want you for my wife.' "

She said that she had two daughters. She said that the most common reaction she got from men was for them to make some excuse to touch her. "I'm used to being the center of attention, and I have a very good sense of humor," she said.

The truest moment of the week for me came one afternoon at the Silverdome. The Cincinnati Bengals had just come onto the field. They had been through their rounds of interviews, and now it was almost time for practice to begin.

A group of about ten of them walked down to the far end of the field. They had a plastic baseball bat and a hollow plastic baseball. Almost as if by instinct, they divided into sides and started playing ball.

I stood among them and watched. They clearly didn't think it was anything special; there was some time to kill, and they were going to kill it this way. Here we were at the site of the Super Bowl, and these young men were playing baseball on the football field. They pitched and swung and caught and ran the imaginary bases, and I thought: This is it. For all the publicity and all the false enthusiasm about the Super Bowl, this is what it comes down to. These men have been remarkable athletes since they were small boys, and what they do when they have a few minutes is revert to whatever it was that brought them onto playing fields in the first place.

Forget the hundred million viewers; forget the network cameras; forget the parties. Of all the young boys who dream of being athletes, these had made it to the Super Bowl. But certain things had not changed; as I watched them laughing and swinging at the ball and arguing over plays, I realized that what I was seeing probably was a more genuine story of sports in America than what would be telecast Sunday.

The winner of the contest for the official drink of Super Bowl week was an alcohol-and-ice-cream concoction called "Referee's Revenge." In the top-floor bar of the Westin it would cost you over six dollars, but you got to keep the glass.

I kept my glass one night, and in the morning I saw it on my hotel-room dresser. Next to it was a pile of press releases from the NFL. My coat was draped over a chair; my official NFL pin, complete with its own number, was attached to the lapel. The pin was my badge of admission to all Super Bowl–week activities in Detroit.

I rode out to Pontiac again. I had obtained permission to enter the Silverdome even though interviews were not being allowed this day. Practice had ended; I walked out to the fifty-yard line and stood on the emblem that had been painted with the NFL's official design.

I looked up to the top deck. I realized that the Super Bowl had become an American secular holiday; people all across the country were covetous of tickets to Sunday's game. And yet, as I stood on the field, I realized that I really didn't want to see it. The holiday was the television show, not the athletic contest on this field. I knew that I would feel closer to the game if I was back home watching it on TV than if I was here. To be here on Sunday . . . somehow it would be essentially false. I would not be one of the hundred million.

I sat down on the fifty. No one came by and told me not to. I just sat there in the center of the field and looked around the Silverdome, and I knew that I was going to go home.

I made my goodbyes to the people I knew in Detroit, and I headed out of the city. I thought of a quotation from Duane Thomas, the former star running back of the Dallas Cowboys: "If this is the ultimate game, then why are they playing it next year?"

On Sunday, I slept late. I took a shower, had a sandwich for lunch, and turned on the pre-game show.

Like the rest of America, I sat and watched for the entire afternoon and early evening. It was sort of strange; every time the teams moved across the fifty-yard line, I saw that painted emblem and thought about how I had sat on it and had decided that I ought to leave.

There was one play—a kicking play for which the 49ers' special team was in—and there was a scramble for the ball down by the goal line, and I heard the announcer say the names of Milt McColl and Rick Gervais. I watched them get up from the pile of players, and they looked like noble and battered gladiators. I tried to put that image together in my mind with the memory of talking to them as they stood like wallflowers at a high school dance, waiting for someone to come up to them.

I went in to work the next day. Someone approached me and said, "I heard you went to the Super Bowl." I didn't know quite how to answer. The person said, "How was it?" and I thought about it, and that's when I said for the first time that, no, I didn't go. Which was true enough, and even if it weren't, it would have to do.

Heads You Lose,
Tails You Lose

NOTHING FASCINATES AMERI-
CANS like a loser, and if the loser is one of monumental pro-
portions, so much the better.

On July 2, 1979, amid much hoopla, a new coin was introduced
to the public. It was the Susan B. Anthony dollar—slightly larger
than a quarter, 8.1 grams in weight, featuring a portrait of the
famous suffragist on one side and an image of an eagle landing
on the moon on the other.

Treasury officials expected the coin to be a hit. They were
hoping, in fact, that people would like it so much that it would
eventually replace the one-dollar bill completely. The reasons
for their optimism were economic and practical ones. It costs
three cents to mint a Susan B. Anthony coin and only 1.8 cents
to print a paper dollar. But the dollar coin will last approximately
fifteen years; the paper dollar will last only eighteen months or
so. Government officials figured that if Americans used Anthony
coins instead of paper dollars, the Treasury would save up to
$50 million a year in printing and processing alone.

Nothing of the kind has happened, of course. The Anthony
dollar has become one of the most miserable busts in the history
of U.S. currency. Most Americans refuse to carry the coins. Bank
tellers and cashiers in stores have learned not to even try to give
them out as change; people won't take them. The most common
complaint is that the coin is hard to differentiate from a quarter
when you're reaching into your pocket, but the dislike seems to

be more visceral than practical. People aren't sure why, but they hate the Anthony dollars; they don't even like to touch them.

When panicky Treasury officials turned to opinion leaders in search of support, they got only ridicule. In Congress, Representative Frank Annunzio, a Democrat from Illinois, said, "If we do eliminate the dollar bill and instead use the dollar coin, the Treasury would be required to issue every American a pair of suspenders." Frustrated by the reluctance of its customers to accept the coins, the Skokie Federal Savings and Loan Association in Skokie, Illinois, sold them for fifty cents apiece one Friday. In Dallas, something called the Bonehead Club singled out the Anthony dollar as the "most monumental goof" of the year.

Meanwhile, the Bureau of the Mint was churning out millions of coins that no one would go near. By the spring of 1980, when production was halted, the Mint had issued 840 million Susan B. Anthony dollars; of those 840 million, 525 million were sitting stacked in federal vaults, in deep storage, untouched.

Without Frank Gasparro, there would be no Susan B. Anthony dollar. Gasparro, seventy-one, is chief designer for the Mint. When his superiors told him that he was supposed to draw a woman for the face of a new dollar coin, he said fine—he would draw Miss Liberty.

"But they told me they didn't want Miss Liberty," Gasparro said. "It had to be Susan B. Anthony."

Gasparro had no idea what Susan B. Anthony looked like. He lives in Philadelphia, so he went down to the offices of the Philadelphia *Bulletin* and asked permission to look in the newspaper's photographic morgue. He found two photographs of Susan B. Anthony. In one, she was twenty-eight; in the other, eighty-four.

"I chose the younger one," Gasparro said. "She was a very attractive woman at twenty-eight."

So he designed the coin with a twenty-eight-year-old Susan B. Anthony on the face. Feminist groups began to complain that Anthony was too "pretty." A fine arts commission objected to it. Even Gasparro's wife said the drawing stank.

"I'll tell you how I feel about my work," Gasparro said. "People look over my shoulder and always criticize everything I make.

Every coin is criticized. It hurts my feelings. I have to watch my step and not lose my composure."

He started over. He drew a new face of Susan B. Anthony, trying to approximate what she looked like in middle age. This new drawing featured a square jaw, a hooked nose, a drooping right eye, and a heavy browline. Gasparro had misgivings about it, but the people at the Treasury seemed to like it fine. So the coin was released to the public and immediately became one of the most amazing flops in the history of U.S. coinage.

"I was listening to a radio talk show one night," Gasparro said. "One caller said the coin looked like it was designed by an Arab. The moderator said it was the most hideous thing he'd ever seen. I called up to defend my coin. I said I drew the picture. But the moderator hung up on me."

The director of the Mint at the time the Anthony dollar was introduced was Stella B. Hackel. She became the chief supporter of the coin. She still doesn't understand what happened.

"It's so practical," she said. "It's easy to use. I do it all the time. I always carry the coins with me, in my purse."

Unfortunately, whenever she pays for something with an Anthony dollar, she has to say, "This is a dollar, not a quarter." She has traveled the country talking about the coin and is flabbergasted that most Americans have never even held one, much less carried one around. From what she can tell, the prejudice against the coin is overwhelming. She went to New Orleans to talk to a convention of bankers about promoting the Anthony dollar more vigorously. Of nine thousand delegates at the convention, fewer than one hundred showed up to listen to her.

"It hasn't worked *yet*," Hackel said. "For over a century people have been used to the idea of a dollar bill, and they're slow to change. But a medium of exchange is a medium of exchange. People can learn."

She knows that all signs indicate they don't want to. With half a billion of the coins in storage, there is no appropriation to mint more of them this year. When Hackel goes to her own bank in Virginia, she knows not to ask for Anthony dollars. The bank doesn't carry them.

"I just don't understand it," she said. "These coins are very nice and convenient and easy to use. They are very clean. A dollar bill gets dirty and messy. Toward the end of its life, it becomes very unpleasant to handle.

"But this coin is shiny and clean. I just don't understand the resistance."

Like private corporations, the Bureau of the Mint has a marketing division. Its function is to smooth the way for its "product" with the people who will help merchandise it—in the case of the Anthony dollar, merchants, vendors, retailers, pinball machine operators, and other significant purveyors of coins.

"Naturally, like all Americans, we like success," said Frank De Leo. "The marketing group can't roll over and play dead. We have to try to figure out what went wrong, and correct it."

De Leo is the Mint's liaison officer to the Federal Reserve, and when he tries to persuade people to use the Anthony dollar in their change drawers, his message is simple: "You carry a dollar bill in your wallet with a ten-dollar bill, and there's no confusion. So if you can tell a dollar bill from a ten-dollar bill, and they're the same size and color, why should it be a problem with this new coin?"

De Leo is getting weary of hearing himself talk. "There is an extraordinary amount of resistance to this coin out there," he said. "The public just doesn't seem to go for it. As far as I can tell, this coin isn't being accepted anywhere."

One of the things that is whispered around the Mint is that some of the negative feelings have to do not with the size of the coin, but with the fact that it has Susan B. Anthony on its face. Some Mint people think the public, perhaps subliminally, associates Miss Anthony with the women's movement, and even with the Equal Rights Amendment—and that the public dislikes the coin for this reason.

"Let's just say that marketing studies have told us not to put too much emphasis on the feminist angle," De Leo said.

In show business, when a performer's reputation is in trouble, his managers often hire a public relations firm. In what is believed to be a first in the annals of government currency, the Federal Reserve hired a PR agency for the Susan B. Anthony dollar: DWJ Associates, located in Manhattan. The fee was $150,000.

"Our job was to get the good story out about the coin," said Michael Friedman, executive vice-president of the PR firm. "But we made a false assumption. We assumed that there would be good stories to get out. There weren't. The negative thing got rolling, and it never stopped.

"We were looking for any little piece of good news about the coin, so we could feed it to the networks and the wire services. The stories didn't have to come from big cities; we were looking for the little town that decided to pay everyone in Susan B. Anthony coins—that kind of thing. We'd take *anything*. Spokane, San Luis Obispo, Dover-Foxcroft, Mobile . . . our feeling was that as soon as something good happened, we could start to build a success. But nothing good ever happened. Anywhere."

Friedman has his own theory of why the coin failed. He feels that, especially in a time of inflation, the Anthony dollar didn't *look* like a dollar; it was so small that people refused to take it seriously.

"Look, I used it, but I stopped after six months," Friedman said. "I got sick of it. I got sick of walking into the bank and having the tellers say 'Here comes that nut.' I got sick of fighting with cab drivers."

DWJ Associates has scrapbooks filled with news stories about the Anthony dollar. Getting space in the papers wasn't the problem. The problem was that people had already made up their minds that they wanted nothing to do with it.

"All the publicity in the world can't sell something that people don't want," Friedman said.

"You want to know what hurt the coin? The coin hurt the coin."

While everyone else can reflect on the disastrous past of the Susan B. Anthony dollar, one man has been charged with the responsibility of planning its future—if, indeed, it is to have one. He is Dr. Alan J. Goldman, assistant director of technology for the Mint. Goldman is a sour sort of fellow to talk to, as well he might be; he seems exasperated and annoyed that he has to fool with this matter.

"I can change the color of the coin," he said. "But I'm not sure that anything will happen."

And that is what Goldman is doing. He has transformed the metallurgic makeup of the Anthony dollar and has determined that he can give it a bronze tint by using a combination of aluminum, silicon, and copper. That will make it look different from a quarter.

"I don't believe it will work, though," Goldman said. "To make this coin fly, you've got to force it into use."

What he means is, you've got to withdraw dollar bills from circulation. Goldman's theory is that if paper dollars aren't available to people, they will have to use the Anthony dollar. That, he thinks, is the true answer to this dilemma. "As long as people are given a free choice," he said, "they will not use this coin."

Making policy decisions is not his job, though; his job is to change the color of the coin. So he is doing it, even though he knows that, somewhere down the line, more complaints await him.

"You see, when the bronze Susan B. Anthony coin tarnishes, it will tarnish to a greenish color," Goldman said.

When he talks to you about his work for even a few minutes, he begins to sigh; you get the impression that discussing the merits of the Susan B. Anthony dollar is not his favorite activity.

"Frankly," he said, "you are wasting my time."

Best not to leave the Anthony dollar on that note, however. The last word should go to Frank Gasparro, the septuagenarian designer who created the coin.

"Sometimes I'll go home at night," Gasparro said. "I'll pull the coin out, and I'll look at Susan B. Anthony. And I'll say, 'Well, you're not Marilyn Monroe, but you're mine.' "

Life of a Salesman

For a while there, before we knew any better, we spoke of them with the deepest disdain. "I suppose I might be a *salesman* when I get out of school," we would say, kidding. Sometimes, in bars, we would continue the joke. A stranger would initiate a conversation and ask what we did; "I'm an insurance salesman," we would say, breaking our friends up.

To a whole generation the very word—"salesman"—conjured up the worst possibilities that life could offer. To be on the street day after day, making business calls trying to peddle a product one did not necessarily believe in—that was the depth of hypocrisy, or so we told ourselves. That was the ultimate in selling out—and boring besides. We were a generation that was going to be creative and alive and free of spirit. We may have been a lot of things, we thought, but we were not going to be a generation of salesmen.

Well . . . I am on the road a lot. One of the staples of my life is the moment when I get off a plane, or arrive at an airport to catch a flight, and spend my spare minutes at a pay telephone. The phones are generally in a line, close together; you are able to hear what your neighbors are saying, to your left and to your right.

And what I overhear, time after time, is one of the melancholy stories of our modern age: the salesman checking in with his home office to confess he has not been able to make the sale he was sent out to consummate.

There is a pattern; I have seen the drama acted out enough times that I can almost tell when it is coming. The man moves the receiver away from the wall, then hesitates before making his call. He is figuratively, if not literally, taking a breath. When his superior back home answers, he begins the conversation in a hearty tone of voice. But soon enough he is required to give the news—it usually comes in some variation of "They think they're going to have to pass on it for now"—and it is not long before the party on the other end terminates the call.

I see these same men at tables for one in hotel dining rooms, on stools in hotel bars. I see them heading out into a city not their own at eight A.M., dressed as if they are expected at a fancy dinner; I see them coming back late in the afternoon, their ties loosened, their eyes distracted.

I see them everywhere, and I have come to understand that they are among the bravest of us. They face on a daily basis what we all dread the most: flat, cold rejection. Even the best of them hears "No" more than he hears "Yes"; the unlucky ones hardly hear "Yes" at all. Yet all of them get up each morning and go out to do it again—move through a world where they usually are not welcome, usually are considered a nuisance. And they dare not ever let their fear show on their faces; once they do, they are dead.

Especially in the current economic climate, their task seems brutal. No one has extra money to spend; individuals don't have it, and corporations don't have it, and everyone has been advised to ride the bad times out and wait for a turnaround. But the salesmen can't do that. If they don't sell, their families don't eat; if they don't sell, they don't live. Before they walk out the door in the morning they know they are probably going to fail. But they have no choice other than to try.

The rest of us can ease through our bad days without being stuck in the ribs. If things are not going well, the signs are usually subliminal. The salesman, though—there is no subtlety in the way he is told the bad news. There are a million ways to paraphrase it, but the basic message never changes: We don't want what you're selling. Go away.

Even on the good days, it is hard to imagine that the salesman's sleep comes easily. Even on the days when someone has said the magic word—"Yes"—the salesman goes to bed knowing that he's got to do it all over again in the morning. Can he feel glory?

Doubtful. The product is never his own. If he is able to sell it, the producer assumes that the product is so good it sells itself. When he is unable to sell it, the producer assumes that the salesman is lousy. Lousy, or getting old and tired.

So I see them everywhere—so will you, if you look. And it occurs to me that the salesmen are no longer only the older men so scorned by a generation. As I hear their tales on the pay telephones to either side of me, I glance over and see that more and more of them are a part of that generation. That generation is aging like every generation before it, and many of its dreamers are now salesmen, dreaming different dreams.

If there is something heroic about them—and I think that there is—it is a heroism that is destined to be felt only in their own hearts, or perhaps in the hearts of their families. They have learned to smile when they feel like cringing; they have learned to hit the streets when they feel like locking the door. Most of them may not have ever imagined they would end up doing precisely this. But as long as there is life and as long as there are businesses, there will be salesmen. When this generation is long forgotten, another generation's salesmen will be knocking on doors and taking a breath before phoning the home office. Trying to find a palatable explanation for that ugliest, most familiar word in their lexicon—"No."

Meeting Them More Than Halfway

THERE IS ABSOLUTELY no news in this story. But if you are getting a little tired of reading about warfare, crime, and meanness, you might want to give it a try anyway.

George and Thelma Washburn, of suburban Hinsdale, met a couple named Von and Lois Cook, of Mishawaka, Indiana, some years ago. Although they live a fairly long way from each other, the Washburns and the Cooks like to get together a couple of times a year, just to say hello.

This summer they decided it might be nice if they had dinner together. The Washburns didn't want to ask the Cooks to drive all the way to the Chicago area, and the Cooks didn't want to ask the Washburns to drive all the way to Mishawaka. So they compromised. They selected a town midway between—the town of Valparaiso, Indiana—and they agreed to meet there for a Sunday dinner.

They asked around, and someone recommended a Valparaiso restaurant called the White House. The food was supposed to be good.

The Washburns and the Cooks—all of them are in their sixties, by the way—decided to make a dinner reservation for five P.M. that Sunday. One of them called to make the reservation. Then they made arrangements to meet in the restaurant's cocktail lounge at three P.M., talk for a few hours, and then eat.

On the appointed day, George and Thelma Washburn drove from Hinsdale to Valparaiso. They found the restaurant, on the corner of Jefferson Street and Route 49. The restaurant was a beautiful old house. The Cooks were waiting for them in the parking lot.

The Washburns were so happy to see their friends that it didn't even strike them as odd that the Cooks' car was the only one in the lot.

"You're not going to believe what happened," Von Cook said as the Washburns got out of their own car.

The Cooks had gone into the restaurant, only to be told that it was closed for the day. Usually the White House is open Sundays and closed Mondays—but this particular week, it was closed on Sunday because the owners were having a private family party. The party was due to start in a few hours, and the guests would be arriving.

"The owners told us to come in when you arrived, and they would recommend someplace else around here," Von Cook said.

So the Washburns and the Cooks went into the restaurant.

The owners—twin brothers, Harry and John Pappas, both fifty-eight—led them to the cocktail lounge and insisted that they have a complimentary drink. The brothers were apologetic; they explained that the woman who took the reservation over the phone must have forgotten that the restaurant was due to be closed that Sunday.

The Washburns and the Cooks drank their cocktails and talked. And then the brothers appeared again.

"We feel so bad," Harry Pappas said, "we want you to stay for the party. We want you to be our guests. We insist."

The Washburns and the Cooks didn't know what to make of this. But they didn't have time to decide. Soon the guests started to arrive. There were seventy-five people in all; they had come to the restaurant to honor the high school graduation of the Pappas's niece, a young woman named Cathy Poulas.

Harry Pappas pulled the Washburns and the Cooks aside.

"I know you probably don't feel comfortable with a bunch of strangers," he said. "Nobody does. So just mingle if you wish—but I'm going to set you up your own table out on the terrace, where you can visit with each other like you planned in the first place."

The Pappas brothers moved a table out onto the back terrace. There were plants out there, and a big back yard and a fish pond. The Pappas brothers said that the buffet was inside, in one of the big rooms; the Washburns and the Cooks were to eat as much as they wanted. There would be no charge.

And so the party started. The Washburns and the Cooks were overwhelmed; they knew no one here, and all of a sudden they were joining people at the lavish buffet table. There was roast beef, and ham with pineapple, and a stew, and salads, and desserts. They helped themselves and went to their private table on the terrace.

They relived old times together, but they were interrupted as guests from the party came out to introduce themselves and welcome them. The Pappas brothers came out, too; they told the story of the White House restaurant—how it had been the family house for years, and how four years ago the brothers had decided to make it into a restaurant. The Pappas brothers explained all about the history of the house, and the significance of each room.

When the Washburns and the Cooks had finished with their meal and their conversation, they walked back into the house. The party was still in progress.

Mrs. Washburn didn't know what to say; she couldn't believe that they had been taken in just as if they had been invited. So she stood in the middle of the room full of strangers and said: "Thank you all. I just hope you had as nice a time today as we did."

The people in the room started to say goodbye to them, and the Pappas brothers got up to show them to the front door.

"Get home safe," Harry Pappas said.

So the Washburns drove toward Hinsdale, and the Cooks drove toward Mishawaka. Mrs. Washburn thought to herself: All you hear about is unfriendliness and nastiness; people are supposed to distrust each other and keep to themselves in a cocoon of self-protection. Once in a while, in a small restaurant off the main highway, you see another side.

Miss McNichol Will See You Now

KRISTY MCNICHOL, a cigarette dangling from her lips, fumed in the lobby of Los Angeles's Century Plaza hotel. America's preeminent cinematic symbol of youthful wholesomeness was clearly miffed.

"I look in my closet at home," she said. "The clothes are on the floor. I look for my Louis Vuitton bag. The Louis Vuitton bag is missing. I look for my two Sony Walkmans. The Sony Walkmans are gone. My videotape recorder—gone. My alarm clock—gone."

"Have you called the police?" I asked.

"No," Kristy said. "I called my accountant."

"You're going to have to call the police if you want to get insurance money," I said. "There has to be a police report."

"My accountant said I didn't have to call the police," Kristy said.

Her grandfather interjected: "If she calls the police it'll be in the papers." Her grandfather's name was Don Corey. A gentleman of sixty-four, he wore brown-and-white-striped pants, a yellow shirt that he had not tucked in, and running shoes.

Kristy took another drag from the cigarette. Her diamond earrings glistened in the artificial light. "I don't have to call the police," she said. "I'm just never going to talk to the person who did it again."

"You know who did it?" I asked.

"Maybe," Kristy said.

"Who?" I asked.

"Maybe an ex-boyfriend," Kristy said.

"Someone you went out with would do something like that to you?" I asked.

"You never know," Kristy said. She ground out the cigarette in a glass ashtray. She was clearly in no mood to chitchat.

Kristy decided that a remedy for last night's burglary of her condominium would be a shopping trip. A baby-blue limousine waited for her outside the hotel. She walked briskly to the car. Her grandfather and I followed.

The driver, a young blond-haired man named Jimmy, said, "Where to?"

"Century City Shopping Centre," Kristy said.

Her grandfather started to tell a story.

"I was a winner on the Arthur Godfrey 'Talent Scouts' program," he said. "It was 1947."

He had to stop his story because we were at the shopping

center. It was directly across the street from the hotel. We could have walked to it in less than a minute.

"Pull into the garage," Kristy said.

The chauffeur did.

In the Broadway department store, we rode the escalator. Kristy seemed to know where she was going. Her grandfather and I hurried to catch up.

In the electronic-entertainment department, she walked up to a salesman.

"Miss McNichol," he said. "How nice to see you."

"I'd like another VHS videotape machine just like my other one," she said.

"The big one?" the salesman said.

"The 250, like I had before," Kristy said. "Is it available?"

"For the next few days we have a special on the 450," the salesman said.

Kristy's grandfather said, "Does it have remote control?"

"That doesn't matter," Kristy said. "Bring me one."

The salesman went into a back room. When he came out he was carrying a videotape machine in a box. Kristy had not asked the price. She handed him her American Express Gold Card.

"Also I have to get another thing," she said. "You know the Sony Walkman with the case on it?"

"I don't believe we carry cases for the Walkman," the salesman said.

Kristy's grandfather said, "Not a Walkman case. The whole Walkman."

"It's nice that you keep us in business during these times of economic stress," the salesman said with a laugh.

Kristy lit another cigarette. "Jimmy?" she called.

The chauffeur appeared.

"I want you to carry this videotape recorder to the car," Kristy said.

"Joey is the person who is closest to me," Kristy said. She referred to Joe Corsaro, a Beverly Hills hairdresser who was twenty-six. Kristy was nineteen.

"Joey knows that I can't be tied to one person, though," she said. "For instance, I just got back from a trip to Hawaii with Tim Hutton."

"What did Joey say?" I asked.

"He didn't say anything," Kristy said. "He knows it's my business. I'm free to be with other people. To meet, and talk, and exchange ideas."

"A trip to Hawaii sounds like quite a way to exchange ideas," I said.

"Yeah," Kristy said. She smiled. "I know."

We were walking through the shopping center. Kristy entered a store called Leather Bound. She walked directly to a large suitcase.

Her grandfather said, "Where do you kill the cow for this?"

"These are almost all calf," the salesman said.

"I love leather," Kristy said. "Don't you have anything bigger than this?"

"That's the largest one we have," the salesman said. "It is three hundred ninety dollars."

"I wish you had a bigger one," Kristy said, and left the store.

She walked into a shoe store. She gazed around for a second or two.

"Nope," she said.

"What didn't you see?" I asked.

"I didn't see quality shoes," she said.

In a clothing store called Judy's, she led her grandfather to a display showing a skimpy garment made of leather, festooned with metal zippers.

"Can you see me in this, Grandpa?" she said.

"Good," her grandfather said.

"It's not good, it's disgusting," Kristy said.

"I was just thinking of your great-looking legs," her grandfather said.

She reached toward her grandfather's mouth. She took the cigarette he had been smoking. She put it in her mouth and inhaled. She handed it back to her grandfather. She also handed him her purse. "Carry this for me," she said.

She wandered around the store. She saw a woman's tuxedo suit.

"Let me have this," she said to a saleswoman. She handed the woman her Gold Card.

"Aren't you even going to try it on?" I asked. "How do you know it fits?"

"It probably fits," Kristy said.

"But what if it doesn't?" I said.

"Usually I can tell," Kristy said.

Kristy was hungry. So the three of us went to Lindberg's, a health-food restaurant in the shopping center. There was a brief wait for a table. A young man who was also waiting, not quite able to believe that he was standing next to Kristy McNichol, got up the courage to talk to her. He asked her what her next movie project would be.

"It's about a handicapped girl," Kristy said.

The boy said, "Do you become handicapped during the movie?"

Kristy's grandfather said, "No, before the movie I break her legs."

The young man blushed. "The only reason I asked is that I work with handicapped people. I work with blind people."

"Is that right," Kristy said.

"Have you ever worked with handicapped people?" the young man asked.

Kristy looked to see if our table was ready. "I've thought about working in an orphanage," she said.

"Do you know places?" the young man said. "Because if you don't, I could suggest some places."

Kristy's grandfather said, "Give us your name, maybe we'll call you."

For lunch Kristy ordered a dish called the Health Nut. Kristy said that she would like to be with regular people more, but that she rarely got the chance.

"I was on a cruise with Joey once, and I wanted to get a little lunch, so I went down to the dining room without him, and some people recognized me," she said. "They asked me if I wanted to join them. They said, 'Sit with us.' That was nice."

"Did you do it?" I asked.

"No," Kristy said.

"Why not?" I asked.

"I was in a hurry," Kristy said.

I asked her why she thought so many people felt such warmth toward her when they saw her on the screen.

She ate. "I don't know," she said. "People say I invite people into my eyes. That's what I've been told. Maybe that's it."

I asked her how she met young men.

"It isn't hard," she said.

I asked her to give me an example.

"All right," she said, "I was at this club called the Lingerie. I saw this guy wearing black leather pants and an Elvis rockabilly shirt. I thought he was hot. I danced with him."

"Did he call you after that?" I asked.

"I called him," she said. "I don't give out my number."

"Was he surprised to hear from you?" I asked.

"I don't know," she said. "I just said, 'Hey, this is Kristy.' We got together."

"So what happened?" I said.

"I think he was trying to get me in the palm of his hand," Kristy said. "I think he thought maybe I would be weak. I'm not."

She said that she almost never read any of her fan mail. I asked her why not.

"I get a lot of feedback just walking around," she said. "I hear so much from people on the street, from my family. I don't need to go home and read letters saying how great I am."

"She doesn't have the time," her grandfather said.

"I just don't feel like reading them," she said.

" 'I adore you,' 'I love you,' 'I want to marry you,' " her grandfather said.

" 'I'll jump out of a window for you,' " Kristy said. "I don't need that."

We were in the parking lot that was constructed beneath the shopping center. Kristy had forgotten on which level the limousine was parked; we had not seen the driver since he had been dispatched to carry the videotape recorder.

All around us people moved toward their cars or toward the

passageways into the shopping center. I suggested that we go down another level to look for the car.

Kristy just stopped walking. She stood in the garage and put her hands on her hips. She began to shout:

"Jimmy!"

There was no answer. She shouted again:

"Jimmy!" "Jimmy!" "Jimmy!"

Still no response. She shot a stare at her grandfather, who had been standing silently. He caught the look. In a second he was shouting, too:

"Jimmy! Jimmy! Jimmy!"

The next day Kristy had a lunch date with Joey Corsaro at Benihana of Tokyo, on La Cienega Boulevard. When I arrived they were already eating.

Joey wore a white sleeveless T-shirt. He was brown and lean and quite handsome. Between bites of food he reached over to rub Kristy's leg, or caress her arm. He said nothing.

I asked her if she ever had trouble with people envying her.

"Not women," she said. "Just the guys. I can see it in their eyes. It's males."

I asked her why she thought they felt that way.

"Probably because I've done more in nineteen years than they'll do in their lifetimes," she said.

She reached over to run her hand up Joey's forearm.

I asked her what she thought the greatest public misconception about her was.

"That I'm the all-American girl," she said. "Perfect and cute and good and level-headed."

I noticed that Joey was wearing a clear jeweled earring in the lobe of his left ear. I asked him if it was a diamond.

"What, do you think Kristy would give me a piece of glass?" he said.

The Jimmie Soules Suite

Decatur, Illinois—The person taking my reservation at the Holiday Inn suggested that I try staying in the Executive Suite. I figured that as long as I was in Decatur, the Executive Suite sounded fine.

But then she discovered that the Executive Suite was already booked for the night.

"We could put you in the Jimmie Soules Suite," she said.

"The Jimmie Soules Suite?" I said.

"Yes," she said.

I wasn't going to argue. When I arrived I took my key and went to the second floor, and there, where Room 227 would normally be, was a door with a big brass plaque mounted on it, and inscribed on the big brass plaque was "Mr. and Mrs. Jimmie Soules Suite."

Now, as you know if you read this column regularly, there is nothing I like better than hotel rooms. They bring me inner peace and grant me sustenance; I prefer being in a hotel room to being in my own home. I am a person who pays close attention to hotel rooms.

But in all my travels, I had never come across anything like the Jimmie Soules Suite. I don't mean the room itself; it was very nice, with a canopied bed and an AM-FM radio and a new couch. But the name of the room—I have heard of Monarch Suites and Presidential Suites and Royal Suites and Regal Suites. But a Mr. and Mrs. Jimmie Soules Suite?

Another traveler might have shrugged and let the matter go. But I lay awake and pondered the perplexing question: Who was Jimmie Soules? Did he own this Holiday Inn? Was he a famous entertainer in Decatur? Was he a former governor of Illinois I had never heard of?

My sleep was fitful. In the morning, as I was checking out, I said to the desk clerk:

"I don't mean to be ignorant, but who is Jimmie Soules?"

The young woman returned a blank stare.

"Hasn't anyone ever asked you that question before?" I said.

"Not that I can recall," she said.

I couldn't continue my life without knowing. Jimmie Soules. Jimmie Soules. I sought out the manager of the hotel—at Holiday Inns they are called "innkeepers"—and requested an audience. The innkeeper's name was Dieter Schultz.

"Who is Jimmie Soules?" I said.

"You don't know who Jimmie Soules is?" Schultz said.

"You mean I ought to know?" I said.

Schultz laughed. "I'm only kidding you," he said. "Jimmie Soules is just a man who hangs around the hotel."

"What do you mean?" I said.

"He's a good fellow who hangs around the hotel, so the innkeeper who was here before I took over named a suite after him," Schultz said. "He's like a fixture here. When I arrived six years ago to take over, this man walked up to me and said 'I'm Jimmie Soules.' His name was already on the suite by then, of course."

I felt a sense of awe. Having a hotel room named after you . . . to me, that is the greatest honor a man could ever achieve. And this man Jimmie Soules had done it just by hanging around the Holiday Inn.

I knew I must find Jimmie Soules.

In Decatur, it wasn't that hard. Jimmie Soules turned out to be an eighty-one-year-old man who was delighted to learn that I had slept in his suite the night before.

"Hope you liked it," he said.

I couldn't believe I was really talking to Jimmie Soules. Stammering and struggling to make conversation, I asked him what he did for a living.

"I'm in the bird-repellent business," he said. "I control pigeons, starlings, and sparrows. I can get rid of them without killing a single bird."

I couldn't think of a follow-up question, but luckily for me, Jimmie Soules was still rolling.

"I can walk out on any ledge at two o'clock in the morning, even if it's only twelve inches wide, and check out the birds," he said. "Some people say I even think like a bird. When a pigeon flies, I can tell where he's going."

I said that sounded great, but my main interest was the hotel suite. Had he really had it named after him just by hanging around the Holiday Inn?

"I'm in there quite a bit," he said.

I said that it must be quite a thrill to sleep in a hotel room with your name on the door.

"To tell you the truth, I have never slept in that suite," Jimmy Soules said. "I used to ask my wife to go stay there with me, but she always said that we had a beautiful home and she preferred to sleep here. She passed away in February, and we had never slept there. But when my grandson was married, I let him sleep in the suite on his wedding night."

I was a little flabbergasted. I said goodbye to Jimmie Soules, and repeated how much I had enjoyed sleeping in his suite.

"Thank you," he said.

In the days since, I have reflected on the experience. Some men want to be president. Some men yearn to win the Nobel Prize. Some men lust to sit in the anchor chair on the "CBS Evening News."

But Jimmie Soules, eighty-one, of Decatur, Illinois, has achieved the only dream that I find thrilling. To have your name on the door of some Holiday Inn somewhere, marking your presence in the hotel even on the nights you are unavoidably detained at home . . . that, to me, is what the promise and possibility of America are all about.

Rush Week

THIS IS A story that happened ten years ago. It bears retelling today.

The story should be repeated because, all of a sudden, fraternities are very big on the college campuses once again. A movie called *Animal House* has a lot to do with it. For a few years fraternities suffered a lull in popularity, but now they are back. National magazines are devoting feature stories to fraternity pranks, and television news shows are filming fraternity parties. The country is being told about the fun and craziness of the college fraternity system.

But there is another side. As long as the fraternities exist, there will be another side.

The boy's name was Jon. He was a bright kid. He came to Northwestern in that autumn of 1968 for his freshman year, and he signed up for fraternity rush.

He had something wrong with the way his body was formed. It made him look unusual. Maybe he didn't know what lay in store for him during rush week; maybe he did know, but had determined that he would do his best anyway.

His best wasn't very good. At the first house where he showed up for a rush date, one of the rush chairmen saw Jon and grinned. Jon didn't look like all of the other freshmen who were going through rush, so he made an easy target.

He was placed in a corner, by himself, and he was allowed to sit there for two hours. No one greeted him, no one talked to him. When the others went downstairs to the dining room for their meal, Jon was left to stay by himself in the living room.

He waited the whole time, and when the meal was over and

all of the other freshmen were leaving the house, Jon got up and walked out with the rest. He went on to the next house on his schedule, and again he was sized up at the door, and again he was shunted aside.

At some of the houses it was more subtle than at others. Some fraternities had entire rooms where young men like Jon were placed, so as not to disturb the other freshmen who were judged to be fraternity material. Not all of them had physical disabilities such as Jon's, of course; most were simply not handsome, or were awkward, or were dressed poorly. They were extraneous; they got in the way of rush week.

At one house, Jon was led out onto a fire escape and made to stand there for over an hour. It was an astonishing kind of cruelty; maybe things are different in fraternity rush now. Maybe things have changed.

And then, one night, two active members of one of the fraternities were assigned to make a rush call on a good prospect in a freshman dorm. The two were seniors; they were becoming disillusioned with the fraternity system, but they were going through with rush week this last time. They looked through the dorm for the boy they wanted, and somehow they went to the wrong room, and there was Jon, crying on his bed.

The two seniors could have turned and walked out, but for some reason they didn't. They sat down and they asked Jon what was wrong. He was reluctant to discuss it, but then he told them; told them what had happened to him during rush week, and how it was breaking his heart.

He told them about how he hadn't been given even a sliver of a chance, even by one house. He told them how desperately afraid he was of college. They listened to him and they understood that Jon's story was the story of so many boys who signed up for fraternity rush, and were then casually humiliated because, for various small reasons, they were not judged suitable. It was a hurt that would stay for years, and they knew it.

The two seniors listened, and they talked quietly to Jon, and after they had left him in his dorm they knew they would have to do something about it. Jon was determined to continue with rush week, and they knew they could not let him go through it alone.

So they went to the central rush office, and they got a copy of Jon's rush schedule for the rest of the week. And that night they started to visit the houses where Jon would be going in the days to come.

At every house, the two of them asked to talk to the fraternity members. They explained what they had come for. They told the fraternity men about Jon, and the way he looked. And they said: We are not asking you to take him into your fraternity. We are just asking you not to hurt him anymore.

Surprisingly, the fraternity men listened. There were a few snickers, but not many, and by the time the two of them were through they had talked to every house where Jon was scheduled to go. The two of them didn't talk much to each other about it; they didn't know exactly why they were doing this. But it was the first grown-up thing they had ever done, and it felt right.

Jon went through the rest of rush week. He was not asked to join a house, but he was treated with decency. The fraternities he visited assigned members to talk to him, to eat with him, and to make him feel welcome. Perhaps the pain was lessened a little.

The two seniors ended up quitting their fraternity. Part of it had to do with Jon, and part of it had to do with other aspects of the fraternity system. They just wanted no part of it anymore.

They lived in an apartment off campus. As far as they knew, Jon didn't know about what they had done. They completed their senior year, and in the spring they prepared to graduate.

And then, one day, a congratulatory graduation card came addressed to them in the mail. They opened it. It was from Jon.

"Thank you," it said. . . .

Targets

I ARRIVED IN Atlanta on a Monday evening. The number of murdered and missing children stood at twenty-three. There had been no arrests.

I did not want to talk to police officials. I did not want to talk to psychiatrists. I did not want to talk to social workers. I had read enough of what they had to say about the case.

I wanted to talk to children. Every time I heard about the Atlanta killings, all I could think about was how they must be affecting the children who were living in the middle of them.

But children do not have press conferences, and children do not have public relations spokesmen. Until they were dead, the children of Atlanta had no way to get people's attention. And it was not the dead children of Atlanta I was curious about. It was the children who were still alive. So I got on a plane.

"I don't go outside," said Denise Durr. She was a tiny girl, seven years old. "He might kill me or my friends."

School had just let out for the afternoon. I had been waiting across the street for half an hour. It was a strange way to be conducting business, but I was finding it was the only way.

The city of Atlanta and the public schools had decided that no one from news organizations would be allowed to talk to children on school property. It was a policy that probably made sense. It ensured that the corridors would not be overrun with camera crews.

But if I wanted to talk to children, I certainly couldn't stop them on the streets individually. Not in the terrified atmosphere in 1981 Atlanta. I had to go to a place where the children would feel safe in numbers, and where they might talk to me without running away.

So that meant spending time standing across the street from elementary schools in black neighborhoods, looking at my watch and waiting for the final bell of the day to sound. A number of motorists slowed down and gave me quizzical glances. It was hard to blame them.

It was working, though. The children, buoyed by the courage that comes from being together in large groups, stopped to talk to me. We talked one at a time; they all stood around and watched. I seemed as much a curiosity to them as they were to me. I got the impression that they didn't see many white men spending time in their neighborhoods.

The worst thing was how normal the idea of random murder had become to such little children. They talked about it easily, the way children in other cities might talk about a favorite television show. If, in the rest of the country, the story of the Atlanta killings was a horrible abstraction, here it was a tumorous part of everyday life.

So my wonder grew as child after child told me of an obsession with the idea of death. "He may get me next," said Roderick Hednut, ten. Troy Lee, twelve, said, "I can't get to sleep. I keep thinking the man may come and get me." Larcquo Sharpe, eleven, put it as a question: "The children haven't done anything to him. So if we haven't, why doesn't he stop?"

It all seemed so out-of-sync. The week was warm in Atlanta, and these children should have been on their way to play. But they weren't; they had orders to be home within fifteen minutes after the end of the school day. If a visitor from another country, or another year, had overheard our conversations, he would have been startled. The boys and girls were healthy-looking and handsome. Nickie Marshall, nine, smiled shyly. She might have been telling me about her first sweetheart. But what she said was: "I think I'm going to get kidnapped or something. I've been having dreams about it. One night I dreamt this man, he was following me, and I ran and he caught me and I was kicking and screaming and he killed me."

Law enforcement officials were speculating that the Atlanta murders might not be the work of one killer, but of several. To the children, though, there was only one person at work. He was a man, and they called him "the Snatcher."

And as the children told me the words their parents were using to warn and discipline them, I had to wonder what future scars these months will leave on their souls. "If you're not in by dark, the Snatcher's going to get you." "You be good, or you're the next one the Snatcher's going to snatch."

Some of the children were full of braggadocio, and it was not hard to understand. In the face of the killings, it was an outlet, a mask. So when a seven-year-old boy named Richie Kraft said to me, "If he tries to get me, I'll cut his nose off," the other children watching us talk started to giggle. And Frederick Williams, seven, seemed to be addressing the killer himself when he said in a defiant voice, "What if someone came up to you and had a gun in *your* face? What would you do then?"

With others, though, it was different. I spoke with a sixteen-year-old boy named Anthony Zachary. "I'm not worried," he said, although his eyes betrayed his words.

I asked him how he could say he was calm, with all the children dying.

"I've got protection," he said, and at the same time he reached into his back pocket, pulled out a switchblade knife, and flashed its six-inch blade in front of me.

In another setting it might have been an ominous moment. But as he postured here, waving the knife before my mouth, he seemed very alone, and very vulnerable.

One of the unexpected things about spending time in Atlanta was the fact that every person on the street did not seem to be the murderer; every face did not seem to conceal the secret of the child killer.

I had expected to presume malice everywhere I turned. In a city where the child killings had been going on for so long, it seemed natural to assume that every stranger encountered would stand at least a chance of appearing to be the one.

But it wasn't like that. If I had believed, from afar, that everyone was going to seem like the killer, I was finding that precisely the opposite was true. The bodies had been turning up for so long, and the person or persons responsible had been evading capture for so long, that now, in Atlanta, it almost seemed as if no one was the killer.

Because the victims had all been black, I had been spending my time only in black neighborhoods.

One afternoon, across the street from a school out of which the children emerged minutes earlier, I stood and talked to the black boys and girls for a long time. I was getting used to hearing their fears and unhappy fantasies; by now the pervasive terror that had at first stunned me was becoming commonplace.

As usual, all the children waited while I asked my questions; they did not break off one by one, but left as a group. And I was getting ready to depart when I noticed that three boys had stayed behind.

They were white. For some reason they went to this nearby all-black school; they were the only white children I had seen in days. Hesitantly, they asked if I would talk to them, too.

Their names were David Stewart, Philip Bailey, and James Koenig. We started to speak, and it immediately became evident that they were every bit as frightened as the black children with whom I had talked. Their fear seemed almost more intense, if that is possible, because they were supposedly safe.

David Stewart was twelve. "The man may change from black to white," he said. "He might come to get me." James Koenig, ten, said, "He might come and kidnap me. I have dreams every night that I might get killed like the other kids got killed." Philip Bailey, also twelve, was too bashful to say much of anything.

I stood there, not knowing what to say to them. It was clear that they just wanted someone to talk to. After a few moments of awkward silence, they left, together.

The fear kept the children virtually locked inside after school hours. The months of this particular kind of house arrest were beginning to wear on them.

Rodrigues Martin, eleven, was an athletic-looking boy who

appeared as if he belonged on a playing field. "I can't shoot basketball, I can't play football, I can't do anything," he told me. I heard this from child after child. They were at the age when they should have been unleashing all of their young energy, and yet it, too, was a victim of the murders. Some of the boys and girls spoke with a kind of depressed listlessness that I had come across before—in prisoners at maximum-security penitentiaries.

One evening during my stay in Atlanta, I went over to the Omni complex. I had learned that I was not likely to see many children after dark; a seven P.M. curfew kept most of them inside, and the reality of the murders was a persuader for those who might not respect mere statute.

On this night, though, I saw a young boy in a sport coat walking along with his father. I introduced myself to the man; I explained what I was doing, and asked if I might talk to his son. He said yes.

The father told the boy it was all right to go with me. We walked about twenty feet away; the boy was still within eyeshot of his father, and shoppers were strolling past us, but we were in effect alone. It was one of the few times during the week when there had not been other children around as I talked to someone.

The boy's name was Tony Smith. He was nine, and quite small. As I talked to him, his voice quavered, and I thought I saw his eyes filling with tears. And then he said it: "Do not kill me."

His voice was so soft that I thought I might have misunderstood. I asked him to repeat what he had said.

"I want to have a family," he said. "Do not kill me."

I had talked with more than one hundred children since I had arrived in Atlanta. Virtually all of them I had met through the random method of waiting for the various black schools to empty out. But there was one child I specifically wanted to meet.

He was Johnathan Bell, twelve years old, whose younger brother, Yusef, had been the fourth child to disappear. Yusef had been missing for seventeen days when he was found strangled.

Many of the children I had spoken with had given me grisly details of what they would like to see done to the murderer if he was eventually caught. Most of the boys and girls wanted him to die, some in gruesome ways. It did not seem particularly bloodthirsty to me; these were little children, after all, and their imaginations had been fueled by dark reality.

So I accepted their judgments, but I wanted to know what Johnathan Bell would say when I asked him the same question. Did he want his brother's killer to die? I went to his home one evening, chatted aimlessly with him for about fifteen minutes, and then asked him. Say the killer was found. What would he like to see done to him?

His answer, when it came, was delivered in a calm voice. Johnathan Bell looked me straight in the eye. It was clear he had thought about it before.

"I think he should be put in a room," he said. "With white all over it. A white room.

"And then they should put pictures of all the children he killed up on the wall. All of those pictures.

"And then they should leave him in there. For life."

When I left it was on a morning flight. I was back in the town where I live by midafternoon.

On the way to my home from the airport, I saw children playing and running in city parks; children walking along the sidewalks together; children talking casually on street corners. Atlanta seemed very far away; like a vivid scene out of a book you only half-remember. Like a flash from a terrible time out of your past. Like a moment from a child's dream.

Bachelor of the Month

ON PAGE 114 of the March 1981 issue of *Cosmopolitan* magazine, in the Cosmo Tells All section, there appeared the magazine's Bachelor of the Month.

The feature is a mainstay of each edition; when a woman purchases the magazine, she knows she will find a capsule description of a real-life eligible male.

The small black-and-white photograph in the March issue showed a handsome, smiling man with dark hair and a moustache. He was wearing a short-sleeved polo shirt and a pair of faded blue jeans, and was gripping a racket with his right hand.

The sketch read:

> Chicago's Jeff Kaiser, 30, owns Lakeshore Centre, a "total athletic environment" where 11,000(!) members can swim, sun, play tennis, even indoor ski. Jeff, whose *other* passions include opera and sailboat racing, wants a "warm-spirited woman who's not always crying 'me, me, me.' " Big-hearted girls may write 1320 W. Fullerton Ave., Chicago 60614.

Men who happen to glance occasionally at *Cosmopolitan* may have fantasized about being stopped on the street by a *Cosmo* editor and offered the Bachelor-of-the-Month slot, and the chance to be displayed before all those *Cosmo* women. In the case of Jeff Kaiser, it did not happen precisely that way.

Howard Bragman, twenty-five, is a publicist with the Richardson & McElveen public relations firm in Chicago. Late last year, he was talking on the telephone with Jane Makley, an editor at *Cosmo*. He was pitching a story idea about one of his firm's clients. Makley was not responding well to the pitch, but she and Bragman were having a pleasant conversation. At one point Makley asked Bragman how old he was—they had never met face-to-face—and when he told her, she said, "Maybe you should be a Bachelor of the Month."

For the briefest instant, Bragman's brain buzzed with the possibilities. Not for nothing is he an ambitious young publicist, though. Immediately all lustful thoughts disappeared from his head, and were replaced by two words: *ink* and *client*.

So it was that the phone rang at the Lakeshore Centre club— a client of Richardson & McElveen—and Jeff Kaiser, who had never heard of the *Cosmo* Bachelor of the Month, took the call and learned that Howard Bragman thought he could get him into the magazine.

Six months later Jeff Kaiser sat in his apartment on the four-teenth floor of a high-rise on the North Side of Chicago. In his hand was a drink; on the table, on the couch, and on the floor were more than seven hundred letters from women.

Howard Bragman had submitted Kaiser's photograph to *Cosmopolitan*; the publicist had also given the magazine some facts about Kaiser's background, and within a month of the first con-versation between Bragman and Jane Makley, Jeff Kaiser had been selected for the March issue.

Now Kaiser—a divorced father of two—picked up a stack of the letters, allowed the envelopes to tumble through his hands and back to the floor, and tried to explain the feeling.

"My PR man told me it would be good for business," Kaiser said. "So I told him to do what he had to do. I had no idea they put your address in until some writer from the magazine called to interview me. When I found out that they actually printed a place where women could write, I almost pulled out, but it did seem like it would be good publicity for the club.

"And then it started. Thirty, forty, fifty letters a day, every day. Phone calls from all over the country at the club. Women would lie, would make up business excuses to talk to me. And I would come to the phone—and here would be some woman calling from South Carolina, and she would say, 'Oh, my God, I didn't believe you were real.' "

Kaiser has been physically attractive all his life, but now, be-cause his photograph had appeared in the magazine, he was learning for the first time what it is to be a celebrity. "It's all a matter of levels of fantasy," he said. "The women who are writing are one level below me. I'm one level up, because I'm in the magazine. And then above me is someone like a movie star. At least that's how I'm starting to think about it; I'm new at this, you know.

"This is what I think it is: the magazine makes you famous, but unlike most famous people, you're accessible. They print your address. See, that's the fantasy: they're telling the woman that here's this attractive man, or this rich man, or this talented man—and here's where you can write him, and he'll get your letter.

"It's like they made me a Playmate of the Month, but they changed the rules. It's like they printed the Playmate's address next to her picture. They could never do that in the case of a woman. But their whole gimmick is that with a man, they can do it."

From Iowa:

Dear Jeff:
    Here goes. This is a first. I've never responded to anything such as this before. But I decided that since you were so nice-looking in *Cosmo*, I would let you know. Probably along with hundreds of other women! I am 5'11", 130 lbs. and 27. I work for the U.S. Postal Service as a clerk-carrier. . . .

From Florida:

Dear Jeff:
    I was just sitting here on the beach reading a *Cosmopolitan* magazine when your beautiful smile caught my attention. And since the article read "Big-hearted girls may write," I decided that I would. . . .

From Wisconsin:

Dear Jeff:
    I have never written a letter like this and I don't know why I'm starting now. I guess because Chicago is relatively near where I live. I'll only be 18 on June 26, but I feel older than that because I feel so stifled in my life the way I'm living. . . . I am waiting to find a two-sided relationship that will remain two-sided and not become one-sided for either side after any amount of time. I have an intense need for hugging and being hugged. . . .

Many of the women enclosed photographs with their letters. The great majority of them were quite attractive; the women writing to Jeff Kaiser did not appear to be people who would have any trouble finding a man. They were professional women and salesclerks; credit managers and students. "I never thought

I would answer an ad in a magazine," wrote a fashion model from northern Illinois. "I hope to God you don't know any of the same people I do." And there was the woman dentist from Georgia; the letter was on her office stationery, and above her signature there was only one sentence: "Why not make your next dental appointment in Atlanta?"

Almost all of the women said that this was the first time they had written to a stranger from a magazine; almost all of them made at least one reference to being "big-hearted" or not being interested in crying "me, me, me." There were the predictable letters from both ends of the spectrum: a few women who included lewd photos of themselves, and a few lost and solitary women whose cries of loneliness were almost heartbreaking.

But all of the others were from women who seemed bright or pretty or both. If one tried to read all the letters—and trying to do so was an endeavor that took many hours—one ended up deciding that these women did, indeed, have ample opportunities to meet men in their hometowns. But their demands were high; they indicated that the men they knew bored them, were dreary. They knew nothing about Jeff Kaiser. Maybe if they met him at their own offices, they would never have thought to approach him. But his picture had been in *Cosmo;* in all America, he had been selected as Bachelor of the Month; thus he was interesting. His appeal had been officially validated.

None of the women mentioned sex in the letters. Not one. Few even hinted at it. At least on paper, they were not lusting for Jeff Kaiser. They were idealizing him.

Brenda Groendyk, twenty-seven, is a receptionist at the Steelcase office-furniture manufacturing plant in Grand Rapids, Michigan. Her letter began: "Dearest Jeff: I saw your picture and description in the latest *Cosmopolitan* magazine and was immediately intrigued. Can we meet?" She signed it "Amour." Stapled to her letter was a color snapshot of herself in a blue bikini, squinting in the sun next to a chain-link fence. Her blond hair curled over her shoulders. On the back of the photo, in blue ink, she had written: "I do not bleach my hair! I have not had a silicone job!"

I called her and explained why I had seen her letter. I said I would like to talk to her. She agreed, and we met for dinner.

"I mainly wrote it to see what would happen," she said. "Most of the men I meet are either boring or married. Grand Rapids is kind of a conservative city, and I'm a little more progressive with my ideas."

She has never been married, but said that the possibility of matrimony was not included in the reasons she wrote to Jeff Kaiser: "When you get married, you think in terms of a normal man. Not someone who's had his picture in a national magazine. That's too unbelievable. I just wanted to meet him and see if we liked each other."

Most of the women I spoke to echoed that. Some were embarrassed, and even angry, that someone other than Kaiser had seen the letters. But when we talked, the recurrent theme had to do with their inability to find someone they considered "good enough" in their own towns. There were plenty of men to sleep with, if that's what the women wanted; but they didn't necessarily want that. What did they want? An "interesting" man. And how were they so sure that this man in Chicago—this man they had never met—would please them where others hadn't? The answer: He had been in *Cosmo*, hadn't he? Out of all the bachelors in America, he had been chosen that month. When I told them about Howard Bragman and his public relations firm, there was often a moment of vague confusion. It had not occurred to them that the Bachelor of the Month might require a middleman, a business partner.

They put that out of their minds, though. The *Cosmo* profile of Jeff Kaiser had been only fifty-four words long, but that was enough to convince the women. Paula Grecco, twenty-eight, of Cuyahoga Falls, Ohio, told me: "If I'm going to go out with a guy, I don't want him to be some factory worker who's making eight dollars an hour at General Tire." When I asked her what was so wrong with her town, she said, "Sucks." She said, "Some days I get asked out five times, but I haven't had a date in a month. I just don't choose to be with these men."

Many of the women used harsh words to describe the men they knew: "hillbillies," "wimps," "losers." The women had put themselves on the line to the man from *Cosmo* because they thought he might be able to rescue them from all that. Every woman I talked to said to me: "Do you know if he's going to call me?" Some of them said it at the beginning of our conversations, and some of them said it at the end, but they all said it.

Three months after he had first appeared in *Cosmopolitan*, Jeff Kaiser had failed to contact a single one of the seven hundred women who had written him. He had not made one call; he had not written one note.

"I don't know how to say this without it sounding arrogant," Kaiser said. "I have a very full life with women as it is. I don't need to meet these women who have been writing. I'm glad that I did this. It was good for the club. And it was great for my ego to get the mail. But I don't have to actually meet the women for my ego to feel good. There's a fantasy here, but meeting the women has nothing to do with it. Just getting the letters takes care of that.

"If one woman lets you know she thinks you're attractive, you might think about it. But when you're getting fifty letters a day, all saying the same thing? Even if you do start to think about one of them, you've forgotten her by the time you open the next envelope.

"This was an interesting experience. But I didn't do it to meet any new women. Maybe someday I'll call one, or write one.

"But I doubt it."

Woody in Exile

COLUMBUS, OHIO—Darkness had just given way to dawn. The visitor waited on the sidewalk outside the hotel. Across Third Street, the sign on the Ohio State

Federal Savings and Loan Building flashed that it was thirty-five degrees.

A gray pickup truck pulled to a stop. The visitor walked around to the passenger side and climbed inside.

"Thanks for picking me up, Coach," the visitor said.

"Well, that's all right," said Woody Hayes. "I'm glad to have the company."

Hayes was behind the wheel of the truck. It has been almost a year since his career as head football coach at Ohio State University was brought to an end when he slugged a Clemson University player during the Gator Bowl. Hayes is a national catchphrase; the words "Woody Hayes" bring nods and knowing smiles whenever they are mentioned. Now there is a new football era in Columbus; a new coach, Earle Bruce, has an undefeated team, and Woody Hayes's twenty-eight-year reign is past tense.

Now the new coach is preparing his team for the season's climactic game with Michigan, and that is the talk all around Columbus; but Woody Hayes still lives. He gets up every morning at his house at 1711 Cardiff Road, and he goes through the day. He is sixty-six years old; behind the wheel of his truck he wore a dark blue business suit and a brown felt hat pulled down hard over his white hair.

"We're going to Westerville, Ohio," Hayes said. "I'm supposed to talk to some high school students. It's . . . what do you call it? When you tell them what they're supposed to do in life?"

"Careers Day?" the visitor said.

"Right," Hayes said. "Careers Day. I'm supposed to tell them about the coaching profession."

A woman in a station wagon backed out of a parking space, causing Hayes to stop. In the front seat the woman's son, a teenager, dozed, his head resting on his chest.

"Look at that kid," Hayes said. "Now there you have a drug victim."

"Oh, come on, Coach," the visitor said. "That kid's not on drugs."

"Well, he's either a drug victim or a lazy son of a bitch," Hayes said. "Yessir. Lazy. I know about these things. Too many people like that out there today."

Hayes headed onto Interstate Highway 71, on his way to Westerville. He talked nonstop; he seemed happy to have a listener. His subjects shifted quickly from international politics to literature to history to women's rights, sometimes with no interconnective phrases. It was cold in the truck, but he did not turn the heater on. He talked all the way to Westerville.

"Now where is this place?" he said to himself as he drove down Main Street. "It's Westerville North High School, but we're heading south. Doesn't make any sense. I don't know why they build these schools so far out into the country. The kids can't walk, and it makes them soft. Wastes gasoline. People don't . . . people don't think."

He found the high school and pulled into the parking lot. He left the truck next to the students' cars; on the way into the school he passed a man, perhaps a teacher, who did not say hello. "Good morning," Hayes said.

When the man had passed from earshot, Hayes said, "They don't even say hello. That stupid. . . . He didn't even say hello. People are so unfriendly these days. Back in Newcomerstown when I was growing up, everyone said hello to everyone. Things have changed. People act stupid."

The speech was in the high school gymnasium. There were several hundred students present; when Hayes talked about coaching, it was in the present tense ("On our team we tell our players". . . . "When we're getting ready for a game. . . ."). Suddenly, though, for some reason not readily apparent, Hayes shifted his talk to United States intervention in Japan following World War II. He was shouting, combative, and he stepped from the microphone, as if it was not loud enough for him. He approached the students in the bleachers, and he bellowed:

"Do you know who that man was? No, you don't want to say his name because you think he was too much a chauvinist! Well that man's name was . . . Five-Star General Douglas MacArthur!"

The students sat in silence, bewildered. Hayes seemed to realize something, and returned to the microphone, where he quickly finished up his talk about coaching.

In the truck on the way back to Columbus, he talked about his pain for the first time. He said that after having Ohio State football be his whole life, he could not bring himself to attend a game this year. Most Saturdays, he said, he spent in a cabin he had built down in Noble County.

"Sometimes I listen to the games on the radio," he said. "But I can't go.

"You know, the worst thing in the world is feeling sorry for yourself. Self-pity will kill you. I can't have it.

"You can't dwell on what used to be. You can't . . . bring it back. The football. . . . I've got to separate myself from it."

For a few minutes Hayes and the visitor rode in silence. Then Hayes cleared his throat, as if to cut off the thoughts that had filled the truck, and he said:

"Do you know what President of the United States I feel the least use for?"

"Who's that, Coach?" the visitor said.

"Woodrow Wilson," Hayes said.

"Why's that?" the visitor said.

"Come on, you know," Hayes said.

"No, I don't," the visitor said.

"Because Wilson wasn't a man's man," Hayes said. "Yessir, he wasn't a man's man."

And on he drove, a legend in exile, heading down I-71 in pursuit of the rest of his life.

"Ever See Your Old Man Cry?"

I TOLD THE man I wasn't a social worker. That usually works. With him it didn't. He was back the next day.

"Look, sir . . ." I began.

"I know," he said. "I know. But honest to God, you got to do it."

"I can't," I said. "I'm not the person you want."

"I wouldn't be here if I wasn't begging you," the man said. "You got to talk to him."

He was a worried-looking little man in a rumpled brown suit. Everything about him said defeat.

"I don't know why you're coming to me," I said. "I just write stories and put them in newspapers. You need somebody with some training in this."

"I tried," he said. "Please. I trust you."

"Well you shouldn't," I said.

"Please," he said.

I said okay. The next afternoon he brought the kid down.

The three of us went into a little office with a long table and some chairs. The kid stared at the floor. The father fidgeted. We could hear people walking around out in the hallway.

"Maybe you'd better wait outside," I said to the man. He left the room, almost apologetically.

The kid and I sat in silence for maybe a minute.

"This is stupid," the kid said.

"Agreed," I said.

"What do you think you are, a shrink?" the kid said.

"I don't want to be here any more than you do," I said.

"Then what are you doing it for?" the kid said.

"Your father," I said.

"What's he to you?" the kid said.

"Nothing," I said.

The kid had bad skin and he picked at his fingernails. I would guess he was seventeen. He was bigger than his father.

"What did he tell you?" the kid said.

"That you're on pills a lot," I said. "That he thinks you're stealing. That he thinks you and your friends are stealing."

"He's lying," the kid said.

"He doesn't think so," I said.

"So he drags me down here," the kid said.

"He couldn't drag you anywhere," I said. "I figured you wouldn't show."

The kid lit a cigarette.

"So why did you?" I said.

"You ever see your old man cry?" the kid said.

We looked at each other some more.

"What are you supposed to tell me?" the kid said.

"I don't know," I said. "I guess I'm supposed to tell you to straighten out."

"You never liked to get high and run around?" the kid said.

"I never stole anything," I said.

"I can't believe it," the kid said. "He takes me to a newspaper."

"Would you have preferred the cops?" I said.

He played with his cigarette.

"I don't even read the newspaper," the kid said.

"Some days neither do I," I said.

"So why does my old man have me here?" the kid said.

"Some people believe in magic," I said.

"Well, tell me whatever you're supposed to tell me," the kid said.

"I'm not going to tell you anything," I said.

"What am I supposed to do?" the kid said.

"You're supposed to sit here for awhile and then you're supposed to go out there and pretend that you're going to try to make your old man happy," I said.

He shook his head.

"Why should I try to make him happy?" the kid said.

"Because he cared enough to come down here," I said.

"Yeah, and you don't even have anything to tell me," the kid said.

"I hate this worse than you do," I said. "I got better things to do."

"Then why aren't you doing them?" the kid said.

"Because I thought your father was going to cry when he was talking to me, too," I said. "I don't see a whole lot of people who care that much anymore."

We wasted about fifteen minutes more. Mostly he smoked and I looked at the wallpaper.

"All right," I said. "Let's go."

The father was waiting on a couch in the hallway. He was up and shaking my hand before we could even get out the door.

He looked at me like he expected me to nod or something. I just motioned to the kid. The two of them, father and son, walked together toward the elevators. They didn't appear to be talking.

I stopped for a drink on the way home. Sometimes it helps me sleep.

Direct Male

T HE AD: IT is probably one of the most famous advertisements in modern American merchandising history. For ten years, it has been appearing regularly in 109 magazines and newspapers, ranging from *Psychology Today* to *National Lampoon* to *Man's Action*. You would be hard pressed to find a male in the United States who has never seen it.

The ad varies slightly: sometimes it features photographs of several attractive young women, sometimes only one. The copy has been refined over the years. But the one constant in all the ads is that the main element on the page, in the biggest type, is the title of the book being marketed: *How to Pick Up Girls!*, by Eric Weber.

And the promise is explicit: "Starting today, you'll be able to walk up to just about any woman who catches your eye, start a conversation, a relationship, maybe even a love affair right then and there. . . . It costs less than a tankful of gas—yet it's so much more of a help when it comes to meeting the kind of beautiful women you've always dreamed about."

THE BOOKS: There are a number of them. *How to Pick Up Girls!* is the bestseller, the flagship; but they all address the same theme. There are *How to Make Love to a Single Woman*, *100 Best Opening Lines!*, *Picking Up Girls Made Easy* . . . inexpensively bound, not sold in bookstores, available only via direct mail from Symphony Press, of Tenafly, New Jersey.

If *How to Pick Up Girls!* has become part of the national mythology through the magazine advertisements, you would still have a difficult time finding an American man who will admit that he has bought a copy. There seems to be a certain shame associated with being an owner.

And yet, someone out there is buying the books. During an economically difficult time for the book publishing business, Symphony Press generates an estimated two million dollars in revenues a year selling *How to Pick Up Girls!* and its brethren. The books' average price is $11.50 a copy; there is no retailer, no wholesaler, no middleman. Symphony Press is Eric Weber, one assistant, and two secretaries. It has developed into a productive and thriving loneliness industry, apparently impervious to the inflationary and recessionary factors that influence the rest of the country's business environment. Symphony Press has tapped a market that seems as if it will never go away.

THE MESSAGE: The Symphony Press books provide a combination pep talk and battle plan. The reader is assured that women really do want to meet him—are sitting home alone at this very moment, in fact, just wishing that a man had picked them up during the day. On the other hand, it is made clear to the reader that women have to be tricked into saying yes—that only the cleverest of men will be quick and wily enough to trap a woman.

The most striking thing about *How to Pick Up Girls!* is its elementary tone. Far from dropping his reader off in the middle of an exotic secret world, Eric Weber almost leads the fellow by the hand and asks him not to be afraid. One chapter, for example, is called "Sure, I'd Get Picked Up!" and features such testimonials as the quote from a woman named "Linda," who says: "Of course I get picked up. How else am I going to meet guys?"

Other chapters include "Women Get Horny" ("Janet" tells Weber: "Sure, women get horny. Sometimes I go home and read a sexy book because I don't have a sexy man around"); "Beauty and the Beast" (Weber's friend "Tom" has a face that is a cross between a gorilla's and a toad's, but he managed to marry ("Laura— one of the prettiest brunettes I've ever seen"); and "Relax" (Weber advises: "Do not, if at all possible, get uptight. You are not on a bombing mission over enemy territory. You're not hunting bull elephants. You are simply going to talk to a woman. That is all").

But if at one moment Weber is persuading his reader that women are not dangerous and threatening, at the next he is cautioning that same fellow to be as devious as possible, lest they get away. Nothing Weber prescribes is straightforward; everything is intended to reel in a girl before she feels the hook. Weber even has advice for his readers about the richest streams to fish. "Pretend you're shopping for a gift for your mother or sister in a fashionable women's clothing store," he writes. "These places can be real gold mines because they're simply crawling with thousands of young, good-looking girls." And, in a passage apparently not revised since the book came out during Vietnam days: "March in a peace demonstration, even if you're secretly for war. I've heard countless stories of guys who've picked up fantastic broads at peace demonstrations."

None of this shows any signs that the author is smirking. Indeed, Weber's "Fifty Great Opening Lines" seem to be offered almost gently to his reader, as if Weber understands that the man has often agonized over what he might possibly say to a woman. The lines read humorously at first, then become almost unbearably sad with the realization that every night there are men memorizing them: "Do you have an aspirin?" "How long do you cook a leg of lamb?" "Is there a post office near here?" "Wow! What a beautiful day!"

Weber seems to understand that many men are sensitive about the way they look; he knows they spend so much time staring at beautiful women that they become self-conscious about what they see in their own mirrors every morning. So he spends an inordinate amount of space trying to convince his readers that their looks don't matter.

A woman named "Connie" is quoted as saying: "I've come to find men attractive who at first gave me the chills I thought they were so ugly. It's amazing how many times this has happened to me."

And Weber advises: "Just what do women find sexually stimulating about men? You'd be amazed!

"Women are nuts. They really are. They're totally unpredictable.

"If a group of guys standing on the corner spots a girl with huge breasts and a deliciously curvy behind, they all go crazy and elbow each other in the ribs.

"Women don't work that way at all. . . . So don't get all neurotic and insecure because you're not the spitting image of Paul Newman. Without realizing it, you may have some incredible feature that will literally drive women wild. . . ."

If the contents—and success—of the Symphony Press books seem to speak unhappily of the state of the American man's psyche, the same assumption cannot automatically be made about the American woman's. Eric Weber has tried for years to market a similar line of books aimed at females (*How to Pick Up Men!*); the books have been dismal failures. The women don't order.

THE MAN: Eric Weber, thirty-eight, has been married for twelve years. He and his wife have four children. He looks like a slightly older version of Joe Rossi, the reporter on the "Lou Grant" television series; he speaks with the hurried authority of a progressive-rock disc jockey who has suddenly found himself on an easy-listening station and has been instructed to tone it down.

Weber was a trainee at an advertising agency when he got the idea to write *How to Pick Up Girls!* from his own history of insecurity with women. Having assembled and marketed the book in his free time, he rose to become vice-president and associate creative director of Young & Rubicam before he decided to run Symphony Press full-time.

"I know what the American male is like," Weber said. "Like him or not, I understand him. He thinks he's looking for instant sex. But that's not really what he's looking for. He's looking for a woman to like him. That's all he wants. Just a companion. Nothing would make him feel happier than for a woman to like him. I understand that. Actually, I feel for him.

"Ninety-five percent of my message is trying to get the man to calm down, to not be so afraid at the idea of meeting a woman.

"I know what men need to hear. They need to be told that women aren't that critical of them. That women aren't that booked up. That women don't mind it if you're a bit of a bumbler; they find it endearing. That the way a man looks isn't as important to women as it seems to men. That the pretty girl in the office isn't having four orgies tonight; she's at home wishing there was a little romance in her life."

Weber is convinced that the average buyer of his books probably doesn't even realize his true reason for making the purchase.

"He probably sees the ad and says to himself, 'I'll meet a girl on a plane and screw her standing up in the bathroom,' " Weber said. "Or, 'I'll meet a girl on the street and take her to a hotel room and then never see her again.' It's acceptable for a man to want that. But the real reason he's buying the book is the one he's afraid to admit. That he just wants to have a woman to be around.

"The so-called sexual revolution is a kind of myth," Weber claimed. "I don't think this alleged sexual sophistication has filtered down to the population as a whole. What the 'revolution' probably means is that boys and girls who are going together are sleeping together a year earlier than they used to. But the typical man is still saying to himself, 'I have five bucks to go to a movie, but I don't have a girlfriend to take.' "

Weber recognizes that the true theme of his books seems to be loneliness—but he prefers a different phrase. "I like the word *fear* over *loneliness*. Because what the men who buy the books are dealing with is a terrible fear of rejection. They are so afraid of women. I pride myself on knowing what's in men's minds and hearts, and that fear is what it is."

Although he realizes he is open to charges that he exploits this fear, Weber denies it. "I happen to be a painfully cynical person about a lot of things," he said, "but not in this area. In this area I am a virtual innocent, a virgin. It is one of the great wounds in a person's life to be shy and fearful of women. I don't take advantage of that. I try to help."

THE MEANING: The men who purchase Eric Weber's books will never have to make eye contact with a clerk in a bookstore. Which is important. As much as the mail-order arrangement is an economic boon to Weber, it is also a psychological necessity to the men who want to read *How to Pick Up Girls!*. Weber realizes that if men had to buy the books over the counter, many probably wouldn't; in our society it is all right to go to a newsstand and purchase a magazine filled with color photographs of wide-open genitals, but it is too embarrassing to purchase a book that is a tacit admission of your solitary despair.

We happily admit our lust; we desperately hide our loneliness. That is the key to the success of the Symphony Press books and the genius of the advertising campaign. Even as a man is slipping his check into the envelope, he can tell himself that he wants a beautiful pickup, while the truth is that he wants only the courage to say "Hello."

We are supposed to be living in an era of unprecedented openness and candor between men and women; but behind the smiling, inviting woman on the cover of *How to Pick Up Girls!* is the story of a society in which making friendly contact with a woman is still considered an almost unreachable victory for a man—a conquest in the most unsexual meaning of that term.

Better not to talk about that; Eric Weber understands that to address the desperation directly would be to unmask the whole charade. No wonder Weber never writes about loneliness. Listen to his code language:

"Do you know that women get just as horny as you do? Well, it's true. They sit home, all by themselves, and think how terrific it would feel to hop in bed with someone. Anyone . . . ."

Rock of Ages

IN THE VAST and echoing emptiness of Detroit's Cobo Arena, Bob Seger walked to the front of the stage. With his guitar in his hands, he began to sing the first words of "Main Street": "I remember standing on the corner at midnight, trying to get my courage up. . . ."

His voice did not carry. This was late on a Saturday afternoon, at a technical sound check, and something was wrong with the microphone. In a few hours the arena would be filled with more than twelve thousand people, but now the doors to the hall were locked, and Seger had no audience.

With his voice reaching only a few feet beyond the stage, he sang a couple more verses, then stopped. He looked out at the thousands of empty chairs. Tonight he was coming home. After fifteen years of struggling to make a name for himself outside small pockets of the Midwest, Seger had the number-one-selling record album in the country. For six consecutive concerts, Cobo was sold out: nearly seventy-five thousand fans were paying ten-dollar top to hear this thirty-five-year-old rock and roll musician from southern Michigan sing his songs.

Seger gazed up at the top balcony. Behind him, his Silver Bullet Band continued to play the chords of "Main Street," but Seger did not resume the lyrics. He kept staring at those faraway seats, and after a moment a smile of the purest joy spread across his face.

We all grew up with the dream. If in the 1940s and early 1950s American boys yearned to become baseball stars, by the end of the Fifties the dream had turned to rock and roll. New generations wanted only to be Elvis Presley or the Beatles or the Rolling Stones. Some even pursued the dream, forming local bands, playing at school dances, maybe doing some club work around the hometown. But then, inevitably, they gave it up. It was a child's dream; if you weren't a rock and roll star by the time you were twenty or twenty-two, you went out and found legitimate work. You couldn't stay a kid forever.

Bob Seger never figured that out. All the signals told him that he was never going to make it; the signals told him to join his contemporaries who had quit believing in Peter Pan, who had invested in the idea of real work, who had to admit that they often didn't even know the names of the new bands who were making it big. Seger was on the rock and roll road when he was twenty and was still on it when he was twenty-five and when he was thirty. Traveling by car, he sometimes played as many as 265 one-nighters a year, and no one outside the Michigan-Illinois-Ohio circuit cared who he was. In a good year he might walk away with $6,600.

He played bars and he played nightclubs and he opened for touring big-name bands who, it suddenly seemed, were younger than he was. His singing voice developed a whiskey-and-cigarettes rasp; the members of his band changed; his record companies had no idea what to do with him; and still he stayed on the road. The boys he'd gone to high school with were making something of themselves, laboring in the real world, their futures laid clearly and neatly out ahead. And Bob Seger, of Ann Arbor, Michigan, was a grown man singing rock and roll songs.

Maybe they wondered—those boys who had known him when they were all teenagers—wondered what Seger thought about when he realized the audience for rock and roll music was now up to twenty years younger than he was. Wondered what it would take before he would learn that nothing was going to happen. Wondered how it would feel when Bob Seger, nearly forty, had to admit the worst and fill out a job application.

Then, in 1980, something changed. Seger finally—almost magically—caught on. The record-buying public seemed weary of New York alienation and Los Angeles slickness. But Bob Seger had never become a part of either coast; he remained, instead, quintessentially midwestern—singing of summer nights in the back seats of cars, and of feeling alone in a small town, and of words spoken to him by girls who had probably long ago forgotten his face and his touch.

By the beginning of last summer his album *Against the Wind* had led the *Billboard* charts for six weeks; it had sold 2.5 million copies at a total retail price of more than $20 million. Virtually every concert on his nationwide tour was a sellout; fifteen-year-old children were clapping their hands above their heads as he sang the hymns of his Michigan boyhood.

The dream had come true, but it had come late. And was it as lovely as he had hoped? Was it worth the wait? Seger is a man sensitive to the slights and small hurts of the world; yet for fifteen years, while no one paid attention, he had refused to compromise. Now, finally, they were listening. What thoughts raced through his mind as, at last, he saw the crowds coming to be near him?

"I always felt I had something to offer," Seger said. "There were times when I was fed up, and I'd find myself playing in a club somewhere, and other bands were making it big . . . and I'd say to myself, 'Well, if you have to play in clubs five nights a week, big deal.' I knew I could always at least do that. I sing pretty good. I could always play a bar gig."

Seger was drinking beer with a lone visitor backstage at Cobo; the third concert of the six-night stand had ended an hour earlier, and now he was barefoot in a small room. His brown hair hung to his shoulders; streaks of gray had begun to come to it. He was stocky, with thick arms in a short-sleeved shirt; he could have been a worker on the General Motors assembly line. He talked with the same constant burr in his voice that was coming out of radios all across the country.

He seemed as bashful as the awkward boy in "Main Street" and "Night Moves," his breakthrough hits about growing up in the Midwest. Yes, he said, the sight of a beautiful woman he's never met before still leaves him speechless, unable to say anything that makes sense. In a crowded room where people want to make him the center of attention, he admitted, he'll grow uncomfortable and "want to move away." But he never moved away from Michigan, he said, because he was afraid that Los Angeles or New York would eat him up. "I never was that good at hyping people or putting myself across. All I could do was write and play, and I figured that if I kept playing away, sooner or later they'd realize I was out here."

The dream had, indeed, started for him the way it had started for the rest of us: listening to songs on the radio and standing in front of the mirror, pretending to be a star. "I'd only do it when my mom wasn't home. I'd be too embarrassed when someone else was in the house."

But why, then, had it stuck with him? When the others with the same dream had long ago given it up, why had he held on?

"I had this rebellion, and I felt very much alone," Seger said. "Maybe I had a larger need for affection than the other people. I don't think it was that I had more ambition. I think it was that need to be liked, to be known. I'm thirty-five years old, and I ache a lot after being on the road so long, and I weigh ten pounds more than I should. But when I go on the stage and I see the people out there and I hear them, all the aches and pains go away. They're saying, 'We accept you.' That's what I hear when they cheer.

"For such a long time, everyone around kept trying to convince me I was going to make it. For all those years, all those people were saying, 'It's going to happen, it's going to happen, it's going to happen.' It got to be so frustrating, because nothing *was* happening. Finally the only thing I could do was to stop listening to them. It got to the point where I didn't think I could believe anybody. I knew it wasn't going to happen, and I lived with it, and now . . . this."

Seger said that he dreads but understands the fate of people who work jobs that bring no satisfaction: "Maybe they decided one day, 'This is as far as I'm going to get, and I'd better dig in for the long, slow fade.' " The specter of the slow fade is something that is constantly on his mind—the image of reaching as far as he can reach and not being able to produce, not being able to deliver any longer.

"I say to myself, 'You're thirty-five and you're rich, can you still rock and roll anymore?' On the real cold dark nights, it goes through my mind: the idea of a grown man in a children's game; the money thing—making a career out of something that was once natural for me. When and how do I gracefully leave off?

"I see the kids out there, and they seem to be enjoying it, but then I think maybe it's just the visceral excitement of hearing a monster guitar riff. As a writer, I'm thinking about the words, but maybe that kid's just thinking of the drum beat. What I'm trying to do is make someone out there feel, 'I'm not alone. Someone else feels the same way.' But sometimes I think that maybe a lot of people can't have the insights or don't really care.

"How long can you maintain? You've got to do what Al Kaline did, I think: he knew he could have played ball for three or four more seasons, but he said, 'Nope, I'm not going to do it.'

"I can't see a fifteen-year-old kid wanting to see me when I'm forty-five. I tell myself to give it two more years and then look at it. But I've been saying that since I was thirty-two. When I decide that I'm not going to do it anymore, though, at least I'll be able to say to myself: 'I liked what I was doing, and I think I was pretty good at it, and I never felt embarrassed by it.' "

The night passed as Seger and his visitor talked. The conversation eventually turned to small things; Seger said that for all the songs he has written, he is unable to write personal letters, even to someone he feels very close to. "I don't want them lying around to haunt me," he said, and laughed.

He said that he never wants to go on television; whatever it is he has to offer, he thinks the camera would kill it. "If I were to go on a talk show, I wouldn't know what to say." he said. "I don't know how I would explain my life in eight minutes. I remember once I heard that Lennon and McCartney were going to be on the 'Tonight' show. I got real excited, and I stayed up to watch it . . . and Johnny Carson wasn't even there that night. He was off, and Joe Garagiola was the guest host, and here were John Lennon and Paul McCartney trying to make jokes with Garagiola. It made me sad to watch it. I don't think I could do that. It would seem to trivialize everything that I think I am."

Gradually, as they were heading home, members of the Silver Bullet Band drifted into the room to say goodnight. Seger waved to them. It was getting very late, and soon only the janitors remained in the arena. Still Seger didn't budge. He was tired, but the memory of the twelve thousand voices in Cobo was still with him. It was as if by staying and talking in this back room, he could make the night go on endlessly.

"I have a cabin up in northern Michigan," he said. "Sometimes I'll tie my hair back and walk down to the bar and sit around in front of the TV set with the old guys there, yelling for the Tigers. They don't know who I am, and that's fine, because that's how it always was before. I'm just some guy."

Finally Seger and his visitor got up to leave. As they headed for the door, Seger had another beer in his hand, and the visitor had one more question:

Now that he had made it big—fifteen years later—did the dream still hold? After wanting the success so fiercely for so long, did he find it as sweet as it was supposed to be?

"Oh, yeah," Seger said. "Absolutely. Terrific."

They walked through the empty corridor, toward the door to the arena, and then Seger stopped.

"Nah," he said. "I didn't give you the right answer. It isn't as good as I thought it would be. I don't guess it ever is, is it?"

He headed for his car, his steps sounding in the deserted parking lot, a Michigan boy come home from the road.

The Truth About 1968

A COLLEGE STUDENT came to see me the other day. The purpose of her visit was official; she was a reporter for her school newspaper, and she had been assigned to seek out certain information.

"Here we are, into the Eighties," she said. "And yet many college students today are still preoccupied with the idea of 1968. We know that 1968 really happened, but from what we hear, it's hard to believe. From everything we've heard, a lot of us would rather be going to school in 1968 than right now. I am working on a story about whether 1968 ever actually existed— and if it did, what it was like."

She explained that hers was a mission searching out history. She had been told to locate relics such as myself, men and women who had actually been college students in 1968, and to ask them questions about what had gone on. Whether the legends were true. Hers was sort of an archaeological expedition into the hazy past.

Well . . . I helped her all I could, providing her with exhaustive information about what the world of the college student had been like in 1968. And after she left, it occurred to me that she probably was not the only person wondering such questions. There are doubtless millions of people out there who were not around in 1968, and who would benefit by a truthful, sober, and frank recall of what happened in those college days.

Thus, just as I helped the student reporter, I will help all of you youngsters who want to know. I will tell you the same things I told her. Here, broken down into specific areas, is the truth about what college was like in that wonderful year of 1968.

HOUSING—There were no dormitories, fraternities, or sororities. Instead, upon arrival on campus each fall, students were assigned to various communes and crash pads with names such as "Peace Farm" and "Hanoi Heaven." Regular meals were forbidden; our diets consisted solely of granola and nuts. Money was outlawed; instead, we lived off the land, sharing all material goods for the benefit of the people. For four years we slept on the floor, because we felt it was more natural, and a symbol of solidarity with our brothers and sisters in the Third World. We often lived fifteen or sixteen to a room; there were no keys or locks, because we were all beautiful and we trusted each other.

VIOLENCE—We all carried guns, provided by the university at the time of registration for classes. Hand-to-hand combat with police officers was a daily occurrence, with the students invariably winning. We received classroom credit for learning to make bombs. Instead of Homecoming, we tore down historic campus buildings brick by brick. Aside from this, we were generally very loving.

SEX—All students had sex in public several times per day. This was often done outside, in the mud. It was not uncommon for a student to have had more than one thousand sexual partners by the time he or she graduated. Birth-control pills were provided free in big barrels placed at strategic locations around the campus. During warm months both men and women usually went naked, including to class.

PARENTS—We all killed our parents.

ATTIRE—Clothing stores as we know them today did not exist. We wore only Army fatigues, available at various trading posts around the campus. Students were required to paint their faces with warpaint. Shoes, of course, were forbidden; we went barefoot on campus at all times.

RACE—It was far more socially acceptable to be black than white. Many students were black during the academic year, becoming white only to go home for Christmas and summer vacations. I, for instance, was black from my sophomore year until the time I graduated and began looking for a job.

DRUGS—All students were heavily drugged all the time. LSD was routinely pumped into the campus drinking water supply, and student assistants handed out marijuana on our way into classes. Vending machines around campus offered mescaline, barbiturates, and amphetamines. Drinking fountains spurted sweet wine for the purpose of washing the pills down. Beer was outlawed; any student convicted of drinking beer was automatically expelled.

POLITICS—We were all, of course, Communists.

MUSIC—Loudspeakers constructed all over campus blasted rock music into every corner of the college, including classrooms. This was constant and at an ear-piercing volume, day and night. When we arrived on campus we were given the home telephone numbers of all four Beatles, whom we were encouraged to call any time we felt like talking.

ACADEMICS—There were no classes as such. Instead we all gathered outside every day and said bad things about Lyndon Johnson while our professors congratulated us for being so young and wonderful. We were all given automatic "A's" just for living in such an exciting and dramatic time.

It does seem like a long time ago. Just talking about it to the college reporter made me nostalgic. She took notes while I filled her in, and then said she had to go back to campus.

"Goodbye," she said.

"Peace," I said.

By Any Other Name

Iɴ 1971, ᴛʜᴇ first year I was writing a newspaper column, a fourteen-year-old girl made an appointment to see me. She came to my apartment on a Saturday afternoon.

She was in the ninth grade and had started using drugs two years earlier. Now, she said, she had stopped; her parents had found out and had gone with her to have a talk with their family doctor. But just as she was giving up marijuana, stimulants, and depressants, her classmates were starting. She felt ostracized. She was thinking of taking up the drugs again just so she wouldn't feel left out.

It was a winter afternoon when we talked; she said she hadn't eaten lunch, and I went to the refrigerator and made her a sandwich. My strongest memory of our encounter is of her overcoat lying on the couch; as she told me of the pills she had been taking, I looked at the coat and saw that her mittens were attached to the sleeves with metal-and-elastic clamps.

We spoke for several hours, and at the end I said that I did, indeed, want to write a column about her experience. I asked her if she wanted me to use her name. She thought about it for a moment, and then she said she would be more comfortable if I just used her initials. Her initials were J. C.

Two days later the column appeared. The headline was ᴀᴛ 14, ᴊ. ᴄ. ɪs ᴏғғ ᴅʀᴜɢs. And two days after that I received a telephone call. It was from the girl's mother.

"I don't know if you'll ever have the experience of having a daughter who is so traumatized that she can't get out of bed," the woman said. "She's been sobbing for twenty-four straight hours."

The girl had gone to school on the morning the column appeared, and immediately discovered that virtually everyone she knew had read it and had easily identified her. They were livid; she had, in effect, told all of their parents about the drugs they were taking. The girl's mother asked me if I understood what this was going to do to the rest of her daughter's high school life, and I said I understood. But I didn't, really; I was brand-new at writing about people's personal experiences for large audiences. I had been given a regular column in a major newspaper in one of America's biggest cities, and the column was being distributed to more than one hundred other papers. I was twenty-three years old.

I've been thinking about that 1971 story because now, a decade later, people are questioning the credibility of reporters, especially young reporters, especially young reporters who write about ordinary citizens, especially young reporters who write about ordinary citizens and do not publish the real names of those citizens. For reasons that have become famous by now, some readers and many editors are beginning to question the practice of writing about people without identifying them precisely; it is occurring to readers and editors both that it is uncommonly easy for a writer to present a word picture of a person who does not, in fact, exist.

The hard thing about dealing with the question is that the skeptical readers and editors are right; it would be easy to fabricate characters. In the case of the fourteen-year-old girl, if I had changed her initials, or merely referred to her as "she," no one would ever have been able to trace her. And I wish I had; I do not know what happened to that girl in the months and years after I published her story, but I do know that I caused her pain when I didn't have to, and that the story wasn't worth it. I have written two thousand newspaper columns since the one about J. C.; I am not twenty-three anymore, and one of the things I have learned is that filling up one's allotted space for a day is almost never worth bringing pain to a person who has done nothing to deserve it.

I am not talking about the kind of work that a Jack Anderson does; I do not deal with politicians who have abused the public trust. In my newspaper work, it is more likely that I will be discussing a man who has just been fired and is feeling the tormenting self-doubt that comes with being told that, in effect, he has no worth; or a woman who has decided, after great debate, to have an abortion and has allowed me to accompany her into the operating room; or a middle-aged wife whose husband has just hired a young female sales associate to travel with him, and whose marriage is being threatened by the pressures that the new situation brings.

Of course, not all of my stories are like that. When I talk to a Richard Speck or a Patricia Hearst, the reader comes into the story with certain images and expectations about the subject; what I try to remember, though, is that famous people share a common humanity with obscure ones, and that no matter whom I am interviewing, the best service I can provide the reader is to let him know what it was like to be there. To the extent I am successful at that, I succeed at my job; to the extent I am not, I fail. And more often than not, the episodes I am relating have to do with people who have never been in the public light before, and whose deeds are private.

For ten years I have been writing stories like those, and it has never occurred to me to discuss in print the decisions I have to make in doing them. But my editors at *Esquire* have asked me to address the question, on the theory that because of recent history, readers might be curious. So, as you may have surmised by now, this month's American Beat is a little different from most. It is not a story; it is about stories.

Almost no one ever asks me not to print their names.

It's not that they are brave; it's just that the experience of talking to a reporter who is taking notes is so foreign to them that they are unable to project forward to the morning when they will see their words in print. They are too busy thinking about what is going on in the reporting process.

But it is not unusual for me to write a newspaper column in which a person's name does not appear. I will not make up a name or use a pseudonym; I will simply use the third-person pronoun, so that the question of the proper name never comes up.

What generally happens is that, at the end of an interview, if I think the topic discussed is especially sensitive or potentially embarrassing, I will say: "Look. I'm glad we talked, but I don't think you want your name connected with this." Often the person will be surprised; there are tricks to the business I am in, and one of the tricks is to make an interview subject feel so comfortable and so warm that he cannot conceive of being betrayed by this nice fellow who is asking the questions and making the notes.

As often as not, though, the person I'm with has never been interviewed before. He is wary at first; it takes a while to make him understand that this is not a surgical procedure. There are tricks to that, too; I will stumble around in my conversation, I will make my questions sound exceedingly dumb, if he is having a few too many drinks I will drink right along with him. I may or may not be a likable person in real life, but I can be a likable person in an interview situation; it's just another trick I have learned.

So at the end of our talk, if I said to my new acquaintance, "You are a fascinating person and people are really going to like and admire you when they read about you," chances are he would willingly give the okay to use his name. What he doesn't know is that the sight of his words and his world in cold print, in front of hundreds of thousands of strangers, is going to jar him; is going to jar him and confuse him and make him wonder why he opened himself up.

I decided a long time ago that in situations like those, I had the obligation to help protect a person even if he didn't know enough to protect himself. In the case of the man who has been fired, or of the woman who is holding my hand as the abortion is completed, or of the wife who is losing trust in her traveling husband, it is not the names and addresses that are important; it is the stories.

Is a reader going to be any more moved by a fired man's anguish if that reader knows how to find him and call him on the telephone? Not if I'm doing my job well. If I can move the reader without subjecting the man to any further personal humiliation, then everyone is served better. If I can't, then I'm better advised to look for another story.

I don't mean to give the impression that these decisions have to be made every day; the great majority of newspaper stories, mine included, feature the names of people who will not be damaged by the reading public's knowing who they are.

But when questions do come up, I think a writer has the responsibility to give them more than a fleeting thought. In one issue of *Esquire*, I wrote about going back to find my first girlfriend, with whom I had fallen in love when I was sixteen and she was thirteen. I learned that she was living in Toledo, Ohio, and I flew there to see her. That month's column was about seeing Lindy Lemmon again, all that time later, now that we were both grown-ups.

The question I was most often asked about the column was: What was Lindy Lemmon's real name? Readers assumed that because the column touched on such a personal subject, I must have used a pseudonym. Well, her real name was Lindy Lemmon, but I didn't just throw it into print. I discussed it with her, and she discussed it with her husband, and then with her parents, and we decided together that it would do her no harm for our story to appear in the magazine.

But in another *Esquire*—in the column about the *Cosmopolitan* magazine Bachelor of the Month—there appeared a list of letters written to the bachelor from women around the country. The letters were real, but at the last minute—after going into galley proofs—we decided to omit the women's hometowns. It was the opinion of *Esquire*'s attorney—and I agreed with it—that to publish the names of the smaller towns might make the women too easily identifiable by people in those towns.

Maybe it was the memory of fourteen-year-old J. C. in 1971, but I didn't think it was worth the chance of having those women's friends and families know that they had written to a man whose photograph had appeared in a magazine, and had offered him their company. The letters were real; it wasn't necessary to identify the writers to make them seem more real.

The business I am in is a strange one. I intrude into people's lives for an hour or a day or a week, and I scrape their lives for what I can, and then I display the scrapings to strangers. I get paid for this; whether it is a moral calling or not, I do not know, but I have no other craft.

When you write about people in a personal way, they react strongly. It is as if you have been to bed with them; the experience stays with them, and often you will hear from them years later. Sometimes at first you will not even remember their names; the encounter you shared that put their names in print was singular to them, but on the next day, while they were still thinking about it, you were having a new encounter with someone else.

The one thing I have not dealt with here is why the people choose to share their lives with a reporter in the first place. I have never known the answer to that, and I don't suppose I ever really will. It probably has something to do with the need to feel special and important, if only for a moment; to validate one's own individuality and uniqueness.

So what do you owe them? Maybe nothing; probably a little kindness. No more or no less than you owe anyone else in this life.

Looking back over this column, I fear it hasn't addressed the specific issues it set out to address. But *Esquire* has a feature called Why I Live Where I Live, and this is probably the closest I'll come to answering that question. I live on the printed page as much as I live somewhere on a map, and maybe that's what this exercise has been all about. I'll be back next month, and with a real story.

Elvis: Visitation

Memphis—For twenty years they called him an idol, but that was just a show-business hyperbole. On Wednesday, in an incredible, frightening, unforgettable way, the term turned literal. The embalmed body of Elvis Presley, displayed in a casket in the foyer of his Graceland mansion, became a frozen idol for thousands upon thousands of hysterical men, women, and children who crushed their way to worship it.

At first the idea seemed impossible: the suggestion by Presley's father, Vernon, that his son's body be made available for a public viewing. No one outside of Presley's inner circle had ever been on the grounds of Graceland before, and the idea of laying the body out there, with any and all fans welcome to attend, brought to mind visions of uncontrollable crowds battling each other and storming the gates.

It happened.

The white gates of Graceland, adorned with green metal guitars and musical notes, were scheduled to swing open at three P.M. The massive grouping began the night before. Three hours before the gates opened, it had become a mob.

When the people finally were let in, single file, this is what they saw:

Elvis Presley, his face puffy and pale, dressed in a white suit, a light-blue shirt, and a white tie. His black hair was brushed back off his forehead. His eyes were closed. The casket was placed just inside the front door of Presley's home, and was open from the top of his head to the middle of his chest. White sheets covered the foyer's red carpeting.

Some wept. Many gasped. Some prayed aloud. Mourners left the casket in tears, unsteady on their feet; some staggered the several hundred yards back to the front gate.

Meanwhile, outside, the thousands who still were waiting charged against that same gate, trying to force their way in every time it would open to let mourners depart. There was shouting and screaming, and scores of people had to be carried away by medics. It was a scene of hysteria that matched the wildest Presley concert.

The setting was unlikely, especially for those who had never visited the site of Graceland before. The estate is on Elvis Presley Boulevard in a section called Whitehaven in the southern part of Memphis. With the exception of Graceland, Elvis Presley Boulevard is a commercial street; the Tuffy Muffler and Brake Shop is one block away, the Mr. Tax income-tax preparation service is across the street. On Wednesday, several blocks down the boulevard, the Bellevue Drive-In Theater was showing a movie called *Autopsy*.

But Graceland sits alone. It is surrounded by a flagstone-and-brick wall, with a red brick guardhouse at the front gate. The temperature in Memphis neared ninety Wednesday afternoon, and the thousands waiting on the street outside began to feel it early. They were crushed behind police lines, with virtually no space between each other, and by noon there were screams of panic every few minutes, as medics rushed to rescue persons who had passed out standing up, and who had no room to fall.

Cars crept by the front of the Presley estate in both directions, slowed by people spilling out onto the street. At one point a woman weaved out of the crowd, seemingly in a daze. A police officer called to a nearby man, "Hey, are you her husband? Better come take care of her before she faints." With that the woman collapsed into the side of a moving Germantown Flowers truck, and then tumbled to the ground.

She, like the others who could not withstand the long hours, close quarters, and intense heat, was carried inside of the gates to Graceland, placed on the grass, and tended to by first-aid workers. Most of the affected persons were women and children. Some were in convulsions.

But the convulsions were minor compared with the reaction that would come when the crowd was allowed inside to glimpse Presley's body—the body of a former truck driver from Tupelo, Mississippi, who was once so poor that he had to sell his own blood, and soon after became one of the most influential figures in the history of popular culture.

Just before three P.M., security officers began to allow small groups from the crowd of eighty thousand onto the property.

The mourners—virtually all of whom were dressed casually, in some cases even sloppily—walked silently up one leg of a long, loop-shaped driveway.

As they approached the main house, the line slowed. There was absolute silence.

Officers from three police forces—the Memphis city police, the Shelby County sheriff's office, and the Presley private security squad—stood at several-yard intervals, making sure that no one broke out of line. Three police helicopters hovered over the mansion. Purses and packages were searched to assure that no cameras were taken into the presence of the body.

A guard driving a baby-blue golf cart with the word "Lisa"—the name of Presley's daughter—painted on the side and a half-peeled "I'm Just Crazy About Elvis Presley" sticker on the back cruised along the side of the line.

The house was made of sand-colored stone, with a white colonnade in front. It sat in the midst of acres of tree-lined grounds. There was a swimming pool off to the right.

Seven steps into the house and there was Elvis Presley, dead.

The mourners were allowed to stare for only a few seconds, but those seconds had their effect. Men, women, and children left the casket as if they had been punched in the stomach. They sucked in air. They cried aloud. They shook with grief. They shook on their feet. In death, as in life, Presley could reduce a crowd to animal emotions.

At the same time, more trouble was developing at the front gate. Those not yet allowed on the grounds were storming the gate every time it would open a few inches. Again and again, a sheriff's deputy made the announcement on a bullhorn:

"Ladies and gentlemen, if you do not cooperate with the officers, we will have to discontinue. If you do not quit pushing and shoving at the front gate, we will shut the gate and discontinue. We will have no alternative but to close the gates."

But the people were allowed to continue coming in. The mourners arriving, giddy with anticipation, marched past the mourners departing, broken with grief. Original plans had called for the viewing to terminate at 5:00 P.M.; the time was extended until 5:30 P.M. when it became apparent that only a small portion of the crowd could be accommodated by that hour.

It was a scene to remain indelible in the memory. The house, with the body of a rock-and-roll singer, dead at forty-two. The grass, filled with weak and unconscious victims of the heat. The driveway, alive with continually moving mourners. The gates, with a riot growing closer by the minute.

It was Wednesday, August 17, 1977, at 3674 Elvis Presley Boulevard, Memphis, Tennessee.

Elvis: "He Would Have Laughed"

MEMPHIS—They entombed Elvis Presley in his family crypt Thursday, and even as his body was being sealed away for eternity, show-business stars, politicians, business leaders, and newspaper editorialists were somberly praising, eulogizing, acclaiming, and sanctifying him.

Elvis would have laughed.

He would have laughed because he remembered how it started— how it was a flood of outrage, negative publicity, and even downright hatred on the part of mainstream America that began his startling rise to a prominence unheard of in the history of popular culture. He would have laughed because he would have known how curious it is, twenty years later, that he had stayed the same while the whole world came around to accept and embrace him.

"We lost a good friend today," Frank Sinatra said on the day that Presley died.

Twenty years ago, asked to comment on Presley, Sinatra said, "Rock and roll is phony and false. It is sung, played, and written for the most part by cretinous goons, and by means of imbecilic reiteration and sly, lewd, in plain fact dirty, lyrics. . . . It manages to be the martial music of every sideburned delinquent on the face of the Earth."

Yes, Elvis would have laughed. He would have laughed because in the beginning it was only the kids who would have him. Now the President of the United States, Jimmy Carter, says, "Elvis Presley's death deprives our country of a part of itself. He was a symbol to the people the world over of the vitality, rebelliousness, and good humor of this country." Elvis would have gotten a kick out of that one. Twenty years ago, if Dwight D. Eisenhower was having any thoughts about young Elvis Presley, he was keeping them to himself.

Newspaper editorials and columns written by music critics this week have placed Presley on a level with fallen popes. Here in Memphis, the *Commercial Appeal* said, "He came out of a mold that the youth of the 1950s comprehended. He communicated, he gave dignity and respect to the pubescent girl or boy who was frightened of growing up, unsure of being loved, afraid of acting natural."

Twenty years ago newspaper editorials were calling for the banning of Presley shows and phonograph records, were warning parents that Elvis would pervert and damage their youngsters. And the entertainment writers—who since Presley's death have strained their superlatives in an effort to top each other in praise—were even rougher on him back then than were the editorialists.

Jack Gould of the *New York Times*, twenty years ago:

Mr. Presley has no discernable singing ability. His specialty is rhythm songs which he renders in an undistinguished whine; his phrasing, if it can be called that, consists of the stereotyped variations that go with a beginner's aria in a bathtub.

Dick Williams, entertainment editor of a Los Angeles newspaper, twenty years ago:

If any further proof were needed that what Elvis offers is not basically music, but a sex show, it was provided last night. The Presley show resembled one of those screeching, uninhibited party rallies which the Nazis used to hold for Hitler.

Columnist Hedda Hopper, twenty years ago:

I applaud the parents of teenagers who work to get the blood-and-horror gangster stories off TV. They should work harder against the new alleged singer, Elvis Presley.

English music critic Tom Richardson, twenty years ago:

I have never met Elvis Presley, but already I dislike him. I know that this man is dangerous.

And if the writers back then were hard on him, his fellow entertainers were harder still. Most of their comments echoed Sinatra. They resented Presley's being a part of their business; they considered him an anomaly who would go away in a few months, and they would denounce Presley in the most sniggering, patronizing terms to any interviewer who would listen.

On the day of Presley's funeral, many of those same entertainers were giving solemn, mournful quotes about how close they had always been to Elvis, what a dear friend he had been, how they felt as if they had lost a brother.

The whole world was behaving that way Thursday. It was a world that Presley had changed forever, while refusing to change one bit himself. And with all the comments being made after his death, it was sort of a shame that he couldn't be around to hear the sober extolling and glorification. He would have had a comment of his own.

It wouldn't have taken him even one word to deliver it.
Elvis would have laughed.
And then sneered that sneer.

Elvis: Bidness as Usual

Acapulco—The correspondent lay in the sun, putting in a hard day's labor. The correspondent's eyes were closed. Next to the correspondent was a portable radio. The voices were all in Spanish. The correspondent did not understand a word of it.

Then a commercial came on the air. The Spanish-speaking announcer said a number of words that the correspondent could not comprehend, and then gave the name of the product: "La Piña Colada Elvis."

The correspondent stirred. He almost opened his eyes. But then he told himself that the heat was getting to him, and that it had been an aural illusion.

But five minutes later, the same commercial appeared: "La Piña Colada Elvis." And five minutes after that. And five minutes after that. And five minutes after that.

"La Piña Colada Elvis" was the most heavily advertised product on Mexican radio. And even though the correspondent was not bilingual, he began to catch on. La Piña Colada Elvis was a soft drink. A soft drink made out of pineapple juice and coconut juice.

A soft drink named after the late Elvis Presley.

"Oh, no," the correspondent said aloud. "Harry Geissler has struck again."

And so the correspondent arose, walked inside to a telephone, and had the international operator place a call to the United

States. Within minutes, the correspondent was talking to Harry Geissler.

"Of course I know about the Mexican Elvis soft drink," Harry Geissler said. "What do you think, I'm not paying attention to my bidness? I'm a responsible bidnessman. I know what's going on."

Harry Geissler is a huge, bearlike, street-tough, gravel-voiced East Coast businessman who is a former steelworker and a third-grade dropout. He also happens to be the man who has the exclusive worldwide concession on cashing in on all Elvis Presley memorabilia. In the months since Presley's death, Geissler has brought in some $14 million selling Elvis Presley products.

While millions of Americans were mourning Presley's death last summer, Harry Geissler was doing something else. He was flying down to Memphis, where he impatiently waited until the funeral was over and then opened negotiations with Colonel Tom Parker, Presley's manager.

"They didn't want to do nothing until after the funeral," Geissler said. "So I waited around. Then I bargained with the colonel. Me and the colonel, we play the same circuit, you know what I mean? He's a hyper and I'm a hyper. We're both in the hypin' bidness."

The result of the bargaining was that Geissler and his company—Factors Etc. Inc.—signed a contract taking over all rights to market the Elvis Presley name and likeness.

And in the time since, the worldwide marketplace has been glutted with Elvis Presley T-shirts, Elvis Presley coffee mugs, Elvis Presley Christmas tree ornaments, Elvis Presley costume jewelry, Elvis Presley bubble gum, Elvis Presley wristwatches, Elvis Presley belt buckles . . . the list goes on and on, and only Harry Geissler knows where it will end.

And now . . . "La Piña Colada Elvis"?

"Nothin' I can do about it," Geissler said. "They're just using the name 'Elvis.' They're not using his likeness, and they're not using the name 'Presley.' I've looked into it. They can claim that their soda pop is named after an Elvis somebody else. As soon as they use 'Presley' or put his picture on the bottle, that's when I sue."

Geissler is, indeed, quite a suer. So far he has launched more than five hundred lawsuits against persons trying to sell Elvis Presley products without going through Geissler. The lawsuits vary in damages claimed, going up to $50 million. Most businessmen stop trying to sell their products as soon as Geissler sues them. The other suits, Geissler wins.

"I know my bidness," Geissler said. "I get the others off the market."

Geissler himself is not an Elvis Presley fan.

"I never seen him perform," Geissler said. "Maybe I seen him once, on TV. Look, I'm not a fan. I'm a bidnessman. I used to sell Davy Crockett hats and Hula Hoops. I am a street man. I'm very crude, very tough, very pushy. This is the key to my bidness. That's why Colonel Parker respects me. He knows I'm only in this for the money. He needs me to protect his boy."

Crudeness aside, though, there are some products that Geissler has refused to let use the Elvis Presley imprimatur.

"I veto products in bad taste," Geissler said.

Such as what?, the correspondent asked.

"Let me see," Geissler said. "I said no to an Elvis Presley air freshener, and I said no to an Elvis Presley pornographic statuette."

The correspondent asked Geissler what new Elvis Presley products had been adjudged to be in good enough taste to market.

"The big ones this year are gonna be Elvis Presley jump suits, Love Me Tender cosmetics, Hound Dog soap, and Elvis Presley bedspreads," Geissler said.

The correspondent said goodbye and hung up. Then, prior to going back into the sun, he called room service.

"One Piña Colada Elvis," the correspondent said.

Elvis: Imitation Blues

THE MANIA OVER Elvis Presley continues, a year and a half after his death. Sometimes the craziness becomes literal. The following pair of conversations may sound like fiction, but they are real.

"He looked just like Elvis. That's what drew me to him."

Yes, ma'am, but what's your complaint?

"He was an Elvis imitator, one of the ones who perform in the nightclubs."

But why are you so upset, ma'am?

"He took my money."

The Elvis imitator?

"Yes, he tricked me into giving him my money."

How much money?

"Thirty-two thousand dollars."

You gave thirty-two thousand dollars to a guy who looks like Elvis Presley?

"It took me twenty years to save it."

May I ask how old you are, ma'am?

"Forty-one."

Why did you do it?

"It started the first day I met him. I was walking down the street to work, and he was sitting in his car. He said, 'Don't I know you?' and I said I didn't know him. But he looked so much like Elvis, we sat in his car and went for a ride."

And then what happened?

"We went up to his apartment. There were pictures of him and pictures of Elvis all over the walls."

What did you do?

"Talked. He had Elvis's habits, his complete habits. He talked just like him."

Did you notice anything else about the Elvis imitator?

"He was a filthy, dirty man. The shower stall was filthy dirty. He would walk around the apartment in his underwear. After a while, when I started doing domestic work for him, I would clean up the shower stall."

And what happened next?

"He tricked me in. He knew he was going to do it. He's done it to other girls, too. He was just like Elvis. He would spend time with me and take me places and make me fall for him. Then, a little bit at a time, he would start taking my money."

What do you mean, taking your money?

"He would drive me to the bank, and he would send me in to get the money. Then he would take it. He would always say he would pay me back. But he knew he was never going to pay me back."

If you really just handed your money over to him, like you say you did—why did you do it?

"I guess I kind of started to dig him. I really did dig him."

Even though you say he was taking your money?

"Yes. I still have pictures of him. I took pictures of him when he was singing, and I took pictures from his apartment."

What would you do when you were together?

"He'd stand in front of the mirror wearing Elvis clothes. He'd talk just like Elvis. And sometimes he'd sing Elvis's songs to me, like 'Blue Suede Shoes.' I know he was only singing them to me because he knew I'd go get money for him."

When did you first sense something was bad?

"He had other girlfriends. He just used me to clean his apartment and pay his rent and give him money."

Did anything make you especially angry at him?

"One day he wanted me to get him money, and I told him that I had to go have mouth surgery, and he said, 'Okay, no money, I don't see you.' "

And what were you thinking this whole time?

"I was trying to win him for the Lord. But I realized that he was just trying to take advantage of me because I liked him so much, and the way he was taking advantage of me was to take my money."

What else could you have been doing with your money?

"I have a ten-year-old son who is living with my parents. I never gave any money for the support of my own son."

Doesn't that bother you?

"I would like to be like Elvis's mother."

So what is it you want?

"My money back. Elvis was always giving money to people. This man is always taking money away. He isn't very much like Elvis after all."

The Elvis imitator was contacted. He was, indeed, a performer who has imitated Presley onstage. He was asked if he had ever heard of the woman.

"Yeah, I heard of her," he drawled. "Why?"

He was told what the woman had said.

"This is one of the fans I've had trouble with over the years," the Elvis imitator said. "Elvis had them, and I've had them."

The Elvis imitator was asked to respond to what the woman said.

"She's got something wrong with her mind," he said. "I didn't take any money from her. I took pity on her, but I shouldn't have. She called me three and four times a day until I had to get my number changed. Elvis had girls threatening to commit suicide. I've had some too, although not as many as Elvis did."

"It's not worth discussing or writing about," he said. "Things like this happen to a performer. It happened to Elvis, too."

Pray for us all . . .

The Voices of Fear

We were on the elevator. This was at the Northwestern University Medical Associates Building in Chicago.

We rode in silence, and then the other passenger—a young black man, perhaps twenty—said my name. That happens sometimes when they put your picture in the newspaper. At first you think it's flattering, and then you come to realize that it has nothing to do with you. If the delivery truck drivers went on strike, or if your bosses decided to take your face out of the paper, people would forget in two weeks.

I asked him how he was doing, just trying to be polite, and he looked embarrassed. In a moment I found out why.

"I . . . can't . . . talk . . . very . . . well," he said. He was apologizing. There was a pause of several seconds between words, and I could see his mouth working, trying to make the sounds.

He said some nice things about what I did for a living, and it seemed to be getting harder for him. I asked him his name, and by that time we had reached the ground floor, and as he struggled to tell me, the elevator door opened. I didn't want to walk out on him, so we stood in the elevator together and the door closed and finally he was able to tell me.

I had some time to kill. I took a seat in the lobby of the building, and looked at my watch. A woman came out of the elevator, and walked to a pay phone. She wore a housedress and moved slowly.

I listened to her conversation. "I'm calling from the clinic," she said into the phone. "They found out what it was. The tube had come out." Her voice was shaking. "They put a new tube in, and they put a bag on it."

There was a silence as she listened to the person on the other end. Then:

"The doctor wasn't as nice as the last one. He did it very quickly. Do you think the tube could come out again?"

Then:

"I told him I rode the bus down here." Her voice was wavering badly now. "He said it was okay to ride the bus. I wonder if I should take a cab home."

Across the way I saw the young man from the elevator. He was looking at me.

The woman hung up the phone. Instead of leaving, though, she put some more coins in and made another call.

"I just saw the doctor," she said. She sounded worse. "He told me the tube had come out. He put a new tube in."

The young man was walking across the lobby, and then sat down next to me.

"I . . . have . . . a . . . speech . . . impediment," he said.

He was wearing nice clothing. The trip to the clinic must have been a big event for him. He had traveled halfway across the city to seek this assistance.

"I'm . . . trying . . . to . . . get . . . help," he said, moving his head jerkily and trying to get the words out. "I . . . want . . . to . . . learn . . . how . . . to . . . talk . . . better.

"I . . . didn't . . . know . . . it . . . cost . . . anything," he said. "They . . . told . . . me . . . I . . . should . . . get a card . . . from . . . Public . . . Aid."

It was very bad with him. This terrible thing that had gone wrong with his ability to speak should have been treated when he was a small child. Now he was an adult. He told me that he lived on the South Side, and that he had come to the clinic because he had heard the doctors could cure people like him.

He was just finding out that it was more complicated than he had thought. He was a stranger in this part of the city, east of North Michigan Avenue. He knew that his odds of competing in the world without being able to communicate were zero, and he seemed near desperation.

"Will . . . you . . . help . . . me?" he said.

I felt lost. Because he had read some of my stories in the paper, he thought I might be able to make some magic for him.

I told him that if he had any trouble with Public Aid, he should give me a call and maybe I could clear a way for him.

He looked down at the floor, and I realized why.

"Do you have trouble with the telephone?" I said.

"I . . . can't . . . talk . . . on . . . the . . . telephone," he said. "If . . . I . . . pick . . . up . . . the . . . phone, . . . my . . . voice won't . . . work."

The woman at the pay phone had dialed again.

"Hello, it's me, I'm kind of scared," she said.

I told the young man to take down a phone number. I told him that if I picked up the phone and there was no voice, I wouldn't hang up, and that I would know it was him. I told him not to panic; I would wait until he was able to speak.

The woman was dialing again. "Hello?" she said. "I'm at the clinic. I rode the bus down here. The tube had come out. A new doctor put a new one in, but he was so quick with me that I didn't have a chance to ask him any questions. Do you think I should go back up there?"

The young man said to me, "I . . . have . . . to . . . have . . . an . . . appointment . . . with . . . the . . . clinic . . . social worker . . . now. Maybe . . . she . . . can . . . help . . . me . . . with . . . the card. I . . . want . . . to . . . thank . . . you . . . very . . . much."

He walked over to the elevator. The woman was still on the phone. She hung up, and hesitated with a coin in her hand, deciding on whether to make another call.

So much fear. The woman turning to familiar voices in hopes that someone will tell her everything was all right. The young man with no voice trying to find one for his own. The elevator door closed and the young man disappeared. The woman put the coin back in her purse and headed back out to the street. So much fear. . . .

Hefner at Home

Holmby Hills, California—
It is the dinner hour. The man of the house sits at the head of the long table. There is no wife. The children are grown. The man reaches over to a small brown box that has been placed a few inches from his napkin. He depresses a button atop the box, and within seconds a butler is beside him.

It is a night for celebration. It is the birthday of the man's girlfriend. She has turned twenty-two today. He is fifty-two. There have been gifts; now the butler has brought the birthday cake, candles aglow.

The man smiles at his girlfriend, and then his voice begins to echo in the massive room.

"Happy birthday to you . . ." sings Hugh Hefner.

It is another night at home. The girl's birthday is not really the one that is on Hefner's mind. After all, she is only twenty-two; his magazine, *Playboy*, has just turned twenty-five. The girl, whose name is Sondra Theodore, was not born when Hefner crafted the famous first issue of *Playboy*, with the Marilyn Monroe nude. There have been many beautiful young women, perhaps thousands of them, in Hugh Hefner's life before this young woman; there will be many more after she is gone.

"But I do fail," Hefner had been saying a few hours earlier. A visitor had asked Hefner about his legendary success with women, and about the popular notion that, at least for Hugh Hefner, there is never a moment of rejection from a female.

"I need the failure," Hefner said. "There are going to be women who say no. The possibility of failure adds something to it. After all, this isn't some fiefdom where I can have any beautiful woman I want."

But, the visitor said, that is precisely what the Hefner legend is about.

"If every woman found you desirable, that would be pathetic," Hefner said. "If every woman desired the exact same thing in a man, then one or two people would be getting all the action. Believe me, women turn me down."

And, when that happens, does it dismay him?

"Depends on the circumstances," Hefner said. "I'm realistic. Everyone talks about the sex symbols created by *Playboy*. Well, the major sex object created by *Playboy* over the last twenty-five years happens to be me."

Indeed. The person most often pictured in the pages of *Playboy* is not a particular beautiful nude woman; it is Hefner. In the current issue, Hefner's photograph appears seventeen times. For a quarter of a century, his personal fantasies have become the fantasies of millions of men around the world, and those men have never been given the chance to forget who Hugh Hefner is.

"It's been a personal adventure, and I've taken people along with me," Hefner said. "Everything that has happened to me has been a product of my own adolescent dreams and aspirations. I have lived out my dreams as a kind of surrogate for a large part of the population."

And his dreams have not changed. Then and now, he has surrounded himself with nineteen- and twenty-year-old girls; the fantasies of the teenaged Hefner have held up. Some ridicule him for this, but he cares not at all. Even though he is a big part of the Southern California celebrity scene now, there remains something about him that is basically midwestern and basically adolescent.

"I've managed to hold onto my childhood," Hefner said. "I may be fifty-two years old, but inside me there is a little boy. I love that little boy. I love him and I keep in contact with him.

"And I'm not sorry about not becoming jaded. Out here, especially in show business, you find people who have spent their entire lives, all their energies, trying to become stars, and then they tell you what a bore being famous is. Punching photographers. Well, fame is wonderful. I love it.

"I suppose I could get tired of what I have, but I'm not tired of it. I have built here what could be viewed as a perpetual woman machine. I don't go night after night looking for a new woman, but the women are here. And one of the things I am finding out is that age doesn't mean anything to women."

That is probably easy for the fifty-two-year-old editor and publisher of *Playboy* to say, the visitor said. But what if he were a fifty-two-year-old shoe salesman?

"If I were a fifty-two-year-old shoe salesman, then I would probably think that girls thought about age," Hefner said. "But I have learned something very interesting. And that is that women, although they say they like a faithful and monogamous man, are very attracted to a man who has . . . had a lot of romantic experiences. The more experienced you are, the more desirable you are to a woman. If a woman knows you have been with a great many beautiful women, she somehow finds that a very attractive thing.

"I think the next ten or fifteen years are going to be the best of my life. My life has never been sweeter than it is right now."

And now it is after midnight. Hefner is in the game house of his mansion. With all the women who have passed through his homes during these past twenty-five years, it is not a woman to whom Hefner has been loyal. The person who has lived with him the longest is a man, a man named John Dante. Dante is Hefner's best friend; they met in Chicago, and Dante has lived with Hefner for thirteen years.

Tonight Hefner and Dante play pinball. Six past and future Playmates, uniformly gorgeous, sit on a couch and watch the endless games. Hefner is in his pajamas. It is two o'clock in the morning, and some of the women are stifling yawns, but they will wait. This is Hugh Hefner's world. The boy survives.

Lines from the Heart

I WAS WORKING on a newspaper story about a person who had reached the heights, whose life had taken a sudden negative turn, and who now had to start over again from the bottom.

I vaguely remembered a line of poetry that applied to the circumstance; I believed it was by William Butler Yeats. I checked several poetry anthologies, with no luck.

I telephoned Northwestern University's English Department. I said that I was looking for a line of Yeats; did they have any suggestions where I could turn?

"Why don't I connect you with Professor Torchiana," the secretary said.

The name jarred my memory. I recalled sitting in a vast lecture hall at Northwestern, fourteen or fifteen years earlier, listening to Professor Donald Torchiana talk about classic poets long dead. It was a required class; I had no real interest in poetry then, and I don't now, and Torchiana's name had not occurred to me in all the years since. I was vaguely surprised to find that he was still at Northwestern.

My musing stopped as he picked up the call. I introduced myself.

"There's this line I'm looking for, I think it's from Yeats," I said. "It has something to do with a ladder and starting over . . ."

Torchiana interrupted, in a deep, rhythmic voice. He said:

" 'Now that my ladder's gone, I must lie down where all the ladders start, in the foul rag-and-bone shop of the heart.' "

"I think that sounds right," I said.

There was silence on the other end.

"I want it to be exact," I said. "Do you want to look it up or something?"

"It's correct the way I gave it to you," Torchiana said.

"Well . . . thanks," I said.

He hung up.

I don't know why, but in the months following our brief conversation, I found myself thinking about Torchiana.

Most of us who go to college check in one September day and check out four years later. College is a phase, a holding area between childhood and adulthood, a place to learn to live outside the constrictions of one's family. When we remember college, it is generally in terms of our contemporaries, the young men and women who shared classes and dormitories with us. In our minds, the colleges we attended did not truly exist before we arrived, and ceased to exist after we left.

The thought of Torchiana stayed with me. It seemed so unusual to consider that for all the years my classmates and I had been out of college he had remained at Northwestern, discussing Yeats and Joyce and Eliot and the other poets with ensuing classes of students who stayed forever young. We who had sat in the lecture halls with him had left the poets behind; we had gone out to pursue money or fame or happiness or any combination of those things.

Torchiana, though . . . he was still at the university. In an age of electronic images flashing across video screens, he apparently was still discussing the merits of dead poets. The life he was leading seemed so far removed from the lives of the students he spoke to, who then moved on into the world of American commerce and industry.

I had never had a private conversation with Torchiana while I was at Northwestern. He had no reason to remember me, or even to recall that I was in his class; I probably got a C, just another young man out in the seats.

But now I wanted to talk to him. I checked the schedule of classes; on a Wednesday evening, I headed for Northwestern and Professor Torchiana's poetry lecture.

I heard the voice before I got to the room. Torchiana was reading aloud from W. H. Auden; the words carried out into the second-floor hallway of Anderson Hall.

There were ten students in the class: nine women, one man. Torchiana, fifty-eight, of course looked older than I had remembered him. He was a handsome, bald man with the countenance of a dignified bulldog. He was wearing a yellow corduroy coat, a blue shirt, a dark-blue turtleneck. He seemed to have a cold; he was coughing and sniffling.

I took a seat. He held a paperback book open in front of him. Now he was quoting from Wallace Stevens. Each word was pronounced with precision, with care; for all these years since I had seen him last, he had been reading these same words aloud for new groups of students. The people in the class did not take their eyes off him. There had always been something in Torchiana's manner, a ferocity, an intensity, that demanded attention.

He glanced at the ten students through black-rimmed glasses. "In a funny way, Stevens is telling us that we love living in a world of illusion," Torchiana said. "It is an illusion that we were ever alive."

I sat in the room while he talked of poetry with this handful of people. I knew that, out in the city, hundreds of thousands of others were staring at movie or television screens.

Torchiana read another line from Stevens, and then said to the class:

"Now, what does he mean by 'the barrenness of the fertile thing'?"

There was silence.

Torchiana spoke softly:

"Ultimately our world is barren."

Class ended just after nine P.M. I waited until the students had left. I approached Torchiana. I didn't quite know how to explain my presence, so I just told him that I was revisiting Northwestern. Did he have time to talk?

He was putting on a heavy overcoat. He nodded. I asked if I could buy him a drink.

"Do you have a car?" he said.

I said that I didn't.

"Well, neither do I," he said. "But we can go to the Orrington Hotel."

We walked along Sheridan Road. It was a frigid, snowy night; we seemed to be the only two people on the street. His cough worsened.

"I'm so broke all the time, I have to teach these night classes," he said. "Night classes and summer school."

On the mezzanine of the Orrington, we found a bar of the kind favored by college students. There were video games and a jukebox playing an old Janis Joplin record. The room was overheated; we were the only people present out of our twenties. We took a table in the corner.

I didn't know where to start; didn't really know exactly what I was doing here. So I asked him about the energy he had put into reading the poetry to the students this night. Surely he had read the poems thousands of times before. Where did he find the will to give each word meaning?

"It's a performance," he said. "It doesn't matter if it's the thousandth time or the tenth time. The kids are out there. They've paid their money."

He told me that teaching poetry and literature at Northwestern was the only job he had ever had. He had come to the school in 1953 and never sought work elsewhere. He had been a B-17 pilot in World War II, flying twenty-four missions over Germany and Austria. Then he had returned to college, and then he had been hired at Northwestern, and here he was.

I asked him what made him do it. His students just drifted through; listened to him read them poetry for a term, then graduated and went out to pursue wealth. But Torchiana . . . he stayed on, with his poets inside of books.

"When you decide that this is how you're going to spend your life, you settle on this early on," he said. "I told myself a long time ago that I'm going to teach and I'm never going to make any money. You deal with that fact at the beginning.

"When I was an instructor, I worked at the Railway Express office at Christmastime. I sold my blood at the hospital on occasion."

He let it drop. He seemed vaguely uncomfortable to be addressing the subject; after a lifetime of doing this, here was a stranger demanding to know why.

He told me that he was divorced and that his children were grown and gone. He rented out rooms in his home to graduate students, for the income.

"I don't go to the movies," he said. "I don't own a TV or a radio. They don't interest me."

I asked him if—with his love of poetry—it ever frustrated him to dwell on the words of others. Didn't he write his own poems?

"Yes," he said. "Right now I'm working on three poems."

Who got to read them?

"Nobody."

I asked him why.

"I don't know," he said. "They're not very good. I just write them, I don't send them out. I never leave them alone. I'm always working on them."

Did he never feel the urge to at least read his own poems to his classes?

"No," he said. "They're not paying for that. They're there for Joyce and Auden and Yeats and Stevens . . . they're there for the curriculum."

I asked him if it was hard, in this world of mass communication, to put out for a room of ten people. When he thought of all the performers with audiences in the millions, did he ever have trouble delivering to so few?

"They're there in good faith," he said. "They've showed up. I do what I can to fulfill that faith."

The jukebox was playing "Every Little Thing She Does Is Magic," by the Police. We each ordered another drink. Torchiana said that if he could afford it, he might consider retiring. But the money was not there.

"You think what you might do," he said. "Give yourself over to reading and writing, without having to worry about grading papers. Perhaps travel more, meet a more varied set of people. But I'm here for the duration."

I asked him if Northwestern had a mandatory retirement age of sixty-five.

"You can stay on until you're seventy, but I don't think I'll last that long," he said. "Frankly, my health is not very good, and I don't think I'll live to see seventy. But I probably have ten more years in me, and I'll spend them teaching here."

There was a line I had heard him quote in the class just completed; he had been reading from Auden, and he had said:

" '. . . for poetry makes nothing happen.' "

I asked him if he thought that was true.

"Auden was going out of his way to play down himself and the importance of what he did," Torchiana said.

But what about the truth of the sentiment? After all these years of teaching the poetry of others, could he candidly proclaim that poetry does, indeed, make things happen?

"If it doesn't make anything happen, then at least it teaches man how to praise," he said. "Maybe that's enough."

The jukebox kept playing hits old and new, and the beeping from the computer games became constant, and outside the storm grew worse. Maybe some of the students in the barroom had had Torchiana in a class, but they didn't come over; we drank by ourselves, and we decided before long that it was time to go home.

We walked down a long hallway toward the front of the hotel. He said that he had papers to grade at home; I still hadn't really explained the instinct that had brought me to see him, and so he told me that he hoped I had enjoyed my trip to the university, and hoped that the memories had been pleasant.

He had his books of Auden and Stevens in his hand. Both of us were supposed to be pretty good with words; and yet there was no way of letting him know that I had come back to Northwestern not to look at the campus, but to find out about him— and that what I had found had moved me, in ways that I had not quite expected. So I didn't say anything. He was going to walk to his house; I was going to call a cab.

I asked him again if he had never considered letting his friends and students see his own poetry, instead of the poetry of others he had been teaching for twenty-eight years.

He didn't answer. He just shook his head no, and before I could make a proper goodbye he walked out into the snow. I watched him pass beneath a streetlamp. You could still hear the jukebox playing down the corridor.

Love Story

TRUE ROMANCES:

John and Mary (names have been changed to protect my health) have been man and wife for twelve years. John is an ironworker. Mary, who stands five foot two and weighs 180 pounds, is a typist. John works days. Mary works nights.

Mary is proud of her family life. "My family has no derelicts in it," she said. "I know karate."

But love, as it will, winked at Mary. It winked in the person of Elroy, a thrice-divorced clerk for the county. He met Mary one night after work, at an informal gathering in a tavern. He asked her to dance. She accepted. When the song ended, she said to him:

"You're a jerk."

Several months passed. Then, one night at work, Mary received a telephone call from Elroy. Elroy wanted to know if Mary would like to go out on a date.

For all the years since her marriage to John, Mary had been faithful. But by this point, according to Mary, "You get aggravated and disgusted and stuff. I was super-bored and not taking part in activities or hobbies." So when Elroy called, Mary was receptive.

"Are you still a jerk?" she inquired.

"No," Elroy said.

"Okay," Mary said. "Pick me up after work."

And thus Mary, a mother of four daughters, began her tempestuous affair.

At first, she thought it would be merely a lark:

"I thought, hey, I'll go out with this dope and spend his money."

But the fling turned into romance:

"He treated me real gentle and all that crap."

Soon they were meeting on the sly three and four times a week. "We'd drink or eat or hit a motel," Mary said.

Love was not blind; Mary knew that Elroy had a few minor character flaws.

"I knew he was a nut," she said. "He'd been married three times, and he mentioned something about being in an alcoholic drying-out ward once, and I knew that he was a home invader. He burglarized apartments. But he told me he was through with all that. Still, sometimes when we were drinking, his pupils would dilate, and he would talk about crazy things, like doing more home invasions to support his habit. He never mentioned what his habit was and I never asked. I was very attracted to him physically."

For a year, Mary and Elroy met in the shadows. Then, on a recent Sunday, Mary borrowed her husband's car and she and Elroy went for a ride. Mary's husband John, who had borrowed another car, saw them cruising and cut them off on a side street.

"John was going to punch Elroy's face in," Mary said.

But Elroy ran away.

That evening, John took his four daughters to a shopping center. While they were inside a store, Elroy came to the parking lot, stuck a rag in the gas tank of John's car, lit it, and tried to blow the car up.

Luckily the wind blew the flame out. But later that night, John and Mary looked out their front window and noticed that John's car had exploded.

After the fire department had doused the flames and the charred hulk of the car remained on the street, Mary went to Elroy's house to confront him.

"Did you go and torch my husband's car?" Mary said.

"Oh, no," said Elroy. "I have been sleeping."

"I do not want to see you again," Mary said.

Several days later, the apartment of Mary's cousin Bertha was burglarized and set on fire.

"I found Elroy with some of Bertha's possessions," Mary said. "He had taken seven bottles of liquor, a pair of handcuffs, and a gold badge that a police officer had given Bertha as a memento.

Bertha works in the Cook County's sheriff's department, in the field of locking up prostitutes."

Mary again confronted Elroy with the evidence.

"I cannot remember," said Elroy. "I must have had an alcoholic blackout."

Mary said to Elroy, "I am giving you the brush-off."

She said to Elroy's brother, "Tell him if he ever comes near me again, I will blow his brains out."

John, for his part, said, "I was going to tear Elroy apart limb by limb. I'm a pretty big boy. But I decided not to, because I might get arrested for it."

Now John and Mary's marriage is on solid ground again.

"We never used to shop together," Mary said. "That has changed."

"There's one thing you can say about my wife," John said. "She is not the worst woman in the world."

The Real News

DELAFIELD, WISCONSIN—In the city where I live, there are four million people. When I woke up on a Saturday morning, much of the news of those people was unhappy. In the criminal courts building, a man was on trial for allegedly murdering thirty-three boys and young men, the most killings charged to one person in United States history. The city's schoolteachers were fighting with the Board of Education; children had not been to classes in two weeks. The firefighters were angry, too; they talked of walking out on their jobs. An arson-for-profit ring was being investigated, in which human lives were traded for insurance dollars.

The choice I had was the choice a newspaper reporter makes every day: which of those big-city crises to think about before the end of the shift, and the deadline for the next column.

But on this Saturday, I chose none. Instead I borrowed a ride just two hours to the north, and here I sit in another world.

The temperature here in Wisconsin is below freezing. I am in the living room of a house where I have never been. Out the window, Lake Nagawicka is frozen solid. There is a small island out in the middle of the lake. In the summer, the townspeople approach it by boat. This afternoon, though, children are walking out over the frozen surface of the lake, their black rubber boots flopping against their ankles, heading for that island on foot.

On a map, I am not far from the big city in which I make my living; indeed, the sounds of the big city's radio stations stayed clear most of the way up here. It was only in the last twenty minutes or so of the ride that the city voices disappeared, and were replaced by the voices of the smaller Wisconsin broadcast outlets.

It is quiet here. I feel like an intruder; I am a stranger in the house, and as I walk around the first floor I realize that this place has nothing to do with the seemingly frantic life I have left fleetingly behind. If I were to talk about the important news stories of the city, the people here would be puzzled, as well they should. Up here, those stories seem to have no true importance, no relation to life as real people live it.

I look at the framed photographs on the wall of this house. Generations of a family I know nothing about, the faces smiling proudly for photographers going back to almost a century ago. The history in this house has nothing to do with stories that once appeared on the front pages of newspapers; the history here is a personal history, and walking in the midst of it I sense a significance that could never be matched by news stories that appear one Monday and are forgotten two weeks hence.

Around the edge of the lake, a number of bait shops that double as taverns peek out over the ice. The Leprechaun, the Light House; to a visitor they look the same, but each has its own clientele, its own personality. There are pool tables, and racks of potato chips and pretzels for sale. The faces, it is easy to sense, are here every Saturday afternoon.

Some of the people of Delafield talk over their beer; some play a hand of cards. A few read the region's daily paper, the *Waukesha Freeman*. There are wire-service stories about the White House and the Kremlin and the FBI, but those are not the ones that have caught the fancy of this afternoon's readers.

Instead, the men and women in the Leprechaun read that Waukesha North High School lost in overtime, 61-55, to West Allis Hale last night. This was not the only important basketball game up here; West Bend East beat Oconomowoc, 67-65, and Kettle Moraine defeated Slinger, 59-56.

And there is other news. Anne Dennis, daughter of Mr. and Mrs. Daren Dennis of Waukesha, is engaged to be married to Richard Jonas, son of Mr. and Mrs. William Jonas of Pewaukee. The prospective bridegroom works at the Quality Aluminum Casting Co.; the wedding will be on July 26 at St. Mary Catholic Church.

Ruth Heinzen of Waukesha has been named the No. 1 Sales Associate of the year by Relocation Realty. James Burmeister will present an organ recital at the North Shore Presbyterian Church in Shorewood. The town's Choral Union will hold auditions in Carroll College's Shattuck Auditorium; the auditions are open to any interested singer.

Surely there is heartache and crime and unhappiness here in Delafield; these are the 1980s, and the plagues of the real world cannot be kept at bay, not anywhere.

But from where I sit on a freezing afternoon, all is quiet. I watch those children tromping out toward the island, over the ice; one pulls a sled behind him. It is silent here in the house; only the sound of the dog pacing around on the wooden floor upstairs provides an occasional interruption.

It is nearing dusk; soon those children will return from the island. Their parents will be waiting. It will be time to go to dinner at Karl and Gretchen's, the restaurant which has served the families of Delafield on Saturday nights for generations.

Dusk; time for me to return, also. In a few hours I will be back in the city of deadlines and crises and news that never stops.

For now, though, the only news that matters is right out that window, over the frozen lake. It is news of another kind; news that there is more than one way to live a life. That is today's news from Delafield.

The Fortunate

IN PRIVATE DINING Room No. 9 of Chicago's Palmer House hotel, twenty men and women are playing a game. They are playing with a certain degree of passion; the room is filled with shouts and groans and shrieks.

On the surface, this is surprising. Nothing exceptional seems to be going on here. There is an old green chalkboard at the front of the room, with letters of the alphabet taped across its top. There is a portable wheel, which, when spun, rotates and then stops at various points denoting dollar denominations. There are three casually dressed people who appear to be in charge.

The atmosphere in the room is unusually tense. And perhaps it should be. For the men and women who are playing, this will be—by their own admission—one of the most important half hours of their lives.

By the time the weekend is over, more than six hundred contestants will have passed through the room. "Wheel of Fortune," an NBC television daytime game show, has decided that its pool of available players has just about worn out in the southern California area. So the show's producers have come here to recruit prospective contestants from the Midwest.

The game, as seen on television, is fairly simple. Three people at a time compete in an electronic version of the old children's game "hangman," in which one attempts to spell words by guessing letters one by one. The winner of each televised round gets to select from an array of merchandise displayed onstage.

"I decided that our viewers had seen enough tanned faces from Los Angeles," says Nancy Jones, the show's producer. "There is a certain California look and attitude we're trying to get away from. So here we are."

Jones has heard all the theories about the greed and money-lust that drives people to try to appear on game shows. She thinks such theories are wrong; according to her, there is a simpler dynamic at work.

"The motivating factor is not money, and the motivating factor is not merchandise," she says. "The motivating factor is that people want to be on television. To be on television is, to most people, the ultimate American experience. Our contestants know that they are unlikely to walk away from the show with very much in terms of merchandise.

"We don't even pay our contestants' way to California. They don't care. They're happy to pay their own expenses. All they want to do is to be on national television once in their lives."

In Private Dining Room No. 9, the three "Wheel of Fortune" staff members who are running the tryouts—Paul Gilbert, Tony Pandolfo, and Reva Solomon—are explaining to the contestants what will happen next.

"In a moment we're going to leave the room," Pandolfo says. "We're going to talk about how you did, and then we're going to come back in and read off a list of names. If you hear your name called, we would like you to stay in the room a little longer. If you don't . . . well, we'd like you to sort of not stay in the room."

A man calls out: "I notice that when someone wins the jewelry, you always say that they get a gift certificate. Does that mean it's not the exact piece of jewelry we see on the show?"

"That's right," Pandolfo says. "You can select your own jewelry. And we deliver our prizes anywhere in the United States. Right to the house. Actually in the house, not out on the curb. The only thing we ask is that all the prizes be sent to one address. You can't have the washing machine sent to your house, and the microwave oven to your Aunt Millie in Cleveland."

The man nods. He does not know it, but he has already lost. During the tryout game, Gilbert, Pandolfo, and Solomon have made notes about which contestants seem best to them: the most enthusiastic, brightest, and liveliest. The man with the question is not one of them.

Mary Farris, twenty-five, wife of a carpenter, mother of two, has paid $118 for a round-trip TWA ticket from Kansas City so she could be here this afternoon.

"I saw them announce that they would be in Chicago," she says. "I always play along with the game on TV, and at home I always win. With the two babies I never get out, but I had to come here to try."

Many of the prospective contestants echo her sentiment. In the main, they are women, the majority of whom spend most of their time inside their houses. This is to be expected; to be a "Wheel of Fortune" fan,, you must be home during the day.

"I know I'm going to be picked," says Sandy Burnell, twenty-seven, of Elgin, Illinois. She has three children, and she stays home with them. "When I came down here to play the game, I knew that I would have to smile a lot and look excited.

"My husband can't afford to leave the city, but I have relatives in California, and so I told him that if I have to leave him and the kids for a few days—hey, I have to go for it."

Mike Maty, a twenty-eight-year-old sales representative from Evergreen Park, Illinois, says, "You have to smile a lot when you're playing the game, but a lot of smiles is something I've got. When I was playing, I made sure I was making a lot of eyeball contact.

"I know the odds are against me getting on, and even if I do get on I know the odds are against me winning. But I'm a media fan, and I'd like to say that I was on TV once."

The Nancy Jones theory of why people try out for "Wheel of Fortune" seems to be holding; virtually all of the people who are asked say that, to them, the prizes are secondary to the chance of appearing in front of a network camera. One man has just found out this morning that he has lost his job. But he has kept his "Wheel of Fortune" appointment anyway.

"You try to be outgoing when you're playing," he says. "You

show a lot of teeth. I have nine grandchildren—I'm fifty-three—
and if they could see me on a game show, it would make their
granddad seem important to them."

Elaine Kloth-Goodman, a thirty-four-year-old flight attendant
for United Airlines, says, "My ultimate dream was to be a stewardess, which I achieved. So I'm here because you always have
to have a new ultimate goal." And Wendy Jurs, twenty-nine,
says, "A person has to have some gratification and achievement
and satisfaction in their life. If someone says to me now, 'What
do you do?' all I can say is that I'm a bartender.

"But if I do well enough here today, then for the rest of my
life I can say that I was on a game show."

Pat Sajak, the sandy-haired thirty-five-year-old man who is
host of "Wheel of Fortune," is not taking part in the tryouts.
But he is in town with the show's hostess, Susan Stafford, to tape
some midwestern-scenery shots for the program's opening and
closing segments.

"All of the people who are trying out are trying to show that
they are enthusiastic, warm people," he says as he sits in a room
of the Palmer House. "It's all great fun for them here. But
sometimes it goes away when they step out there in front of five
cameras and two hundred people in the studio audience. Their
confidence wanes. This is real. This is television.

"Why are they here? I've tried to come up with philosophical
answers—you know, looking into the heart of America. But I
don't think there are any big answers.

"It's a simple target if you want to make fun: middle-class
Americans jumping up and down. But I don't think this has
anything to do with people's desire to see other people feel
foolish. We're not doing *Macbeth*. We're not trying to be uplifting.
This is just a case of people trying to prove they can be as smart
as people on television. People like the idea of having a moment
in the sun; there's nothing so terrible about that."

Back in Private Dining Room No. 9, a new batch of contestants
is getting acquainted with Paul Gilbert, Tony Pandolfo, and Reva
Solomon.

"I'm scared that if I get on, you'll have a hard puzzle," a woman says. "Remember when the answer was 'Massachusetts Institute of Technology'?"

"Yes," Gilbert says. "But most of our answers are much shorter."

"One thing you should remember," Pandolfo says, "is that when you are actually on the show, you can get nervous and make mistakes on even the obvious answers."

"I remember that one show," a contestant says. "I'll never forget it. There were only two letters left, and the person said she was ready to solve it, and she said, 'A bird in the hand is worth two in the dish.'"

In the hallway outside Private Dining Room No. 9, Susan Stafford has arrived. A roomful of contestants is inside trying out, but here in the corridor the next group is waiting, and the sudden appearance of the hostess of "Wheel of Fortune" takes them by surprise.

Most stare in silence. But one—a woman who has attempted twice to qualify for the show, and who has been told that she will not be allowed in the room a third time—moves toward Stafford almost involuntarily.

"Susan . . ." she says, and begins to cry.

Through her sobs she says, "I'm so embarrassed to be like this. But it's been such a terrible year. I lost my mother—she was seventy-eight years old, but she was so youthful, she looked like sixty—and nothing seems to be going right, and now I can't even get in and try again."

The tears well out of her eyes. "I'm sorry, Susan, I know there's nothing you can do," she says.

Stafford puts her arms around the woman. "I can hug you," she says, and in the middle of the crowd they embrace.

In an anteroom down the hall from Private Dining Room No. 9, Gilbert, Pandolfo, and Solomon are deciding which members of the latest group will get to make it to the next round. They are referring to a seating chart filled in with the first names of the people in the game room.

"I like three of them," Pandolfo says.

"What did you think of Pam?" Solomon says.

"I don't know," Pandolfo says. "She started out strong, but she got kind of quiet in the end."

"Anyone else?" Solomon says.

"Karen I didn't like at all," Pandolfo says.

"Is that the one with her foot up on the chair in front of her?" Gilbert says.

They are running late. Pandolfo is clearly in charge. He begins to read names from up and down the rows on the chart:

"Dan, yes. Joel, no. Leslie, no. Karen, no. Alice, no. Janet, no. Vickie, yes."

They have been in the anteroom for less than five minutes when they leave to give the news to the contestants.

The wheel is spinning. Outside the Palmer House, darkness has come to Chicago. The losers are already on the way back to their homes around the Midwest. But here in the room the day's last group of contestants is playing the game.

"Spin, spin, spin!" shouts Debora Adrian. Her fellow players cheer her on. In the questionnaire she filled out, she noted that she is twenty-seven; that she lives in Fairfield, Iowa; that she is married with two children; that she works as a dental assistant; and that her hobbies are "making jewelry, traveling, and raising hogs."

Now Paul Gilbert calls on her to pick a consonant. "I'll take a *W*," she yells.

But there is no *W* in the correct answer. Another contestant is selected to make a choice of letters; he does well, and comes up with the solution: "Liver and onions."

The three "Wheel of Fortune" producers leave the room. Debora Adrian—who has driven five hours from Iowa to Chicago for this tryout—waits for their decision.

"The day they announced on the show they were coming to Chicago, I asked my husband's permission to call long-distance to make a reservation to try out," she says. "He said he didn't care. I called straight from eleven-thirty in the morning till four-thirty in the afternoon before there wasn't a busy signal, and I finally got through.

"What an experience this has been. If I get to be on the show, it's great. But even if I don't, I'll have this day to remember for the rest of my life."

King of the
Wild Frontier

IN THE MIDDLE of the 1950s, when television was just passing the stage of being a novelty in American homes, something important happened.

People had already become used to the idea of the TV set introducing strangers to them. What had been inconceivable only a few years before—the concept of moving pictures appearing in one's own home, inside an electronic box—was on its way to becoming commonplace.

So people were adapting to the idea of men and women dancing into their living rooms. What they weren't prepared for—because it had never happened before, there was nothing in history to prepare them for it—was the phenomenon that occurred when the TV camera and a specific performer mutually discovered an almost perversely magical chemistry.

When that happened, the result was instant folk-hero status for the performer. In a moment's time, he was part of tens of millions of lives. He became something that had no antecedent in the world.

In its most extreme sense, this phenomenon happened to only two people. One we all remember with no prodding. Elvis Presley, because of the jarring way his physical presence carried over the airwaves, changed the country's social history. Because of the publicity given Presley's sad end, we tend to think of him as the only man with this visceral power. When we recall television during those days, it seems that Presley was the one male figure who affected Americans—especially American children and teenagers—so strongly.

But there was another. If you think back, you may recall a television show known as "Davy Crockett, King of the Wild Frontier."

Finding Fess Parker in the 1980s is not an easy task. Unlike Presley, Parker did not remain an American institution; following his portrayal of Davy Crockett, he reverted to his status as a journeyman actor and then seemingly disappeared.

But when Walt Disney's "Davy Crockett" shows were being broadcast, the response to Parker was astounding. In its fury and its scope, it was every bit the equal of what was happening with Presley. In his portrayal of Crockett, Parker brought to the small screen a presence that was palpable; people looked at him, and they listened to him, and they tingled.

The face and the voice combined to represent everything that was ideally male in the United States. Davy Crockett coonskin caps were seen in every elementary school in the country; there were trading cards and lunch boxes and dolls. "The Ballad of Davy Crockett" was the number-one-selling record in the United States for sixteen consecutive weeks. Columnist Hedda Hopper wrote that Parker was "the greatest he-man find since Gary Cooper and Clark Gable."

But twenty-five years later, Fess Parker seemed impossible to locate. The standard Hollywood reference points—agencies, studios, celebrity services—said they had not heard of him in at least a decade. Some ventured that he might be dead.

So it was intriguing when I was put in contact with an attorney in Santa Barbara, California, who acknowledged that he represented Parker. Not as an actor; Parker didn't do that anymore. Now, I was told, Parker dealt in real estate, including mobile-home parks. He was just another American businessman trying to make it.

I waited in room 640 of the Beverly Hilton hotel. Parker had agreed to meet me; he had said he would call as soon as he arrived in the lobby.

When the phone rang and he said he was there, the voice was

startling. All this time later, it was that voice of Davy Crockett at the Alamo. I sat there with my *Los Angeles Times* and the remains of my room-service breakfast, and I felt like I was nine years old.

The room had a balcony overlooking the Hollywood Hills; Parker had driven two hours to meet me, so I asked him if he felt like riding the elevator up and just relaxing out on that terrace, instead of going to a restaurant. He said that sounded good.

Several minutes later he knocked on the door, and when I opened it Parker stood in the hallway, six feet six, fifty-seven years old, wearing a brown suit and carrying a briefcase. His hair had gone completely gray, but he wore it long, as in the Crockett days. Most of all, he had that unforgettable squint that had mesmerized and haunted so many million living rooms.

We shook hands and I led him to the balcony. We sat out in the warm morning air; he looked like nothing if not a successful executive in the first-class cabin of a jet. And yet he had known a part of the American dream that few others will ever know. I asked him about it.

"Well . . ." he said. He spoke slowly. "It's an interesting thing to live with."

He told me the story: how he had been a young actor with sixteen or seventeen movies to his credit when, at the age of twenty-nine, he had been offered the part of Crockett in the Disney productions. How he had shot all three segments—"Davy Crockett, Indian Fighter," "Davy Crockett Goes to Congress," and "Davy Crockett at the Alamo"—in 1954. And how he had no idea of what effect the programs were going to have on the country, or on his life.

"The first episode showed at the end of 1954," Parker said. "And the first idea I had of the impact it was having was when I went to a little town in Texas to visit an old friend of mine and he asked me to go to a dance class his wife was teaching to say hello to the children. And when I walked in that room . . . it was as if every child was gravitating toward me. I still remember them automatically moving toward me."

He said the fame, when it started, was impossible to contain.

All it was was three television shows, and yet television was so powerful that nothing more was needed.

"There was a dinner in Washington honoring a retiring assistant secretary of defense," Parker said. "I was invited. I walked in wearing that coonskin cap and buckskin outfit—Mr. Disney required that I wear it everywhere I went in public. This was a formal dinner. Everyone was in tuxedoes or evening dresses.

"So there I was at the head table. Some of the most important people in the government were there. Senators, generals, admirals. And I sat at that head table with that getup on, and people tried to make speeches. And suddenly this line began to form in front of me. People just stood there staring. They weren't listening to the speeches. They were just looking at me.

"Mr. Disney sent us on a tour of forty-five cities to promote the shows. I remember arriving at the airport in New Orleans. For twenty-five miles the route was lined with cars, people waiting to see me. They said it was a bigger reception than Eisenhower got when he was there. I grew accustomed to things like that. In Scotland, people pushed through the glass in a department-store window. In Holland, they chased me down the street. There is nothing that prepares a man for something like that."

Parker said that the experience began to affect him. "When I started to do that job, I had never had a filling in any of my teeth," he said. "Within three years, I had thirteen. I think it must have been the tension. I was pulled off the set once, because it was some sort of Walt Disney Night at the Hollywood Bowl. They drove me to the Bowl, and they put me onstage in my Davy Crockett cap and uniform, and they handed me a guitar. The Los Angeles Symphony Orchestra was behind me, and the Roger Wagner Chorale, and I was supposed to sing 'Farewell to the Mountain.' There were twenty-five thousand people in the audience.

"It wasn't fun. It was awesome, but it wasn't fun. It had gone beyond the dream. I wasn't allowed to go out and eat. I was kept practically like an animal in my room."

Unexpectedly, that was all going to end soon. At the height of the success of Davy Crockett, Walt Disney grew bored with it. He had determined that he would film no more Davy Crockett adventures, even though he had created the most popular character in America.

"I don't claim to have known Mr. Disney that well," Parker said. "I was never even in his home. From what I could tell, he was like an artist who didn't want to paint the same picture over and over again. All he was interested in at that point was Disneyland. He was pressured into making a two-part show that second year—'Davy Crockett and the River Pirates'—but that was it.

"He was always very polite to me. If I wanted to see him, the secretaries let me walk right into his office. I would ask him about various opportunities, and he would hear me out. But I got the impression that by this time he was thinking about other things. People I knew pointed out to me that the attention span of the American public is very short, and I tried to make Mr. Disney understand that I was concerned about how that applied to me.

"I was under personal contract to him. I still harbored some illusion that I was going to have a well-rounded film career. But it wasn't to be. I remember I went out and bought a copy of the play *Bus Stop*. I thought if I could appear in that movie with Marilyn Monroe, it might give me a new career. I asked Mr. Disney if I could do it. I think I still have my copy of the play in my library at home, with his note in it: 'I don't think this is a picture you ought to do. Walt.' "

Parker said that he finally got out of his contract with Disney, then became involved in other television and movie projects, including a Crockett-like portrayal of Daniel Boone. None of it approached what had happened to him with the Davy Crockett programs. His counterpart, Presley, had become an American icon; Parker was finding that he was just another actor again.

"I never met Presley until years later," he said. "Our images were vastly different, but with what was happening to us so suddenly, I suppose the same possibilities for self-destruction were there. When I did meet him, it was after all of this was over. He was appearing in Las Vegas, and I went to the show and I was led back to his dressing room to meet him afterward. I was in a business suit and he was in the white jump suit. I shook hands with Elvis and his father, and that was about all there was to it."

By that time Parker had decided that if there was any future for him, it was in the field of business. He tried out a few theme parks, then settled on the mobile-home-park idea. He said it has worked well for him.

"In my community I'm thought of as a controversial character," he said. "A rich man who isn't against hurting the environment because I'm a developer. I suppose some people there think that I'm greed personified."

I looked over at Parker. He was staring out at the Hollywood Hills.

"It's different, trying to be a successful businessman," he said. "Even after Davy Crockett, when I would meet people—merchants, executives—I could tell that they thought what I did wasn't worth much. They knew that what I had done was transitory, fading, momentary. They didn't sense any accomplishment.

"But whatever I do now, I will make it or not make it as a businessman. I had something very unusual, but that was a long time ago. It's over. Out is out."

We sat for a while in the sun. Parker said that it was rare for him to be in Beverly Hills; he had once lived there, but now preferred to remain in Santa Barbara, away from the entertainment community.

"There probably isn't a day when I don't get some reminder of what happened to me," he said. "When people find out who I am, they tell me how much I meant to them when they were children.

"But then there's the other side of it. I'll call some businessman, and I'll try to leave a message with his twenty-one-year-old secretary, and she'll say, 'Wes Parker? How do you spell that?' "

I told him that, whatever becomes of the rest of his life, he is doubtless destined for an obituary that begins, "Fess Parker, who in the 1950s achieved superstardom as the frontier character Davy Crockett . . ."

Parker squinted again as he looked out at those hills.

"That's fine," he said. "That's fine."

The Prettiest Girl in Kanawha County

SAM HINDMAN, THE executive editor of the Charleston, West Virginia, *Daily Mail*, was on the phone.

"How would you like to come down here and pick the prettiest girl in Kanawha County?" he asked.

"Yes," I said.

"This is the thirty-sixth year for the Miss Kanawha County Majorette Festival," Hindman said. "I know you're busy, but I really think . . ."

"Sam, I said yes," I said.

"Our paper sponsors it, and if you would just think about it for a couple of days . . ."

"Sam," I said. "Yes."

An official of the Miss Kanawha County Majorette Festival called me several days later. He stressed that my only function was to select the prettiest majorette in the county. High school marching bands and majorette corps would be competing in skill categories, too; I was to ignore those. All I was required to do was catch a Piedmont flight to Charleston, show up at the proper time, and decide who was prettiest.

Just to make sure I was not missing the point, a letter soon arrived from Mel Verost, who handled promotion for the festival. He outlined where I was supposed to be and whom I was supposed to meet. Then he emphasized my duties:

"The selection is based purely on your ideas of beauty, stature, poise, and personality.

"It's best to ask contenders to say something so you can see their teeth."

I arrived at Laidley Field just after dark. The temperature was in the forties, but that was not stopping some seven thousand residents of Kanawha County from showing up and selecting seats in the grandstand.

I was wearing a coat and tie; a young man stopped me and asked me if I was the judge. I confirmed that I was.

He introduced himself. He said that he was Ivan Fraser, seventeen, a senior at South Charleston High School.

"We have a pool to see who's going to win," he said. "I bet two dollars."

I asked him who he had his money riding on.

"Two long shots," he said. "Lisa Barker and Lisa Bianconi. They have short hair, so the odds are against them."

The marching bands and majorette corps were arriving. The young men and women represented eleven high schools: East Bank, Stonewall Jackson, Dunbar, Sissonville, George Washington, South Charleston, Herbert Hoover, Saint Albans, Nitro, DuPont, and Charleston. They took preassigned seats in the bleachers on the opposite side of the football field.

My official judging duties were not scheduled to start for another fifteen minutes, so I talked to some of the majorettes. "My whole family is here," said Kim Canterbury, sixteen, of Charleston High. "The rules are really rough. You're not allowed to use curling irons or blow dryers. Last year they blew a fuse in the locker room."

Vanessa Jones, seventeen, of DuPont, said, "Every girl in Kanawha County sets her goal on being Miss Majorette from the time we're in Little League. That's when we start cheering for the peewee football teams. I was Little Miss Majorette when I was five years old. You're well aware even back then how important it is. All the little boys say 'hi' when you're a majorette."

Terri Busby, seventeen, of Stonewall Jackson, said, "Being

Miss Majorette is the best thing that can happen to a girl. It's the biggest thing you can be."

But Beth Bruney, seventeen, of Nitro, said, "A lot of the time Miss Majorette becomes disliked because people say she thinks she's the queen of everything. Every girl wants to become Miss Majorette, but I hear it's not so easy once you get the title."

Our idle gossip had to stop because a voice on the stadium's public address system announced that the majorettes were supposed to take to the field. A pageant official was impatiently motioning to me; I walked over to him, and he handed me a clipboard with a score sheet on it.

"Walk slowly past them and examine them," he said. "Narrow them down. You'll make your final selection later."

The majorettes—ninety-nine of them—were lined up in a giant U-shape on the football field. The stands were filled to capacity. I waited for someone to tell me to start, but no one did. So, under the lights, I began to march past them, like a general reviewing his troops.

As I reached the beginning of each high school's corps, the young women snapped to attention. All wore short skirts, tall hats, and knee-high white boots. As I walked past, some raised their legs in a kicking motion.

It had rained in the afternoon, and the dampness of the field, combined with the rapidly falling temperatures, caused a number of the majorettes to chatter their teeth as they flashed wide, glistening smiles. Traffic whizzed by on I-77 behind the stadium. In the distance I could see a RED ROOF INNS—SLEEP CHEAP! sign and the dome of the West Virginia state capitol.

Each young woman wore a big number pinned to her chest, so that I could identify all of them easily. I jotted down the numbers of the ones I found the most strikingly attractive; I noticed that all of the majorettes were looking at me as I walked, so I pretended to be writing something down on the clipboard even when I wasn't. I didn't want to hurt anyone's feelings. Also, I was worried about snipers among the family members up in the stands.

When I had reached the end of the line, pageant officials looked at the clipboard and remarked that I had not done a very good job of narrowing the contestants down. I apparently had been taken with too many of the young women; my list was well into double figures. So I was directed to make another swing past them and to work on winnowing the list. I was informed that this was the first time in the history of the pageant that a judge had been required to walk by the majorettes twice.

The Reverend Ross Harrison of the Good Shepherd Southern Baptist Church, in Scott Depot, gave the invocation. "Lord, these young people here on this field represent the happiness of Your creation," he said. "Smile upon them tonight." Then the combined bands of the eleven high schools played the national anthem.

The marching and twirling competition began. I was seated at a table on the fifty-yard line; police officers stood between me and the crowd. I leaned back to watch the precision routines, but I was quickly handed a pair of binoculars. I was instructed to single out the young women who still remained on my list; by the time the competition was over, I was to have examined them through the high-powered lenses and to have finished with just one majorette from each high school.

The bands' routines were intriguing. The majorettes from East Bank appeared dressed as rabbits in front of a wood-and-cardboard representation of the Playboy mansion. Then, as the band played "The Stripper," they removed their rabbit suits to reveal homemade Playboy Bunny costumes. As the band played "Centerfold" in the cold West Virginia night, they danced around with champagne glasses balanced on waitresses' trays.

This routine had barely ended when master of ceremonies John Barker intoned, "The Sissonville majorettes will appear as the Fruit of the Loom gang dancing to 'Tutti Fruitti.' Then they will peel off their fruit skins and dance on top of boxer shorts to the music of 'Short Shorts.'"

Robin Toner, a reporter for the *Daily Mail*, was sitting next to me. I sneaked a look at her notes. She had written: "George Washington High—Mixed tribute to Walt Disney and world peace."

I fixed my binoculars on the undulating numbers.

There are probably many parts of America where something like the Miss Kanawha County Majorette Festival would not fit in. Certainly the routines that were going on out on the field were lacking in what some people would describe as world-weary sophistication.

But I couldn't help thinking, as I watched the Charleston High School majorettes pretend to drive a cardboard eighteen-wheeler while their band played "On the Road Again," that this probably was not the worst way in the world to grow up. Forget about the rightness or wrongness of selecting a bona fide beauty queen this far into the Eighties; the real point was, for whatever reasons, all of these West Virginia teenagers had decided to opt for the discipline it took to participate in this exercise. Put aside the grand meaning of it all; they were fifteen and sixteen and seventeen years old and, instead of swallowing Quāāludes behind the school or trying to slip backstage at the Civic Center to hook up with the lead singer of AC/DC, they spent their time practicing and getting ready for this.

That may not be such a bad thing. I had to quit my musing, though; the last band number of the night, "Ease On Down the Road," was concluding, and the majorettes were scurrying off the field. It was time for me to make my choices.

I walked back ten feet to the pageant officials' area. I handed my selections to the chief official; he gave me a somber look and offered his hand, which I shook.

John Barker announced: "Here are the semifinalists for the Miss Kanawha County Majorette title." The stadium grew silent.

"We will call the young ladies by number first, and ask them to come forward and line up on the west side of the platform. Then we will introduce them by name."

He called the numbers. Each school exploded into cheers as the numbers were announced. The majorettes came running to the center of the field.

"For a closer look at these beauties," Barker said into the microphone, "we will now ask each one to walk onto the platform . . . go to the center for a brief pause . . . then return to her corps."

I was led to a spot next to the platform. Each majorette walked up a flight of steps to the platform, struck a pose, smiled, stared at me, then walked down the stairs. Behind me the stands were in turmoil. Once in a while you pause and reflect on what factors have led you to this precise point in your life.

One of the majorettes looked at me directly and winked at me. I felt quite old. I may be easy, but not that easy. She wasn't going to seduce this geezer with a bat of her eye. I smiled back at her and she pranced down the stairs.

I handed my final selections to the pageant committee.

The trophies for marching and twirling excellence were handed out. Then John Baker announced, "Now we will see who is the fairest of them all." I felt someone standing next to me; it was Kelly Ellis, last year's Miss Kanawha County Majorette, who was returning to help crown her successor.

Barker spoke: "The second runner-up is . . . from George Washington High, Blaire Bartrug!

"The first runner-up is . . . from Nitro High, April Lawhorn!"

I looked behind me. Seven thousand people were on their feet. Someone handed me a bouquet of roses from Dudley's Flowers. "And now, ladies and gentlemen," Barker announced, "the new Miss Kanawha County Majorette, who will hold the title for the next year . . . I give you . . . from DuPont High School . . ."

The stadium erupted.

". . . Karen Persinger!"

She came running across the field toward me. I walked out to meet her. From the stands, her parents were running, too. The bands were playing; the drums and horns were sounding.

"This isn't happening!" Karen Persinger screamed at me. "This isn't happening! This is not happening!"

"I think I know what you mean," I said. I looked for the majorette who had winked at me, but she was lost in the crowd.

Blue Eyes and Cancer

I MEET PEOPLE when I'm on the road. It's one way to keep travel schedules and airports from driving you crazy; if you allow strangers into your life, even if for only a few hours, then your trip is never wasted.

In Dallas I met a woman named Tressa Hawkins. She was twenty-two; we were having a drink in the barroom of the Amfac Hotel, out by the airport. We were telling each other the things that strangers generally do, and I guess it was during our second round of drinks that she told me she had cancer.

I was startled; she was an exceedingly attractive young woman, bright and vital and the picture of health. She pulled her collar back and showed me a three-inch scar at the line of her collarbone. It had been left there after a biopsy.

When she was sixteen, she found out that she had Hodgkin's disease—cancer of the lymph system. Now she was in remission, but she knew that the cancer could become active again at any time, without warning.

"The subject will generally come up without my bringing it up," she said. "I'll say that I have a doctor's appointment, or that I'll be at the doctor's all day, and people will ask me what's wrong.

"I used to just say I was sick. It was like I was protecting them, and I didn't really like that. So then I would say that I had Hodgkin's disease. A lot of people don't know what that is. So I guess I shock them now, but I just say that I have cancer."

Because she would seem to be just any pretty young woman in any office building, people are often confused when they find out she has cancer. They have cancer-ward stereotypes, and

Tressa certainly doesn't fit those images. The only thing different about her is her matter-of-fact attitude about the chance she may die younger than most people.

"It'll be seven years in July since I found out," she said. "I pass each year. I'm always aware when one more year has gone by and I'm okay."

She said that one thing having cancer has taught her is not to be afraid to take chances, to go after things that she otherwise might be too shy to attempt. And she realizes that one of her biggest potential problems is that some people aren't sure about how to react to her.

"I don't whisper that I have cancer," she said. "I just say it: 'I have cancer.' I have blue eyes and I have cancer . . . it's just another thing about me.

"If people can't handle that, that's their problem, not mine. If you like someone and they like you back, then it's not a problem. I just find myself a lot quicker to let someone know that I like them than if I weren't in this situation. I find myself not wanting to pass up opportunities."

She told me a couple of stories that illustrated how afraid people who don't have cancer can be of people who do.

"People wrongly think that it's contagious," she said. "I know one woman who has cancer, and she went to another woman's house. The hostess served them coffee. She served herself in a regular cup. She gave my friend a paper cup. The message wasn't very subtle.

"And one night I was at a bar called Friday's. I walked past a group of men, and they started talking to me. This one man kept asking me what the scar on my throat was. I guess he was just trying to make conversation. I'm not ashamed of what's happened to me, and I'm always ready to acknowledge it, but standing up in a bar full of people didn't seem like the place. He kept asking me and he kept asking me, and finally I said, 'Look, will you just shut up? I have cancer. I had a biopsy.'

"And do you know what he did? He moved about three feet away from me. I'm sure he didn't even realize he was doing it. But the word 'cancer' made him back away."

She told me that she was not afraid to begin relationships with people, but then she told me a story that contradicted what she was saying. It was about a man named Jerry she had known; a man who, it so happened, also had cancer.

Theirs was mainly a long-distance relationship. She lived in Dallas, he lived in Houston. They talked on the telephone and wrote often. She called him one day, and there was no answer at his apartment. She called his parents' house.

"I'm so sorry," the man's mother told Tressa. "His funeral is Tuesday."

Tressa was able to finish the telephone conversation before breaking down. She was surprised; mixed with her grief was an unexpected kind of anger.

"It was a case of 'How dare you,' " she said. "I was thinking, 'How dare you die without telling me. Couldn't you have at least picked up the phone and said, "Tressa, I'm dying"?' "

It has been almost a year since I met Tressa Hawkins. The reason I am telling you her story now is that I called her apartment in Dallas the other day, to wish her a happy new year. The phone rang twice, and then a recorded voice said the number had been disconnected.

I called her mother's house. I was expecting the news. But her mother said that Tressa had just had her phone number changed; she gave me the new number, and when I called, Tressa answered.

She laughed when I told her what I had been afraid of. So I reminded her of the story she had told me about her friend who had died, and who had not let her know.

"Hey, I'm okay," she said. "I'm sorry to laugh. I just don't think of people thinking of me dying. *I* don't think of me dying."

She laughed again.

"Very much," she said, and then she changed the subject.

Dance Card

I WAS NURSING a late-evening drink in the top floor barroom of a hotel called the Red Lion Inn in downtown Omaha when a local woman made a terrible mistake.

She came up and asked me to dance.

I looked her in the eye. I smiled. I slid from my chair and rolled underneath the table. I curled up into a ball and began to sob and chew on the leg of the table.

Other than that, everything was okay.

I'm sure there are many men out there who share this problem. Dancing is just something that never worked for us. We could play baseball, we could do pullups, we could run around a track, and no one noticed anything wrong. But when we stepped onto a dance floor, it was as if we were in Portugal. That is, something was vaguely out of place.

It's not that we were aggressively bad dancers. It's just that we felt stupid even trying to do it. The legs and arms might have been going in the proper direction, but we couldn't stop asking ourselves what business our legs and arms had doing that in the first place.

My dancing history is not a happy one. It started when, as a mere lad, I was enrolled in something called Mrs. Potts' Dancing School against my will.

Every Friday afternoon I was put in a tiny suit, a tie was jerked up against my little neck, and I was dropped off at the YWCA, where other children of my age were waiting.

The enterprise was conducted by Mrs. Potts herself. Mrs. Potts was a dead ringer for Queen Elizabeth, and she always wore an evening gown. Her assistant, a fellow named Doc Hyatt, was clad in a tuxedo. The boys and girls were taken into an anteroom where they were directed to pair up. Then—under orders from Doc Hyatt—we were led into the main ballroom, where the boys were ordered to present their "dates" to Mrs. Potts and say, "Good evening, Mrs. Potts. May I present to you my companion for the evening, Susie Snowflake."

(By the way, "Susie Snowflake" is not some pathetic literary device I have chosen to use here. "Susie Snowflake" is the precise example that Doc Hyatt used every week when instructing us on the proper comportment in front of Mrs. Potts.)

Elvis Presley had burst upon the national scene by this time, and Mrs. Potts realized that she was risking a revolt if she confined us to the waltzes being played on the record player at the far end of the YWCA ballroom. So, to keep in step with the times, once each evening she would allow us to attempt a dance referred to by her as the "Chicago Rock and Roll."

I remember it still. It went toe-heel, toe-heel, back-forward; toe-heel, toe-heel, back-forward. Little suburban rebels without causes, that's what we were; and had I not been apprehended attempting to kiss Betsy Cook on the dance floor one night and watched very closely thereafter by Doc Hyatt, I might have been relaxed enough to improvise my own steps to the Chicago Rock and Roll.

As it was, I was a miserable failure.

Soon enough I was a teenager. On weekend evenings we would drive to a place called the Whitehall Recreation Center, in the next town over from ours. We told ourselves that the girls in this town were of looser morals than the girls in our own; thus, for some reason that escapes me right now, we made certain to use false names when we introduced ourselves to them. (The name I always used—I swear this is true—was Mike Holiday.)

The biggest hit record that winter was "Louie, Louie." But at the Whitehall Recreation Center, it was felt that a better dance song was the number on the other side of "Louie, Louie"—if memory serves, it was called "Haunted Castle."

The biggest studs at the Whitehall Recreation Center knew how to do a dance called the Skip. We thought we were pretty cool, but we hadn't a clue about how to do the Skip. We would hang around the periphery of the dance floor, trying to look sullen, dark, brooding, and sensitive. Then we would spend the rest of the weekend in front of a mirror, trying to perfect the Skip.

When your self-image is sullen, dark, brooding, and sensitive, it is difficult to reconcile three hours of jumping in the air in front of a mirror, flailing your arm to the right, jumping in the air again, flailing your other arm to the left, all the while trying to keep a bored, worldly look on your face. By the time we had mastered the Skip and had returned to the Whitehall Recreation Center, the Skip was obsolete; now the other people were doing a dance called the Pony, and we couldn't have seemed to be bigger fools if we had come in the door doing the minuet.

Things only got worse. Gradually, as we grew older, we could pretend that we didn't dance because we had disdain for the whole process. When *Saturday Night Fever* came along, we could sneer at its followers and say that disco made us sick; the truth was, we knew that if we had been unable even to master the Skip when we had been in much better physical condition, we had no chance of duplicating what John Travolta was doing on the screen.

Once in a while a symbolic gift from heaven came along. Crosby, Stills, and Nash were on a tour of the United States; it was reported that, in a Washington club, a woman asked Graham Nash to join her on the dance floor, and Nash coolly replied, "Musicians don't dance."

I guess when you're Graham Nash you can get away with that. I could have used him in Omaha. Good evening, Mrs. Potts.

Twenty-seven-
twenty-two

Bexley, Ohio—It was a vacation of sorts, perhaps the strangest I have ever taken. And, although it had none of the glamour of a flight to Mexico or Europe, it turned out to be one of the most satisfying few days I have had in years.

Of all the places I have dreamed of visiting, I have been lucky enough to visit most. And yet the place that is always most on my mind always seemed an impossible destination. Not because it is remote; it is not that far a journey from Chicago to central Ohio. Not because it is expensive, either; money is not even a factor.

But it remained unlikely because people just don't do things like this. What I wanted to do was go back to the house in which I grew up; not just look at it from a car driving by, but spend time there, visit it, remember it as it was. Several families have lived there since my own family moved away; often I have thought about what the reaction would be if I just showed up unannounced someday, but I always rejected that as a fantasy.

This time, though, I did it. I hadn't the nerve to simply knock on the door. But I found out the names of the people who now live in the house—Stanley and Elaine Shayne and their children—and I wrote them a letter asking if they'd mind. Mrs. Shayne called me and said it would be fine with them.

So I found myself on Bryden Road in Bexley, Ohio, again. The street is still made of red bricks, and when I walked up to the front door, I had a feeling of anticipation that couldn't be equalled at Buckingham Palace or the Ritz Hotel in Paris. To be granted leisurely time again in the most important place in one's memory—that is a true luxury, and I was prepared to savor it.

The Shayne family couldn't have been more understanding; they let me know that it was okay for me to be there (they even put a "Welcome Home" sign on the big tree in the front yard), and yet they realized that it was not them I had come to visit, but the house. They went about their daily business and let me wander. For the better part of three days, I lived at 2722 Bryden Road again.

It was jarring, moving, weird. Think about what it would be like if you were turned loose in the house where you grew up. You would find that it had been redecorated several times as families had moved in and out; you would find strangers living in the rooms you always associated with your parents and brothers and sisters. Everything would be different, yet everything would be the same. One moment you would feel a thousand miles away, the next you would feel as if you had never left. It would be confusing and exhilarating and happy and sad, all at the same time.

My visit was all of those things. I found myself climbing the front stairs countless times, looking into bedrooms, sitting on the front stoop waiting for the paper boy to arrive. The Shaynes got used to me soon enough; they had their meals, and talked in the living room or the back yard, and just allowed me to have the run of the place.

It was like being in a movie you half-remember; it was like you had seen it a long time ago, and now you weren't really seeing it, you were inside of it. You recognized the set precisely, but you didn't know the actors, and even as you moved among them they couldn't really see you.

So I went to my old room, and the boy who lives there now was lying on his bed listening to music. What a feeling. That might have been me in there when I was his age, but now I was standing in the doorway, an observer, almost afraid to step inside.

In the upstairs hallway was a little cranny built into the wall to hold a telephone. I had forgotten about it completely, but seeing it again took me back to all the nights I had pulled the cord into my own room and locked the door for privacy. And sure enough, on this evening the phone had been pulled away, and was locked in one of the children's bedrooms.

The interior of the house looked completely different, but every few minutes I would come across a touch that almost made me shiver. The front door, for example; it had been painted and refinished, but when I went to open it, the knob and latch felt so familiar in my hand; I looked at them, and although I hadn't thought about them in years, I knew immediately that they were the same ones. When you spend all of your growing-up years coming through the same door, you don't forget something like that so quickly.

And the wooden bannister that runs up the stairway and then curves around next to the bedrooms—as I walked I found myself letting my hand glide across the top of it, and I realized that this was a habit I had ever since I was a child. Everywhere I turned there was something like that; the bathrooms had been refurbished and decorated, but in the children's bathroom the old-fashioned heater was still built into the wall beneath the window; you wouldn't imagine that something like that would affect you, but believe me, it does.

The house seemed very small to me. Which is inevitable, I guess; when you are growing up, your house is your whole world, and once your world becomes the real world itself, one building can never seem quite so imposing again. As I stood at the top of the stairs I realized that, of course, there was nothing inherently romantic in this structure; it was just one house on one block in one small city.

Still, when the three days were over, I had a feeling of satisfaction that is hard to describe. I hope, someday, the people in the Shayne family will look back on their years at 2722 Bryden Road with the same warmth and joy that I do; and I hope, if they ever get the urge to come back, they won't be too shy to ask, and that the people who live there in that future summer will not be too protective of their privacy to say yes.

Because I can promise them this: it may not be the most lavish vacation they will ever spend, but it will surely be one of the best.

Arnold Zenker
and "The Way It Is"

IN THE PERIOD of one week, Dan Rather did three things. He got Walter Cronkite's job; he was given a contract for $8 million; and he appeared on the cover of *Time* magazine. In the United States, those are probably the three nicest things that can happen to a person.

And of the three, the most impressive is getting Cronkite's job. By now it has been said so many times that Cronkite is the most trusted man in America that you don't even listen to the words as someone says them. Since the 1950s he has sat in that "CBS Evening News" anchor chair; there has been no one else as the official nightly voice of CBS than Cronkite.

Well, that's not precisely true.

There was Arnold Zenker.

You probably have forgotten his name, but for thirteen days in 1967, Arnold Zenker found himself in the unusual position of having to be the most trusted man in America.

What happened was, the American Federation of Television and Radio Artists—Cronkite's union—went out on strike. Cronkite would not go on the air; neither would the other big-name CBS correspondents. Frantically, the CBS bosses looked around their headquarters in Manhattan. They needed someone to broadcast the news.

They found Arnold Zenker, a bespectacled middle-management executive who had once done a little radio work. He had never appeared on television.

For thirteen nights, Arnold Zenker became Walter Cronkite. His face and voice were beamed into every town and hamlet in the nation. He received thousands of fan letters. And then the strike ended and Cronkite came back to work and the "CBS Evening News" with Arnold Zenker became kind of a dim memory.

Listening to all the talk about Cronkite and Rather, I found myself wondering how Arnold Zenker was reacting to it. After all, it could have been him with the $8 million and the cover of *Time*. I decided to track him down.

"I've gone on with my own life," Zenker said to me. "I live in Boston; I haven't worked for CBS in years. I own a company that trains business executives how to communicate better. I have absolutely no desire to be on television again."

Zenker said that when he was recruited to sit in Cronkite's chair, events moved too quickly for him to panic.

"First they told me that because I had done radio before, I should do the radio news, so I did," he said. "Then they told me that I might as well do the morning news on television. I said that I had never been on television, but they said to go ahead and do it anyway. Then I stayed around and did the noon news on television. Then I went home and went to bed.

"But the telephone rang. They said they wanted me to come back and do the evening news, Cronkite's news. So I took the bus back to work and I did it. I guess I was too dumb to be nervous, because I just wasn't nervous. I had never been the focus of that kind of publicity and attention before, but I just sat in that chair and read the news every night.

"The funny thing is, I was appearing in all those millions of homes all over the country every night. And yet I walked the streets and rode the buses during those thirteen days, and no one recognized me. People think that if you're on television one time or even three times, you're famous. But from my experience, you have to be like a chewing gum ad, on there over and over and over again, before people start to remember your face."

When the strike ended, Zenker went back to his middle-management job. He said that he passed Cronkite in the hallways of CBS several times, but Cronkite never spoke to him. And his own co-workers seemed a little wary of him; they didn't know how to treat him now that he had become a nationwide star—and now that the stardom was over.

"A very unusual thing happens to people who have been on television," Zenker said. "When you go off television and people see you, they act as if you had died. It's as if when you're not on television, you're dead. You go on living your life, but it doesn't count because you're not on TV anymore."

With all the news of Rather's ascension to Cronkite's job, Arnold Zenker said that he has been feeling no remorse about what could have been.

"I don't think about it at all," he said. "It's as if the star of a Broadway play got sick, and an understudy had to go on for thirteen days. You don't think you're Laurence Olivier because of it. It's just something interesting that happened to you.

"I suppose my story is a vicarious thrill for a lot of people in America, because we seem to like stories about the underdog, the kid who's thrown in when the star is sick and who does all right.

"But honestly, I don't think about it. Walter Cronkite and Dan Rather have nothing to do with my life. I'm just Arnold Zenker, and that was just something that happened to me for thirteen days in my life thirteen years ago."

Date

A FEW BLOCKS from Rush Street in Chicago there is a video dating service known as Sneak Previews Inc. Its purpose is simple: single men and women pay its owners a fee; they are interviewed on-camera, and their tape cassettes are kept on file. Then, as members of Sneak Previews, they have the right to examine other people's tapes, and decide if they would like a date with any of those people.

It is an enterprise for the modern age. Men and women are able to decide on a person's attractiveness within seconds of when the person appears on the screen. As the owner of Sneak Previews, Joseph De Bartolo, says, "Our members generally have very high self-esteem. You're usually an attractive person or you wouldn't come in here."

And indeed that seems to be true. When you join Sneak Previews, you are putting yourself on the line. You know that other people will be looking at you, judging your appearance and the visible aspects of your personality. Those people will be making a decision about you.

And so a visitor to the offices of Sneak Previews is struck by the self-confidence, the smoothness, of the members. On videotape, an attractive blond woman says that she works out with bodybuilding equipment in her spare time; she describes herself as "spunky; I'm crazy." She says she is looking for a "successful" man with "charm, charisma, and class." A handsome young sales executive says, "I don't have much trouble meeting people," and it is easy to believe him. The people on the Sneak Previews tapes, in the main, seem to be young, attractive, and well-off.

So it is somewhat of a shock to browse along the shelves in the Sneak Previews offices, and to select a cassette marked simply, "Nancy." That's how all of the cassettes are marked; first names only.

With most of the cassettes it is a matter of slipping them into the playback machine and waiting for a new youthful, attractive image to appear on the screen. With Nancy's cassette, though, something different happens.

Nancy is an elderly woman; the off-camera interviewer asks her her age, and she replies that she is seventy.

The interviewer asks her why she has come to Sneak Previews. "Why?" she says. "Because I'm very lonely. No other reason."

She is wearing a simple green dress; her hair is close-cropped. The interviewer asks her what she hopes to do on a Sneak Previews date. Most of the respondents on the other tapes have mentioned nights on the town, racquetball, Sunday brunches.

"I just want to meet someone to share dinner with," Nancy says. "To talk with on the phone. To pass the time."

It is clear, from the tone of the off-camera interviewer's voice, that he is vaguely uncomfortable. With most of the other Sneak Previews members, it is almost a lark for everyone involved, a little adventure. This Nancy, though . . . she has come here to pay her money because she really is hoping for something.

"If I just had someone to sit and watch TV with," she says. "I don't go out to shows anymore. But I do enjoy the TV. I like that doctor who comes on at nine o'clock. What's his name? Quincy."

The interviewer continues with his questions; they come from a prepared list, and each person hears the same ones. Nancy begins to talk as if she has forgotten she is on-camera, though.

"My husband died seven years ago," she says. "You get so lonely when that happens. Every year you get lonelier."

She says that she has a grandson who is a Chicago police officer; she says that she has come to Sneak Previews because her daughter told her that she had to start getting out of the house. The interviewer finishes up his list of questions, and then the tape ends.

A visitor to Sneak Previews, after coming across Nancy's tape, asked Joseph De Bartolo how it had happened to be in his files.

"She called up and made an appointment," he said. "She lives in Berwyn. She took the train down here and paid her money. I tried to be gentle with her. I said, 'You know, ma'am, we really don't have a lot of people who it might be appropriate for you to choose.' "

"And she said, 'That's okay. I don't expect to walk out with a date today.'

"I didn't want to just take her money and give her nothing in return. But she said she was lonely, and she wanted to try. So I keep her tape on file just in case an older gentleman comes in here some day. I don't know what else to do."

The visitor left Sneak Previews. A few hours later, though, he found that he was still thinking about Nancy, and what it must have taken for her to bring herself downtown to the video dating service on the periphery of Rush Street. De Bartolo had given the visitor her address and phone number; the visitor called her and explained that he wrote a newspaper column, and that he wondered how she was doing since she had been to Sneak Previews.

"They were very nice to me down there," Nancy said. "But I haven't received an offer for a date as a result of it. They were honest; they explained that they don't have many older people on file."

She said that she used to go to the Melody Mill Ballroom, near her home, but that now she just stays around the house. She said she knew that going to the video service was a long shot; she said she realized it probably wasn't designed for people like her. But it is so hard for her to meet people; she felt it was worth a try.

"Companionship is a very important thing for anybody," she said. "Not just people my age. But if it doesn't work out, that's all right, too. I'll just do without."

The Sky's the Limit

AT GATE D-11 of Chicago's O'Hare International Airport, a voice was sounding on the public-address system: "Outbound passenger Clarence Waldron, will you please return to the gate and see an agent. Outbound passenger Clarence Waldron."

The announcement was going largely unnoticed, because directly next to gate D-11 was Ella Fitzgerald, who was singing "Give Me the Simple Life." Miss Fitzgerald was backed by a three-man combo.

An elderly woman was being pushed through the gate area in a wheelchair. She glanced over at Miss Fitzgerald. Someone handed the woman a plastic cup filled with champagne. The woman's companion continued to push her. The woman stared at Miss Fitzgerald, then at the cup of champagne, then at Miss Fitzgerald again, evidently bewildered.

The idea was this: Continental Airlines was reintroducing the Pub compartment on all of its wide-body aircraft. The Pub was a bar-and-lounge compartment located between the first-class section and coach.

The flight that was about to leave from gate D-11—a DC-10 bound for Denver, and then for Los Angeles—was going to be the official inaugural flight for the Pub compartments. To introduce the new service, Continental had hired Miss Fitzgerald and her combo to perform aloft, in the Pub, all the way west. For her day's work, Miss Fitzgerald was to be paid fifty thousand dollars.

Some sixty-seven members of the news media had been invited to be passengers on Flight 17. Added to the regular passengers on the flight, this placed the load on board at well over two hundred.

Some of those regular passengers were annoyed by the commotion at the gate. Flight 17 was already almost an hour late leaving Chicago, and Miss Fitzgerald was still performing at O'Hare. When the passengers had bought their tickets, they had not been informed that this would be a special flight.

"I have a connection to make in Denver," said Gene Collerd, a clarinet player. "I have an audition to get to in San Francisco.

"I like Ella, but I really have to make my plane in Denver. I'm shelling out my own money for this audition."

As the day grew later and Miss Fitzgerald continued to perform, a truck rolled up to the DC-10. It was a snowy, frigid day in Chicago. Men from the truck began to de-ice the airplane's wings.

Leroy Neiman, the artist, had been commissioned by Continental to do a painting of Miss Fitzgerald in performance. A Continental press release said that Neiman "was on hand to capture the one-of-a-kind performance with initial sketches which he will use to complete a painting in his unusual and colorful style."

But as the passengers finally were allowed to walk through the jetway and onto the plane, Leroy Neiman came rushing off the plane. There was no explanation; he did not reboard, and was not seen again for the rest of the flight.

Once in the air, virtually all of the reporters and cameramen on board left their seats and pushed their way up the aisles toward the Pub compartment, which had seating for only ten persons.

Denis Quinlan, a publicist working for Continental, got on the plane's public-address system. "Please," he said. "Please . . . bear with us for just a few minutes."

The rush to the Pub continued, though, and soon flight attendants were ordered to draw curtains so that it would be blocked off.

"Please," Denis Quinlan said over the PA system. "We've got a little bit of weather here. The captain would like you to remain seated until he turns the seat-belt sign off."

Miss Fitzgerald, sixty-four, began to sing "You're Driving Me Crazy" in the Pub compartment. She stood in front of her combo—a drummer, a bass player, and an electric-piano player—who in turn stood in front of one of the DC-10's exit doors. She wore a dark-blue dress with gold jewelry.

Reporters, photographers, and TV camera crews jostled to try to enter the Pub.

"Please," Denis Quinlan said. "Everyone will get a chance."

Miss Fitzgerald sang "Blue Moon." As she surveyed the scene in front of her, her face showed confusion.

In the back of the plane, the regular passengers were also confused. Slowly word was spreading among them about what was going on. There would not be room in the Pub for them to see Miss Fitzgerald singing; flight attendants passed out Ella Fitzgerald albums to them instead.

A voice on the public-address system told these passengers

that if they looked at the screen at the front of their cabin, they could see Miss Fitzgerald's performance. If they put their headsets on, they could hear her on channel one.

They looked at the screen. There was a glimpse of Miss Fitzgerald in the Pub, but then Barry Bernson of WMAQ television in Chicago walked in front of the lens. When Bernson eventually wandered away, Miss Fitzgerald appeared again momentarily. Within seconds, though, the shot of her was blocked by *Time* magazine photographer Arthur Shay.

Channel one was broken; the passengers in the back of the plane attempting to hear Miss Fitzgerald sing got only static.

Stephen Wolf, the president of Continental Airlines, was on board, sitting in the first-class cabin. I slipped into the seat next to him.

"Are you a nervous flier?" I said.

"A nervous flier?" he said. "Not really. Are you?"

I confessed that I was.

"To tell you the truth," Wolf said, "I was on this small airplane out in California the other week, and we hit some turbulence, and the wings started shaking, and I thought my goddamn stomach was going to . . . but you don't want to hear about that, do you?"

"Well, I guess it's reassuring that you're not a nervous flier," I said. "I mean, you fly all the time, and you're the president of a whole airline."

"I've only been president for six weeks," he said.

Miss Fitzgerald was singing "All of Me." In the back of the plane, the paying passengers searched through the dial to try to find a sound track on their headsets to match the performance on the screen. They could not. On the screen, Miss Fitzgerald was a dull shade of green.

The plane rocked slightly. Flight attendants tried to edge past reporters in the aisles to serve a meal. The Pub was filled past capacity, and the curtains had been drawn again to keep people away. Back in the cabin, all that could be heard was the sound of cymbals.

"I'm going to go out on a limb," said Paul Galloway of the *Chicago Sun-Times*. "I don't think airplanes are ever going to make it as an entertainment medium."

A young public-relations aide walked up to Denis Quinlan. "The NBC crew has requested that they be upgraded to first class on the way back," the aide said.

Quinlan looked around the cabin, as if seeking a doorway.

Miss Fitzgerald and her combo took a break. She returned to her seat in first class. I followed her.

"So," I said. "I imagine this is a lot of fun for you."

She looked up. She seemed not quite to believe where she was. "Yes it is," she said.

She turned to her companion in the next seat and said, "My stockings are starting to fall down."

"So," I said. "I guess you probably haven't done anything like this before."

"There's a first time for everything," Miss Fitzgerald said.

"I imagine the acoustics on an airplane aren't as good as the acoustics in a concert hall," I said.

"We are trying the best we can," Miss Fitzgerald said.

Back in the coach section, Kimberly Mayer, a business reporter for the *Rocky Mountain News*, was hunched over a legal pad. She was writing out her story in longhand.

It began with a dateline that was the stuff of newsmen's dreams: "SOMEWHERE OVER NEBRASKA—. . . ."

The airplane landed in Denver. Passengers got off; passengers got on. Miss Fitzgerald was led out to the concourse in Stapleton International Airport. In front of gate C-11, a temporary stage had been set up for her.

Passersby in the airport stopped to see what was going on. Miss Fitzgerald seemed not to want to think about it. She simply stepped up to the microphone and began to sing "The Lady Is a Tramp."

The airplane took off for Los Angeles. Miss Fitzgerald sang "Blue Moon" again.

A paying passenger managed to get into the Pub section. Somebody handed him a glass of champagne. He looked around. He stared at Miss Fitzgerald. He stared at the videotape crew from "Entertainment Tonight" that was photographing her. He stared at the reporters who were crouched in every nook of the Pub.

The passenger stared at Miss Fitzgerald's drummer, Bobby Durham.

"Did anybody ever tell you that you look like that guy on 'The Jeffersons'?" the passenger said to Durham.

The captain of the flight, Bud Kootz, fifty-two, turned the controls over to his first officer and wandered through the cabin.

"Do you feel nervous flying with the president of the airline looking over your shoulder?" I asked.

"Nah," Kootz said.

"When you're taking off, you don't think about the president of Continental sitting in the first row of first class?" I said.

"Nah," he said. "One takeoff's pretty much like another. I just get her up there."

"Did they tell you about this flight way in advance?" I asked.

"I didn't know about it until yesterday," he said. "Someone told me that Ella Fitzgerald was going to be singing on board. I didn't know what they meant."

"But one flight is just like any other flight to you?" I said.

"Oh, I guess when we get to the hotel tonight I may call my wife and say, 'Honey, guess what?' " Kootz said.

Miss Fitzgerald sang "They Can't Take That Away from Me." She seemingly had decided to put out of her mind where she was and how she had gotten there. With a handkerchief in her left hand, she began to scat-sing. She closed her eyes and tilted her head toward the ceiling of the airplane, and did about thirty seconds of the most magical jazz singing one could imagine. Then someone dropped a bottle of beer, and a flight attendant knelt down to wipe it up. Miss Fitzgerald scrutinized the scene in front of her and returned to the traditional lyrics of the song.

"Ladies and gentlemen," came a voice over the public-address system, "as you can tell by the angle of the plane, we are in our descent to Los Angeles International Airport."

The floor of the DC-10 was, indeed, beginning to point in the direction of the ground.

"Please return to your seats," the voice said. "Please make sure your seat belts are fastened, your seats are in the full upright position, and all carry-on luggage is stored safely beneath your seats."

Miss Fitzgerald was singing: "You can take the 'A' train, if you want to get to Harlem in a hurry. . . ."

Outside the windows were the night lights of southern California.

Fatal

T HIS IS HOW it happens.

On a recent Sunday afternoon, a brother and sister named Robert and Wendy Muchman drove out to suburban Flossmoor, Illinois, to visit their parents. Robert Muchman, who was twenty-four, was a law student at De Paul; Wendy, who was two years older, was an attorney in Chicago.

Their parents, Irwin and Beatrice Muchman, had just returned from a vacation trip to Italy. So the children welcomed them home. Because their parents were tired from the trip, Robert and Wendy left for the drive back downtown early, around dinnertime.

Robert was driving. In his car, a 1980 Toyota, he pushed the buttons to the radio. There was a new song by Supertramp he wanted his sister to hear; he thought she would like it. But no station was playing it as he looked.

They were on I-57, heading toward the city. They talked easily; unlike some brothers and sisters, they were very close and were comfortable in the company of one another. Robert worked full-time at the Harris Bank; Wendy was proud that he was able to be earning a living at the same time he was completing law school. Robert was engaged to be married in January; the money he was earning at the bank was being put away to start his new life.

So Robert drove, and the two of them talked, and the radio played. It was a normal Sunday, dusk in Chicago, and Robert said, "Oh, my God," and Wendy saw the other car jumping the median from the other side of the highway.

Just before the car hit, Wendy could see the driver. He appeared to be unconscious as he slumped over the wheel. His car slammed into Robert's, and when Wendy opened her eyes she saw that her brother was probably dead.

He was bleeding from a severe head wound, and blood was coming from his mouth. Almost without thinking what she was doing, Wendy reached inside her brother's mouth to pull his tongue out; if there was any chance he was still alive, she wanted to make sure he could breathe.

"Robbie," she called. She said his name again and again. He did not answer.

A Chicago police officer named Ron McAuley arrived at the scene of the accident and radioed for an ambulance. Wendy ran up to a nearby house and said, "We've been in a car accident." The owner of the house let her come inside to use his phone.

She called her parents. She couldn't allow herself to tell them that she thought Robert was dead; so she said, "There's been an accident. Please meet us at Roseland Hospital."

"Are you all right?" her parents asked.

"I hope so," she said.

"Is Robbie all right?" they asked.

"I don't know," she said.

Down on the highway, a nurse had stopped to try to help.

One of those terrible city scenarios was taking place; for some reason no ambulance had responded to the officer's call, and he was trying again to get some help.

"What time is it?" Wendy kept asking. She looked at her brother, who had not moved. She was wearing a watch, but she was not aware of it. "What time is it?"

An ambulance finally arrived. Wendy said to the nurse who had been helping, "Please . . . please ride with us to the hospital." The police officer told the nurse he would take care of her car if she rode with Robert, so she said that she would.

At the hospital, Wendy saw her mother waiting by the emergency entrance. She hurried to move her mother out of the way so she would not see Robert when he was carried out of the ambulance. But Wendy's father was right there when they carried his son into the emergency room. He saw his son's face and he slumped down.

The hospital personnel carried Robert into a treatment room. Wendy wandered around the emergency area; she looked into a room and saw the driver of the other car. His name was Ronnell Reynolds, of Calumet Park; later, the police would charge him with reckless homicide and driving under the influence of alcohol.

Wendy Muchman looked at the man. She had read dozens of articles about drunken driving, seen dozens of television reports. She could think of only one thing: she wanted to kill the man. She wished she had a gun so she could kill him. For twenty-four years her brother had built a life; now, with his impending marriage, the most important part of that life was about to begin. Had Robert and Wendy left their parents' house five minutes earlier, or five minutes later, their car would not have been in the path of Ronnell Reynolds's car when it jumped the median. She wanted to kill him, but instead she walked away from the room.

A woman came to the area where the Muchmans were waiting. The woman didn't have to say much. Just two words: "I'm sorry."

The Muchman family went to look for a telephone. Ever since Robert's engagement, his mother had been keeping a scrapbook and filling it with news of the wedding plans. Now they had to call his fiancée and let the phone ring and explain that Robert was dead.

These things happen every day. Cars collide, and drivers are charged with being drunk behind the wheel, and lives are changed forever. It's so common that no one considers it to be a big deal. Usually it doesn't even make the paper; this one didn't. Robert Muchman's parents went back to their home, the son they had raised now gone; Wendy Muchman went back to her apartment. This is how it happens.

Rejection

THIS IS MY favorite story of the year. Maybe of any year.

Chuck Ross is a young free-lance writer who is anxious to get his first novel published. Like many aspiring authors, he has sent his work around to different New York publishing houses, hoping that an editor will see it, like it, and decide to bring it out in hardcover. And like many aspiring authors, he has received nothing but rejection slips.

After a while, though, Ross began to wonder if his writing really was unpublishable—or if publishers are just prejudiced against unknown authors who have yet to have a book in print.

So he decided to conduct an experiment. He sat down at the typewriter, and copied the entire text of *Steps*, by Jerzy Kosinski, onto white paper. *Steps* won the National Book Award for Kosinski in 1969; since its publication in 1968, the novel has sold more than 400,000 copies. Not only has it proved itself to be a work of high quality, but it has established itself as a big seller in the marketplace.

Ross then decided to submit the manuscript to a number of publishers—but not to call it *Steps*, and not to say it was by the well-known Kosinski. In other words, he wanted to see if the publishing houses would accept the award-winning *Steps* if they did not know that it had been written by a prominent, proven author.

He thought he would probably get caught. And well he should have. Four of the publishers he sent the manuscript to—Random House, Houghton Mifflin, Doubleday, and Harcourt Brace Jovanovich—have published books by Kosinski, and Random House was even the original publisher of *Steps*.

In addition to those four publishers, he also sent the manuscript to The Atlantic Monthly Press; Farrar, Straus & Giroux; Harper & Row; Alfred A. Knopf; Seymour Lawrence; David McKay; Macmillan; William Morrow; Prentice-Hall; and Viking.

Then he sat back to wait and see what would happen.

And what did happen?

All fourteen distinguished publishing houses rejected the manuscript—including the four that had published works by Jerzy Kosinski.

None of the houses thought that the book was worth publishing.

Harcourt Brace Jovanovich—which had published Kosinski's *Being There* and *The Devil Tree*—wrote:

> While your prose style is very lucid, the content of the book didn't inspire the level of enthusiasm here that a publisher should have for any book on their list in order to do well by it.

Random House—the original publisher of *Steps*—sent a form rejection notice.

Houghton Mifflin—which had published Kosinski's *The Painted Bird, Cockpit*, and *Blind Date*—sent a letter that said:

> Several of us read your untitled novel here with admiration for writing and style. Jerzy Kosinski comes to mind as a point of comparison when reading the stark, chilly, episodic incidents you have set down. The drawback to the manuscript, as it stands, is that it doesn't add up to a satisfactory whole. It has some very impressive moments, but gives the

impression of sketchiness and incompleteness. . . . We do not see our way to publishing this particular work as it is, but if you should ever have other manuscripts in progress now or in the future, we would be happy to consider them.

In other words, Kosinski's book sounded like Kosinski, but wasn't as good as Kosinski.

After all fourteen publishers had turned the book down, Ross did some thinking. He knew that most publishers will give a book serious consideration only if the author has a literary agent, and Ross didn't have an agent.

So Ross sent the manuscript to thirteen prestigious literary agents, with a letter asking the agents to represent him in selling the book to a publisher.

All thirteen agents turned him down.

Julian Bach wrote:

Thanks for having sent me your untitled novel. You write clearly and well, but I felt that the novel jumped around so much that it did not hold interest, and I would not be the right agent for it.

Lurton Blassingame wrote:

From the section I read of your untitled novel, it seems too fragmented and dreamlike to be a good commercial bet. Of course, I may be wrong. Good luck with it.

Helen Brandt Literary Agency said they were not "sufficiently enthusiastic" to try to place it.

An agent at Curtis Brown wrote:

I'm afraid the novel's episodic nature and the lack of strong characterization would not allow this book to compete in a very tough fiction market.

Candida Donadio & Associates wrote:

We have read your novel with great interest, and although we found the style quite intriguing, we have decided to return it. When all is said and done, we felt the manuscript lacked that all-important dramatic tension for us to consider taking it on.

Ross knew he had discovered something important about the publishing industry, and the chances that an unknown writer has of breaking in. He wrote an article about his experiment for *New West* magazine, and went on the "Tomorrow" show to talk about it. He thought the publishers might learn something from his experience.

"But I guess not," he said the other day. "I went to the American Booksellers Association convention to talk to the publishers about what I did. They all thought that it was very amusing or silly. They agreed that it probably could happen again tomorrow. But the attitude was, 'So what.' They didn't think it proved anything."

So Ross is back at his typewriter again, working on his own novel. He still thinks it's worth trying.

"If you're a writer, you have to hope," he said.

Scot's Tap

WE WERE DRIVING around the North Side, looking for a place to eat. I don't know what made me think of Scot's Tap.

"I never heard of it," my companion said.

"On Clark Street," I said. "Just south of Howard."

There was a time when Scot's Tap represented everything that was Chicago to me. I was in college, and every night my friends and I—fraternity brothers, co-workers on the student newspaper—would go to Scot's Tap for dinner. True, it was only about

300 feet inside Chicago, just over the Evanston line, but as soon as we walked into Scot's, we knew that we were in the big town.

No college kids eating wheat germ in Scot's Tap. At Scot's, the lights were dim and the decor was red and the patrons were served steaks. Sinatra was on the jukebox, and Sinatra's pictures were on the wall. The waitresses brought us cocktails—at the time, you couldn't even get a beer in Evanston. For college seniors anxious to get out, Scot's Tap offered a welcome preview of a world beyond milk shakes and marijuana.

The real draw at Scot's Tap though—the real clue to us that this was, indeed, Chicago—was Scot himself. Not that we ever met him; we were too intimidated. Scot was a savvy-looking guy with a pencil-thin black moustache, a sharp dresser, a man who looked like he would be at home making trips to Las Vegas. He would hang out at the end of the bar, talking business with men in expensive suits. To us, he seemed to be glamorously notorious—we didn't know what his past was, but it had to be full of intrigue. He was Chicago, all right. Scot didn't seem to be a man you would want to cross.

On the wall, Scot kept a framed black-and-white photographic portrait of himself, looking dapper in a dark suit. Next to it was another framed portrait, this one of a beautiful blond woman in a low-cut dress. We always assumed this was Scot's wife or mistress. We were afraid to ask anyone.

Once, one of us got a little drunk, and got up the courage to approach Scot. Scot was at the bar, and our friend walked up to him, waited until Scot turned around, and then said, "Cash a check for me?"

Scot looked him in the eye.

"No," he said.

The food and drink were always good, Sinatra's voice always filled the room, and soon enough I was, indeed, living in Chicago, which on a good night sometimes lived up to the smoky, unspoken promises of Scot's Tap. I had not been back in years, and so it was that I told my companion to take me there.

But when we arrived, Scot's Tap was gone—replaced, in 1979, by a Greek family-style restaurant. We went inside. There was no sign that this had ever been Scot's. It was bright and bustling and full of people with children. Scot wouldn't have been caught dead in the place. We ate our dinner there, and then drove away.

I was lamenting the loss of yesterday's dreams. We were driving through a residential neighborhood in Rogers Park, on our way back downtown, when, like a mirage, a recently constructed building appeared on our right. On its front was a sign that said, "Scot's Restaurant."

"Quick," I said. "Pull in there."

We got out of the car and walked through the front door. The voice of Frank Sinatra sounded throughout the room. The carpets were red. The lights were low. On the wall were framed black-and-white photographic portraits, all in a row—Sinatra, Richard J. Daley, Maurice Chevalier, George Raft. And, at the very end of the row, the portrait of Scot, looking every bit as cunning and worldly wise as the rest.

I went to the bar and ordered a drink.

"Scot here?" I said.

"You just missed him," the woman bartender said. "He's back in his office."

"Could you get him for me?" I said.

She pointed to a telephone, with two buttons lit. "You see those lights?" she said. "He's on the phone. No one interrupts Scot when he's talking business."

"He's talking on two lines at once?" I said.

"Sometimes he talks on four lines at once," the woman said. "Scot talks a lot of business."

So I waited. Thirty minutes passed. I ordered more drinks. Finally, a pleasant-looking man wearing a green golf shirt and a pencil-thin moustache walked up to the bar. It was Scot.

I was confused. He looked like any of a hundred men I had met over the years in Chicago. He smiled and introduced himself. A pleasant man who happened to own a restaurant. I started to jabber about the college days at Scot's Tap, and the mystique we had built up, and the amazing circumstances of finding Scot in this new place on this different street.

He looked at me as if I were a little crazy.

"Yeah?" he said.

I wanted to tell him what we had thought of him, and what he had represented to us, and how to us he had embodied so much of the Chicago legend that we had built him into an ominous icon. He was smiling at me, puzzled, and I pointed at the picture by the front door, the picture of the beautiful blond woman in the low-cut dress.

"Scot," I said. "We always wondered . . . is that your wife?"

He looked over at the picture.

"Nah," he said. "That's Julie London."

I paid for the drinks and motioned for my companion to leave with me. Sinatra was still on the jukebox. Scot said to come back soon, but sometimes there's no going back.

Island of the Lost Boys

ALL YOU HAVE to do is walk in the door to know that something is wrong.

The men in the office are dressed in business suits. If you extend your hand, they will shake it and say hello. Once they have been introduced to you, some of them will even fall into casual chatter.

But something stays amiss. There is the undeniable feeling that the men in this suite of rooms have been harmed. They are wary; they are not young men, and yet they seem to be lacking a certain self-assurance that typically comes with age. There is something in their eyes that advises you to be careful in here; these people are more fragile than most you will meet. They seem to have been wounded.

The office is the headquarters of the Chicago chapter of an organization called Forty Plus. The qualifications for membership are simple. You must be at least forty years old. You must have earned a salary of at least $25,000 a year. You must be unemployed.

The office is in the basement of the Illinois Athletic Club, on South Michigan Avenue. The Athletic Club leases Forty Plus the space; up one floor, executives of Chicago business and industry gather for lunch, for drinks, for a workout or a massage. Down here the members of Forty Plus keep to themselves. They are not considered a part of the Athletic Club; they are merely tenants.

Most of them have been let go by the businesses for which they worked. The problem of unemployment in America has become stereotyped; our quick reaction is to think of auto workers or factory laborers standing in line at a government office building, waiting for a check. As unpleasant as that is, it is an image that the country has learned to live with.

There are others, though. There are these men. They have been executives and managers for most of their working lives; now they have been fired. Each of the men here has heard about Forty Plus and has gravitated to it.

The purpose of Forty Plus is to help these men find employment. Notices of openings are posted, mailings extolling the members' strengths are sent out, job-counseling sessions are held. But those don't seem to be the real reasons the men keep coming to this basement every day.

They come because, after all these years, they need a place to go when the working day begins. They have been going to the office for all their adult lives; now they can't stop. They never expected to be put out on the street; as often as not, they were the men who did the firing. Now, out of work, they sit in the basement and talk with one another. Their old colleagues might not understand, but the other men here surely do. In an eerie way, you feel as if you have found yourself on some sort of island of lost boys. They are all waiting to go back home.

One afternoon I sat and talked with them. I took notes and wrote down all of their names; I think I will not identify them, though. One day soon, perhaps, some of them will be back at work, and they do not need an announcement in a national magazine that they were once here.

Here is what some of them said.

A sixty-year-old engineering executive: "I think we all go

through different stages when this happens to us. We get up in the morning and get ready for the day, but there is really no day to get ready for.

"It calls on every resource you have. All your life you have been a productive man; you have done your best. And when this happens, a certain unreality sets in. Every morning you tell yourself you have to keep going. Somehow or other you are going to make it.

"The predominant feeling is that you have let your family down. Your wife and your children have depended on you and taken you for granted. And now you aren't bringing anything home. You feel very guilty for putting them through this."

A forty-six-year-old financial manager: "It's very difficult to leave the business that fired you. When you are an executive, the place really begins to feel like your own; you take a personal pride in the company, and you feel a personal identification with it. It just doesn't occur to you that they are going to fire you.

"Twenty years ago, if you had told me this was going to happen someday, I probably wouldn't have believed you. Managers were just not let out of work. It happened to lower-echelon people, but not to the managers. Today, because of the economy, there is no longer quite the stigma to being unemployed. At least that's what I tell myself.

"But when the boss calls you in and informs you that you will be leaving, it's still a terrible shock. You try not to take it personally; you tell yourself it's because of what the economy has done to the country. But your self-esteem can't be unaffected by it."

A forty-seven-year-old vice-president of a chemical company: "The day it happened I came home early and called my wife and two daughters together, and I told them that I was now unemployed.

"Looking back on that day, I guess I was in total shock. It probably took me an hour after I was fired for it to sink in. I live in a suburban area; on the days that I come downtown, I ride the train, and I see everybody else carrying their briefcases, and here are all these folks going to their executive positions. It gives me a lot to think about.

"You are used to running your own life, and suddenly you

have no control. You go through moments of real self-doubt. You can't predict when things will happen, and you're used to making things happen. You sit at home, and you get filled up with hope every time the phone rings. And then it turns out to be for your wife or for one of your daughters."

A forty-six-year-old general manager of a manufacturing firm: "When I go to work again, I'm going to be a little different than I was the last time around. That's one good thing that will come out of this. I'm going to have a little more compassion for people, because I'm finding out that compassion is sometimes in short supply.

"I never needed compassion before. Because I was never unemployed. But next time I will answer my own phone. Since I've been out of work I have heard too many secretaries say that a man is in a meeting, when it would have meant a great deal to me if he would just have taken the call. And I will see as many people as I can who are looking for work, even if I have no specific job open at that moment. I'm learning that it doesn't cost anything to show people a little kindness. I'm not sure I ever would have learned that if this hadn't happened."

Forty Plus is open to both men and women. But on the days I was in the office, there were no females present.

That's probably not surprising. We live in an age in which the idea of working women has become normal. Women in positions of responsibility are no longer uncommon; women compete with men for jobs at virtually every level of the marketplace.

But somehow there is a difference. Somehow there is no shame for a woman to be unemployed; if a woman, especially a married woman, finds that she is going to be staying home full-time, she can be safe in knowing that no one will be whispering about her or avoiding her gaze on the sidewalk.

That is not the case with men. I got the impression that one big reason they came to Forty Plus was that they didn't want to be at home when the mail carrier or the dry cleaner showed up at the door. One of the men told me that a neighbor of his, who had been fired by his company, never told his children about it. He got up every morning as usual, shaved, put on a suit and tie, rode the train downtown, and just killed the hours until it was time to take the train home. This was less painful for him than admitting he was unemployed. He did it until he found a job again.

One morning, after one of the men from Forty Plus had gone downtown to look for a job, I rode out to his house to talk with his wife.

She led me to their back yard; we sat on a terrace and she brought out coffee and cups. "It's been a very painful thing to watch," she said. "He is a very ambitious, creative man, and when a man like that is denied work, it kills him. He wants to go to work in the morning, and this is the first time in his life he hasn't been able to do it."

She said the day it happened, he had called her and said he had to talk to her right away. "I knew something was wrong," she said. "But he wouldn't tell me over the phone. He said, 'It's not the kids,' and that set my mind at ease a little bit. But I couldn't imagine what it might be.

"It slices right through your life. Suddenly your world is completely different than it was the day before. Six weeks after he was fired, and there was still no sign of work, I think his ego hit rock bottom. For a man who has always been an achiever, something like this is literally devastating."

I asked her what the most noticeable change in him was. "The sleep pattern is different," she said. "When he's awake, he can put on a brave front. But now he'll wake up in the middle of the night and just stare at the ceiling. I can tell that he's close to panic, thinking about what he's going to do.

"I'd like to roll over and tell him, 'I understand; I'm here; I care for you.' But I don't let him know that I know he's awake. I just lie there and pretend to be asleep.

"When he comes home from a job interview, I know how it went before he's even in the house. I can tell by the way he's walking from the car. By the way he's holding his shoulders, and the look on his face.

"I don't ask him questions. I don't want to put that kind of pressure on him. I just try to make him feel that he's welcome at home. It's the best I can do."

At Forty Plus there is no paid staff. The members run the organization themselves; when and if they find work, they graduate from "active" to "corporate" status and are invited to continue to help out.

On a normal day, though, it is only the active members who are present. The ones who are lucky enough to have secured employment are at their offices. The Forty Plus members in the basement divide up responsibilities: a man with a background in publishing helps put together the brochure that promotes the virtues of the brethren to prospective employers. A man with experience chairing meetings plans formal get-togethers for the membership. A man with a deep, resonant, confident voice answers the telephone.

The men of Forty Plus are constantly checking the phone-message center. This is their business number now, and they know that at any time the message may be waiting that will set them free. In most offices, if you are visiting and there is a phone call, your host will have his secretary take a message so that he can call the person back. Not at Forty Plus. When it is announced that a man is wanted on the phone, he breaks off his conversation to take it immediately.

Sometimes there is good news. One day while I was there, a bell clanged. I was informed that this was the signal that one of the members had found work.

It was one of the men I had spoken with on a previous visit. He had come downtown to announce his new job; he had brought a box of doughnuts for the others. He had literally changed in physical appearance since I had seen him last; his face looked more alive, he carried himself with a new sense of strength, he somehow even seemed larger.

I congratulated him and asked him how it had happened.

"I had my fifth interview with this company, and they offered me a job," he said.

I asked him when he would be starting work.

He smiled and looked me in the eye. "Tomorrow," he said.

The others in Forty Plus lined up to shake his hand; he told them that they, too, would soon be back at work. What he did not say, of course, was that this was goodbye; he was no longer one of them.

The change I saw in that man was startling; it seemed to symbolize the unparalleled importance that work has in a man's life. Family, friends, and home may have their niches; but without work, a man loses an irreplaceable part of himself.

One of the Forty Plus members, trying to explain it to me, said, "Self-confidence is about as easy to lose as a dollar bill, I guess." It is a lesson that these men learned late; sitting with them in their basement office, I doubted that they would soon forget it.

Gangs of Princes

ONCE UPON A time, twelve years ago, there was a world that had never been seen before, and may never be seen again.

At the beginning of the 1970s, the executives who ran the popular-music business were discovering something intriguing. Rock and roll, which had been a steady money-maker for them ever since its inception in the 1950s, suddenly had become a growth industry that knew virtually no bounds. Rock and roll was bringing $2 billion a year into the national economy. Young entrepreneurs with no show-business credentials at all were instantly transformed into the elite of New York and California entertainment society.

There was a curious aspect to all of this. Even though the financial rewards available through the rock and roll business had no discernible limits, the general-circulation press had been slow to pick up on the news. This bothered the music entrepreneurs; the surest way to place a band into the public consciousness was through publicity, and yet there were no established conduits into the mainstream media. Opportunities were being lost.

Coincidentally, a new generation of reporters was coming along at precisely this time. We were just out of school; we had not gained the seniority to cover national politics or global crises, yet we had potential access to great numbers of readers.

So much money was available in the rock and roll industry that it became common practice for the managers of prominent bands to invite various young reporters to accompany the groups on national tours. As often as not, much of the expenses would be picked up by the bands. This worked out for everybody. The reporters got into print, bringing to their publications news of a social phenomenon that had gone all but unnoticed by older editors. The bands got widespread publicity, and made more money. And—most interesting of all—we outside observers gained regular access into a netherworld that we had scarcely imagined to exist. We wrote stories filled with quotes and impressions from arenas; but we often failed to tell how affected we were by what we had become a part of.

Now, all this time later, we are different, and so is the entertainment world. The era of the all-aboard rock and roll show is over; the unlimited money has dried up, and the same blockbuster philosophy that rules the literary world applies to the rock world, too. A decade ago, any number of bands, both established and brand-new, traveled first-class with room for any journalistic stowaways they could induce to join up. Now such a luxury is only for the few groups at the very top of the music business; for the rest, the road is a no-frills highway delineated by ledger sheets and absolute budgets. The music world, like the rest of the world, has turned cautious. And with the caution has come the end of that bizarre landscape we were allowed to glimpse—and which, often enough, we did not even recognize for the improbable, previously unobserved American territory that it was.

It was simplicity itself. On a Friday morning, if you were bored, you could place a long-distance call to one of the rock and roll public-relations firms that had blossomed to meet the needs of the booming business. You might call Gibson and Stromberg, a

California agency with billings all over the music community (their slogan was "Six Flacks; No Waiting").

"What's going on?" Gary Stromberg would say.

"What have you got this weekend?" you would ask.

And he would check his list of itineraries, and by dinnertime you would be in the front cabin of a jet bound for some medium-sized city in the Northern Hemisphere, where a chauffeured limousine would be waiting for your flight, and a room on the band's floor of the town's best hotel would be waiting for your presence. By the end of the night you would be drinking champagne with the members of the group, consorting with the most beautiful women in the state, and recovering from the screams of thousands of teenagers and the voltage of towering banks of speakers. Remember, the night before you had slept in your own bed; that morning you had reported to work in your regular news office; and on Monday you would be back in that same office. For the weekend, though—any weekend you wanted—you would live like a twentieth-century prince.

In Montreal late one evening, I sat in a hotel restaurant with members of the Guess Who, a band that had scored a hit with the song "American Woman." Tom Jones, the Welsh torch singer, was in town also, and the restaurant had been kept open for our entourage and his. The people in the Guess Who party and the people in the Tom Jones party had little in common, other than that they were used to this kind of deference. We sat on opposite sides of the dining room, while waiters three decades older than us stayed up all night to do our bidding. Late in the meal, an elderly couple appeared at the maître d's desk; they wondered if they could get a cup of soup before bed. They were summarily turned away; for them, the restaurant was closed.

The amazing thing was, no one seemed to resent this. The presumed story on rock and roll was that adult America despised it; but in all the hotels and all the airports and all the restaurants I passed through, I saw nothing but envy and curiosity in the eyes of the citizens. The bands would walk into an airport drunk at eight in the morning, making rude noises and cursing aloud; the men and women on the way to their breakfast flights would often come up for autographs, even though they had no specific idea who these young men were. It was as if they were immeasurably pleased to see that someone was allowed to live totally free of constrictions; if it couldn't be them, it might as well be us.

The availability of women was beyond normal comprehension. Teenage girls, college co-eds, married women—they were all there. In an era when young people were reputed not to respect anything, they were in awe of the traveling bands. The bands represented money, fame, freedom, an escape from the hometown—everything young America wanted. The women were part of the reward.

It was the time when the feminist movement was making its most important inroads in the United States, but you couldn't tell it on the rock and roll tours. Women willingly were treated as currency. Girls who had slept only with their boyfriends eagerly teamed up and went to bed in pairs with anyone from the tour party who beckoned them. Young wives lied to their husbands and sneaked out to cruise the bands' hotels. In other parts of American society, maybe, young men had trouble finding female companionship; not in this world. In Norfolk, Virginia, one night after a concert, there were so many women in the hallways of our hotel that the police had to come in with dogs to drive them out.

The attitude of the bands was the same as if the women had been room-service food. There was always plenty, and you could get it at any time, so why give it any thought? At the Clemson, South Carolina, Holiday Inn one warm spring night, I was in a room with Rod Stewart's band of the time, Faces. A young woman had been hanging around the group all evening, making it apparent that she was willing to go off with anyone who would have her. But that was too conventional for the men in the band. Instead of making love to her, they gathered around her, stripped her of her clothes, and placed her on the floor of the room. Then, methodically, they began to take objects and insert them into her. Bars of soap from the bathroom, room keys, a banana, the banana peel—they laughed as they gorged her. And the woman laughed, too. She lay spreadeagled and talked to the band as they did their work. Faces was one of the biggest draws in the world; the woman was clearly honored.

With another band, en route to a concert date, we sat on the plane near a young woman of extraordinary beauty. Almost always, women on the commercial flights would come over to talk to the groups, if only to find out who they were. But this woman was reticent. So the musicians approached her. It turned out that she was going to her father's funeral; he was to be buried that afternoon. One of the guitarists slipped her a piece of paper. Early that evening I saw the young woman arrive at our hotel, the piece of paper in her hand. She had come straight from the cemetery. She went to the room of the lead guitarist and the drummer, and she stayed locked up with them for two days.

With the Alice Cooper group in Sacramento, California, one evening, we returned to the hotel to find dozens of the town's teenage girls waiting. They were decked out in glitzy finery, and they obediently went to the rooms of whoever motioned to them. I never discovered how so many young girls managed to stay away from home overnight so often, but they always did. In the morning the members of the tour party went to the waiting cars for the trip to the airport. The girls from the night before lined up in the parking lot. In the early daylight, they looked far less exotic than they had the previous evening; their makeup was rubbed off, their faces were pale, and their clothes were wrinkled. Who knew what they thought they had gained from the night? They stood several feet from the cars, wanting only a goodbye. And the members of the band, on cue—they had done this many times before—looked at the girls and, Bob Hope–style, began to sing: "Thanks, for the memories. . . ." The girls still stood in the concrete lot, watching the laughing musicians drive away.

There were chartered airliners with built-in bedrooms and showers, and butlers aboard to serve multicourse meals. There were Hawaiian luaus in the dressing rooms of the arenas after the shows, with grass-skirted dancing girls to hand-feed us our supper. There were employees of the record companies to go out day or night to procure any amusement.

The ironic thing was, most of the fans who paid for the records and the concert tickets were unaware of the scope all this had taken. It was a time when a so-called social revolution was in vogue; the rock and roll stars were supposed to be the ultimate people's people. They dressed in jeans and T-shirts and boots, as if they were one with the audience; the boys and girls out in the seats did not comprehend that their money was going toward the bands' oil tax shelters and shopping-center investments.

The clearest example I saw of the attitude of the bands toward their fans came one night in Madison Square Garden, when Jethro Tull was performing before a packed house. Ian Anderson, the band's lead singer, was into the encore, and the audience was surging toward the stage. Some managed to reach the bottom of the wall that led up to the stage itself; by standing on one another's shoulders, they could boost each other up so that they were close to their heroes.

I stood by an amplifier on the stage and watched. Ian Anderson kept singing, and you could see the young fans getting nearer. You couldn't see their faces; but you could see their fingers reaching up over the front edge of the stage as they prepared to pull themselves up.

Terry Ellis, the manager of the band, was watching, too. Very calmly he picked up a hammer and walked over toward Ian Anderson and the microphone. Ellis knelt down. Coolly, every time he saw a set of fingers reach up onto the stage, he brought the hammer sharply down on those fingers. A youngster would reach up blindly to the stage; Ellis would smash his hands with the hammer. The effect was the same as touching a match to a tick; as soon as the hammer came down, the fans would drop back down into the audience. We would never see a whole person; the fingers kept inching onto the stage, and Ellis kept cracking the fingers with his hammer, and eventually the concert ended.

It was a way of life I do not expect to see again. Parts of it I will always remember; parts I am unable to forget. I am not sure if it is something I will tell my grandchildren about.

Bar Child

WASHINGTON—The first time you saw him, you wondered what he was doing there. The tavern was south on Pennsylvania Avenue, in a dying neighborhood where the tourists never come. He was perhaps eight years old, no older, a little kid in cut-off pants and sneakers and a T-shirt.

It was one of those nights that have been plaguing Washington, with the temperatures staying in the nineties, the air full of moisture and filth. You had been wandering, and you had ended up in this part of town and you had decided to look inside.

The television set over the bar was turned on. A few men sat staring at it. The booths were full of people out to slake their thirst on a cruel summer night.

And there was the bar child, sitting by himself at a table too tall for him, looking across the pale Formica top, talking to no one.

The one waitress moved past him, and he didn't look up. You figured that he had wandered in off the street, and that no one had had the time to tell him that he shouldn't be here, that bars were for grown-ups. You chuted a fistful of quarters into the juke, and when the songs had run themselves out you left. It was ten o'clock at night, and the bar child was still there.

In the nights to come, you found yourself returning. Maybe it was because you couldn't stomach the happy bars of Georgetown, and maybe it was because this place didn't seem like Washington at all; maybe it was for no reason, just a habit that you were falling into quickly. The pattern fit: you were most comfortable in a place where you knew nobody and nobody knew you.

The bar child was there every night. He always seemed to be wearing the same clothes, and sitting at the same table. Now you saw that the waitress would stop and smile at the boy once in a while, but the boy did not smile back. One night he had a comic book; mostly, when the TV wasn't on, he played with a tattered menu.

You make your living intruding into other people's lives, so for a while you didn't ask. You figured that you did enough of that kind of thing during the working day, and that at night you should leave alone something that was none of your business. But one night you walked toward the tavern, and the bar child was outside, almost as if he was waiting for you.

He had a crushed beer can, and he kicked it along the sidewalk, metal scraping concrete. He was careful not to wander far. The neighborhood is bad; he knew not to kick the can past the boundaries of the building housing the bar. The street was raucous, but the sounds were not joyful. Up to the north, shimmering in the dirty haze, bright through the distance and the hot grime, was the dome of the Capitol of the United States.

You walked in, and the bar child followed. He walked to his table. He had his crushed beer can in his hand. You got some quarters at the bar and played your music, and when the waitress came to get your order you hesitated, and then you asked her.

"Oh, it's such a shame," she told you. "His father is the cook here. The mother ran away. There's no one to take care of him. So he comes to work with his father every night, and he sits out here while his father is back in the kitchen. This is no place for a little boy, but there's no one else to look after him. He just sits here in the bar until eleven o'clock every night."

The drinkers were loud this night, but the bar child did not seem to mind. Nothing that happened in the tavern affected him; laughter or shouting, they were all the same. The waitress would stop to talk to him, but if he said anything back, he didn't bother to lift his head.

You looked over at him, and thought of saying something, and just then he turned and looked at you and his eyes had nothing in them. The bar child didn't want to be bothered, not by a stranger, not by another face that came into his world uninvited every night. You had been fooling yourself outside;

he had not been waiting for you. He knew better than to wait for anyone.

So you kept quiet, and you finished your drink and you let your music play out and when you left, he was still there. He was there when you went back the next time, and he has been there every time since. And you found yourself wondering: How long until the bar child leaves? How long until he grows old enough to walk away from his father and become a part of the streets that will swallow him up? How long until he is a little boy no longer?

One night you stayed late, and as you left you took one last look at the bar child. His head was down on the table, and the noise wasn't touching him. He was sleeping. . . .

Getting to the Heart of a Man Named Veeck

B Y NOW IT's old news that Bill Veeck has lost the Chicago White Sox; it happened last Friday, and already the papers have been filled with tributes written about Veeck by sportswriters who know him well.

I have never met Bill Veeck. Like everyone else, I was aware of his impeccable reputation for decency and class, but I have never had a chance to shake his hand. Last May, though, something happened. I didn't write about it at the time, because Veeck didn't want me to.

But now—because it looks as if Veeck will be disappearing from the Chicago scene—I want to do it.

It was May 27, a Tuesday. I had written a column about a

thirty-five-year-old man who had four children—boys fifteen, fourteen, and ten, and a girl seven. His wife had left him, and eight months earlier he had lost his job.

Every day since then, he had looked for work. There were no jobs. The gas had been shut off in his apartment; he and his children had no hot water, and could not bathe.

The man told me, in the flattest and saddest of voices, that he had decided to start committing crimes to feed his family.

"I never committed a criminal act in my life," he said. "I never even thought about it. But now I'm starting to see it in a different light. I'm starting to think that most people out there robbing are probably people just like you and me. They just can't see any other way out.

"God knows that I don't want to hurt anyone. I wouldn't take money from an innocent person on the street, like those thugs and bums. But now I can understand what goes through a man's mind when he goes into a grocery store or a bank and says, 'This is a stick-up.' That person knows that he doesn't have anything to look forward to. He's doing it because he has to."

It was a story that belonged in another country, in another century. But it was happening in the economic environment of the United States in the 1980s.

That morning, the phone didn't stop ringing. People had read the column, and wanted to help.

Every caller offered to send money. And to every caller, I explained that the man was not looking for a handout. The gift would be gone in a few weeks. What he wanted was a job. Could the caller ask around and see if there was a job for the man?

That took the callers by surprise. There were no jobs. I became resigned to it as I answered the phone all morning: this was another case of a newspaper column that would stir people's emotions for a few hours, and result in absolutely no change in the life of a man in trouble.

Around noon, the phone rang again.

"This is Bill Veeck," the caller said.

We had never spoken before. Veeck got to the point immediately.

"Is this fellow willing to work?" he said.

I said I believed he was.

"Well, I've got a big old ballpark out here," Veeck said. "I could probably use another hand to help keep things up. It's just manual labor, but if he wants work why don't you send him out here and let us talk to him."

I said I would call the man right away. But I wondered something. All the other callers had been full of sympathy, but no one had been willing to give the man a chance at a job. Why was Veeck doing it?

"Oh, I went through the Depression," Veeck said. "I've seen this before. Sometimes when a fellow is in trouble you want to go out on a limb for him."

I called the man; I told him not to get his hopes up, but that if he went out to Comiskey Park, there might be the possibility of a job for him.

The rest of the week went by; I work every Sunday, and so on the following Sunday I was in my office, writing a column.

I got a call from the security desk. The man was downstairs; he wanted to see me.

He came up. He was nervous and apologetic about taking my time. He was a big man with the softest of voices.

"I just wanted to thank you," he said. "I wanted to do it in person. I would have been here sooner, but when I got to Comiskey Park they hired me right away, and I've been working there ever since."

I said that I was glad to hear the news, but that I wasn't the person to thank. I write newspaper columns all the time and nothing happens. The person who mattered was Bill Veeck.

The man began to cry. "I'm sorry to be like this," he said. "But I was just out of hope, and it looked like nobody in the world cared, and then this happened. It's saved my life and the life of my family. I'll never forget that somebody was willing to give me a chance. I didn't know that people like Mr. Veeck really existed anymore."

Neither did I, I said. Neither did I.

He Was No Bum

A BUM DIED. That's what it seemed like. They found his body in a flophouse on West Madison Street, Chicago's Skid Row. White male, approximately fifty-five years old. A bum died.

They didn't know.

He was no bum. And his story . . . well, let his story tell itself.

The man's name was Arthur Joseph Kelly. Growing up, he wanted to be a fireman. When he was a child he would go to the firehouse at Aberdeen and Washington, the home of Engine 34. His two sisters would go with him sometimes. The firemen were nice to the kids. This was back in the days when the neighborhood was all right.

Arthur Joseph Kelly became a teenager, and then a man, and he never quite had what it takes to be a fireman. He didn't make it. He did make it into the Army. He was a private in World War II, serving in the European Theater of Operations. He didn't make out too well. He suffered from shell shock. It messed him up pretty badly.

He was placed in a series of military hospitals, and then, when the war was over, in veterans hospitals. Whatever had happened to him in the service wasn't getting any better. He would be released from a hospital, and he would go back to the old neighborhood in Chicago, and suddenly the L train would come rumbling overhead and Arthur Joseph Kelly would dive to the ground. Some people laughed at him. He didn't want to do it. A loud noise and he would drop.

He walked away from a veterans' hospital in 1954. He decided that he had to live in the real world. But he was in no condition to do that. He tried for a while, and then he went back to the only place that he remembered as being a place of happiness.

He went back to the fire station at Aberdeen and Washington.

Some of the men of Engine 34 remembered Arthur Joseph Kelly from when he was a boy. They remembered him as a bright-eyed child wanting to be a fireman. And now they saw him as a shell-shocked war veteran.

They took him in.

They fed and clothed him and gave him a place to sleep and let him be one of them. He wasn't a fireman, of course, but he lived in the firehouse, and he had the firemen as his friends. The military people didn't know what to do with his veterans benefits, so some of the firemen went to the Exchange National Bank and arranged for the benefit money to be paid to a special account. The firemen of Engine 34 took it upon themselves to become Arthur Joseph Kelly's conservator and guardian.

The years went by. Some of the firemen were transferred, and some retired, and some died. But there was always at least one fireman at the station who would take responsibility for Arthur Joseph Kelly. The firemen didn't ask for anything in return, but Kelly would stoke the furnace and clean up and help out as much as he could. There were maybe a dozen firemen over the years who became his special guardians—the ones who would deal with the bank and the military, and who would make sure that no harm came to Kelly. For a long time it was the Sullivan brothers; when they left Engine 34, another fireman willingly took over, and then another.

Once Arthur Joseph Kelly went to a Cubs game. A car backfired. He hit the ground. There was some snickering. But an older man, who had been in the service himself and was familiar with shell shock, helped Kelly up and said, "That's all right, fellow. You'll be all right." After that, Kelly stayed close to the firehouse.

His mind and his nerves were not good. The firemen had to remind him to bathe, and to change clothes, and to eat properly. They did it, for twenty years and more, without anyone asking. "He's an easygoing fellow," one of them said. "He doesn't harm anybody. It's not so hard for us to take care of him."

Then the firehouse closed down. The firemen were transferred to another station house, at Laflin and Madison. Arthur Joseph Kelly went with them, but it wasn't the same. It wasn't the firehouse he had loved as a child. He didn't want to live there.

So the last fireman to take care of him—George Grant, a fifty-one-year-old father of eight—found Arthur Joseph Kelly a place to live. It wasn't much—it was the room on Madison Street—but every month Grant would take care of the financial arrangements with the bank, and would go to Madison Street to give money to a lady who ran a tavern near Kelly's room. The understanding was that she would give Kelly his meals at the tavern. No liquor. The firemen didn't want Kelly to end up as a Madison Street wino.

"The firemen had started taking care of Art way before I even got on the force," Grant said. "I just happened to be the last in a long line of men who took care of him. I didn't mind."

When Arthur Joseph Kelly was found dead in his room, they thought he was a bum. But they should have been at the funeral.

Arthur Joseph Kelly was buried with dignity. He was carried to his grave by uniformed firemen. They were his pallbearers. Most of them were not even born when, as a boy, Kelly had started hanging around the firehouse. But they were there at the end. The firemen never let Kelly live like a bum. They didn't let him die like one, either.

Bait

WE WERE DRIVING along the Northwest Tollway, just outside the Chicago city limits. Darkness had replaced daylight.

"All these people worrying about Tylenol," said Tony De

Lorenzo. He was driving. "It doesn't have to be Tylenol next time. Whoever is doing it could put the poison anywhere. He could inject it into a pickle."

De Lorenzo was an FBI agent. We had just met.

Earlier in the day I had received a call at home from Jim Squires, the editor of the *Chicago Tribune*. The *Tribune* is where I work. Squires said he had something important we had to discuss, and he asked me to come in right away.

When I got to his office, he said he had had two surprising visitors. One was Edward Hegarty, the head of the FBI's Chicago office. The other was Richard Brzeczek, the superintendent of the Chicago police department. They had arrived together.

Hegarty and Brzeczek had an unusual request. The search for the Tylenol killer was getting nowhere. Seven people were dead. The Chicago area was in a panic; the rest of the nation was also frightened. The FBI had sent in one of its top criminal-behavior analysts from Quantico, Virginia. He was convinced that if the killer was made to feel some sort of human identification with his victims, the killer might surface.

Hegarty and Brzeczek wondered if I would be willing to write a column that might elicit that response. They realized they were treading on uncertain ground; they made it clear to Squires that they were not attempting to dictate what I would write, or even to suggest what form the column might take. But they thought we should know what their man from Quantico was saying.

Squires and I sat and talked about it. We are both part of the reporting generation that was taught to get queasy at the idea of journalists working hand in hand with law enforcement agencies. We both remembered stories of police units trying to infiltrate antiwar groups during Vietnam days. This, though . . .

"God, I'd like for that guy to be caught," Squires said.

"I know," I said.

We agreed that I should at least talk to the agent from Quantico. Then I would decide what to do.

Tony De Lorenzo pulled into the parking lot of the Mount Prospect Holiday Inn. John Douglas, the FBI criminal analyst from Quantico, was registered in room 215.

We rode the elevator upstairs. John Douglas was a dark-haired FBI man in suit pants and a vest; he had taken off his jacket. He motioned us into the room. There were a few uncomfortable moments of silence, and then he began.

"We've got an attorney general out here who's going on television every night calling this guy a 'madman,' " Douglas said. "That may be true, but calling him that isn't helping anybody."

He said that his specialty was studying the criminal personalities of multiple-murderers. He said that it was closer to an exact science than many people might believe; men who killed more than one person had certain things in common, and one of those things was that they became intensely curious about their victims in human terms.

"If this guy with the Tylenol considers his victims to be only numbers, then he'll never show himself," Douglas said. "But if he starts thinking of them as people . . . then we've got a chance."

He explained that he had followed my newspaper column in his hometown paper, the Fredericksburg, Virginia, *Free Lance-Star*. He said he felt funny proposing that I help him; but had I considered writing about the Tylenol case?

I told him that there was one story I thought was potentially a great one. A twelve-year-old girl named Mary Kellerman had been the youngest victim of the Tylenol killer; she had had a cold, and she had taken a Tylenol capsule from a bottle her mother had bought at the grocery store the night before, and she had collapsed in her bathroom and died. The Kellerman family had talked to no reporters; nothing was known of what they were going through.

"That's a story I would want to write even if I had never heard of you," I said to Douglas. "If you can get me into that house, I'd like to talk to her parents."

He said he thought it could be arranged.

"They have refused to talk to anybody," I said.

"If you knew how much they want the person who killed their daughter to be caught . . ." Tony De Lorenzo said.

We talked for about an hour. Douglas said he knew it was a long shot; but if I decided to write about Mary Kellerman, the FBI would place the Kellerman house under surveillance and would place Mary Kellerman's grave, in a nearby cemetery, under twenty-four-hour surveillance, too.

"Stranger things have happened," Douglas said. "You'd be surprised how many times these guys go to look at the grave or to look at the house."

Tony De Lorenzo picked me up at home the next morning. We drove out to the Colony Square shopping center in Mount Prospect; there we were met by another FBI agent, LeRoy Himebauch, who had been in contact with the Kellerman family. Himebauch was to take me to their house. De Lorenzo would wait for me in the shopping-center lot.

The Kellerman house was about a fifteen-minute drive away. Dennis Kellerman answered our ring. His wife, Jeanna, was waiting in the living room.

I invited Himebauch to listen in on the interview. Normally I like to do them alone. But I wasn't fooling myself; the Kellermans had allowed me in here because the FBI had told them it might help to find their daughter's killer. I thought they would be more comfortable with the agent in sight.

It was about as difficult as these kinds of conversations get. Mrs. Kellerman wept as we spoke; she kept blaming herself for purchasing the bottle of Tylenol. She said she had reached for a smaller bottle in the grocery store; but then, because she had thought she might need a Tylenol even after Mary's cold was better, she selected the bigger bottle. The bottle with the cyanide in it.

Dennis Kellerman's voice faltered as he recalled the morning Mary died:

"I heard her go into the bathroom. I heard the door close. Then I heard something drop. I went to the bathroom door. I called, 'Mary, are you okay?' There was no answer. I called again, 'Mary, are you okay?' There was still no answer. So I opened the bathroom door and my little girl was on the floor unconscious. She was still in her pajamas."

Mrs. Kellerman told me that Mary had been their only child; she was unable to have any more children. Mary had been born one month premature; as she entered the world she did not cry, and Mrs. Kellerman had been afraid. But the doctor had smiled and had said "It's all right; she's only sleeping." And she had been; from then on she had always been a quiet child.

I finished with the interview in about an hour. I thanked the Kellermans. I told Dennis Kellerman that I was curious about one thing.

"I think if this had happened to me, I wouldn't want to help with the investigation at all," I said. "I think I would just want everyone to go away and leave me alone. I wouldn't care if the guy was ever caught. I would just want to hide and be by myself."

"No," he said. "It's not like that. I can't even tell you. I can't even tell you what I would give for that guy to walk in my front door right now. Because once he walks in that door, he's mine."

LeRoy Himebauch and I walked out to his car. He unlocked the door on the passenger side for me. Then he walked back up to the house.

I saw him talking with Dennis and Jeanna Kellerman. They were listening intently.

When he returned to the car I asked him what that had been all about.

"When I was listening to you doing your interview, I kept thinking that they're going to crack up if they just stay in the house looking at each other," he said.

"So what did you do?" I said.

"I told them about groups that help out the parents of young children who have died," he said. "I told them if they contacted any church, they would probably be put in touch with one of the groups."

"But I saw you give them a piece of paper," I said.

Himebauch hesitated for a second.

"I gave them my number," he said. "I told them that if they couldn't find a group to help them, then I'd find one for them."

We rode toward the shopping center.

"I had to make them understand that I wasn't trying to help them as an FBI agent," he said. "They had to understand that it wasn't part of my official duties. It's just that . . . I don't know. Sometimes if you let your business define everything you do, you end up not doing the things you ought to do as a person."

When I got to the paper, the column came quickly.
It began:

If you are the Tylenol killer, some of this may matter to you. Or it may make no difference at all.

If you are the Tylenol killer, your whole murderous exercise may have seemed beautiful in the flawlessness of its execution. You doctored the capsules, and the people died, and you put fear in hearts all over the nation. If you are the killer, the success of your mission may be sustaining you.

If you are the Tylenol killer, though, you may be harboring just the vaguest curiosity about the people on the other end of your plan: the people who were unfortunate enough to purchase the bottles you had touched.

If you are curious, come to a small house on a quiet, winding street in Elk Grove Village. Come to 1425 Armstrong Lane. The people who live there, Dennis and Jeanna Kellerman, feel you have already been inside anyway. . . .

Every copy editor who handled the column questioned me about whether I really wanted to include the address. They pointed out that printing the address would make it simple for anyone to find the house.

I couldn't tell them that that was precisely the point. I simply asked them to leave it in.

The column ran and was widely reprinted around the nation. Squires and I did not discuss with anyone the details of how it had come to be written; we decided that if the word got out about the FBI's interest in the story, then whatever we were trying to accomplish would be undermined.

I have my own questions about the propriety of all this. As journalists, we are supposed to be independent agents. If this episode were to appear in an ethics of journalism textbook, I do not know how I might react to it. It is one thing to say that a reporter should never cooperate with a law enforcement agency; it is quite another, when seven people have been poisoned to death in the area where you live, to say that no, you will not help.

As I write this, the Kellermans' house is under FBI surveillance; so is Mary's grave at the cemetery. The killer has not shown himself. With each passing day it seems that he will not. It is far from certain whether the Tylenol killer will be apprehended. If he is, there is no guarantee that the arrest will have anything to do with what you have read here.

Because of the time between my *Esquire* deadline and the publication of the magazine, this story will not appear until the February issue. By then the case may be resolved. If it isn't, at least enough months will have passed that I will be sure the original newspaper column will have outlived its usefulness in luring the killer. And I don't want to keep this whole thing to myself any longer.

You get up every morning and you go to work and you try to do your job. Sometimes you wonder if you're doing it right. In the end, as always, here we are. You put words on paper and you hope they reach somebody.

His Name Is Sam Brooks

I GIVE UP. Sam Brooks wins.

Sam Brooks is a lumbering, annoying sixty-seven-year-old man from Brooklyn whose entire life is devoted to getting his name in the newspaper. I met him two years ago in New York.

"Put my name in your newspaper," Sam said.

I politely told him that a person had to do something newsworthy to get his name in the newspaper. It was as if I were talking to a wall.

"Put my name in your newspaper," Sam said.

I explained again why I could not do it. I went out to dinner

with some friends. I went back to my hotel room and got in bed.
There was a knock at the door. I opened it.

"Put my name in your newspaper," Sam said.

I slammed the door. I went to sleep. Several hours later, the
telephone rang.

"Put my name in your newspaper," Sam said.

Most people are nicer to Sam than I have been. So far, he has
gotten his name into 149 newspapers. You have to understand
that this is a fairly estimable feat, seeing as how Sam doesn't
even pretend to have anything going for him other than wanting
to get his name in the newspaper. He has a personality reminiscent of the old Jackie Gleason character the Poor Soul, or
maybe Duane Doberman on "Sergeant Bilko." A lot of people
feel sorry for Sam just looking at him. He kind of mopes into
the room, and says, "Put my name in your newspaper."

He travels the country by bus, carrying his moldy old clippings
in a sack. Several times since I met him two years ago, he has
taken the bus all the way from Brooklyn to Chicago in order to
ask me to put his name in the newspaper. A couple of those
times Sam was thrown out of the newspaper building by security
guards. When he finally did get to me, I said "Sam, I'm not going
to put your name in the newspaper. If you wanted to talk to me,
why didn't you just call me from Brooklyn? Why did you take
the bus all the way out here?"

"I don't have a phone," Sam said. "Put my name in your
newspaper."

Some newspapers give in to Sam quite easily. The *Houston
Chronicle*, for example, ran a story on its weather page last month
with the simple headline, THIS IS 148TH TIME SAM BROOKS HAS
GOTTEN STORY IN A NEWSPAPER. Others are less kind. At the *New
York Times, New York Daily News, and Chicago Tribune*, security
guards have standing orders to throw Sam out whenever they
see him.

And Dick Hitt, a columnist for the *Dallas Times Herald*, did a
whole column about Sam—but didn't mention Sam's name. Now
that's pretty mean. Sam bent over backwards for Hitt. "What I
gotta do," Sam said to Hitt, "say something newsworthy? Okay,
Joe DiMaggio's a moron."

A newspaperman in Buffalo shoved Sam out the door of his office. Sam yelled back at him, "I meet lots of young runaway girls on the buses. I hope one of 'em is your daughter on her way to join the Manson gang!"

Sam has developed a certain strategy. He tries to find cub reporters or interns who are eager to get bylines. Or he goes into newspaper offices on Sundays, when there aren't so many security guards around and the news is generally slow.

Sam is a retired mailman and he lives on his pension. He spends virtually all of his time riding the buses and asking people to put his name in the newspaper. The other day a fellow reporter came up to me and said, "There's some crazy guy out there who's getting thrown out. Definitely crazy."

At first I didn't think of Sam. After all, one never knows when he's in town. But about three hours later, as I was leaving the building, I got on the elevator and there, clutching onto the sleeve of one of the newspaper corporation's vice-presidents, was Sam.

"Put my name in your newspaper," he said.

I looked at him.

"Remember me?" Sam said. "We met in New York . . ."

"Yes, I remember," I said.

"I rode all the way from Brooklyn to see you again," Sam said. "All the way from Brooklyn to Chicago."

"Well, you'd better go back," I said.

"Put my name in your newspaper," Sam said.

"Go home, Sam," I said.

"Put my name in your newspaper," Sam said.

I ran away. Sam ran after me.

"Put my name in your newspaper," he yelled.

I escaped. He is gone now. I have just arrived at work. There was a letter from Atlanta waiting. It was from Sam.

"Put my name in your newspaper," the letter said.

I give up.

Damn it.

Audition

He CAME INTO the theater out of the rain, and he waited. He was carrying a bag in his right hand, the kind of bag that you might take to a gymnasium.

Auditions had been called for ten A.M. The musical was casting for actors and actresses, and the word had gone out among the theatrical community. By the time the doors to the theater opened, there was a line.

The young actors and actresses waited in the lobby. The man with the bag did not fit in; most of the other men and women were in their twenties, and he was at least twenty years older than that. There were curtains that led into the theater itself; one at a time, the applicants were called.

Once they got inside, they found a stage set like a bedroom suite. Placed rudely near the bed was a piano; here the audition pianist would lead each one through the two-minute tryout. Each had been instructed to bring a ballad and an uptempo song; if he or she were lucky, another two minutes would be allotted and the second song would be heard.

The director and his associates sat in the second row of plush red seats, clipboards on their laps. It was a beautiful theater; each man and woman seemed to hesitate for a moment upon entering.

The routine was simple. "Good morning," the director would say. "Good morning," the actor or actress would say. "What do you have for us?" the director would say. And the man or woman would hand the sheet music to the piano player.

There was no conversation. The person auditioning would sing a song. The director would say "Thank you, that was nice."

The singer would say "Thank you," and leave. The stage manager would bring the next one in.

The fear of rejection was everywhere, you could almost smell it, but it was lost behind the smiles. The ones with a chance would be telephoned that evening and asked to return; this was never mentioned. It was all very polite. No one revealed that he had a dream.

This had gone on for hours, when the stage manager said to the director, "Watch out for this next one. He's got bells."

It was the man with the bag. He came into the room, and he was jingling. He had bells in the bag.

The first thing he did was to fall down. It happened right by the edge of the steps. He meant for it to happen. He crawled over the stage, hand over hand. Some of the director's associates were stifling laughter, but it was not funny.

The man brought the bells out of his bag. He began to shake them. He handed his music to the piano player, and then, to the tune, began to prance in slow motion around the stage.

No one knew what to make of it. All of the others had stood in place and let the director judge their voices. The man with the bag spotted the bed on the stage; he slithered onto it, tried to crawl between the sheets. There was silence from the director and the others.

The man with the bag started to sing the words to "Brother, Can You Spare a Dime." Without a warning he began to strip; he unbuttoned his shirt, very slowly, bottom to top. His voice began to shake as he sang the song. It was getting uncomfortable in the room.

"Thank you, that was nice," the director said.

The man with the bag, his chest bare, stopped in his tracks. It was as if he had been electrified.

There was no motion in the theater. The director and his associates stared at the man. The piano player paused with his fingers over the keys.

"May I at least ask you something?" the man said.

The director said yes.

"What did you think of me?" the man said.

Of all the people who had come to try out that day, he was the only one to ask. He, the strangest and most puzzling of them all, was the only one to verbalize the question that was in all of their hearts. At first glance he was so different from all the others because his actions seemed to indicate something wrong with him, a certain madness; but really he was just a permutation of the rest, all of their dreams stretched beyond the breaking point and laid bare and quivering for the world to see.

The director hesitated.

"Well . . ." he said, "to be honest with you, we were looking for more of a traditional audition than something . . . ah . . . improvisational."

The man with the bag stood in place.

"Oh," he said.

Then:

"I guess that's what it's all about, isn't it? I mean, doing it in front of people. I can only do it in the basement in front of the mirror so many times." His voice was shaking terribly.

He buttoned his shirt. The piano player handed him his bag, and he put the bells back in.

"Maybe someday someone will want me," he said.

And then, on the way out:

"It's always easier in the basement."

And then he was gone. For the rest of the afternoon the actors and actresses came and went, but somehow there was a chill in the theater that would not go away.

After the Last Knockout

THE LAST WHITE heavyweight boxing champion of the world finished making his final bed of the morning. He swept up in front of the motel, then waited to see if any more guests would be checking in.

It was a balmy day in Pompano Beach, Florida. The motel was not one of the fancier ones in the area; called the Sea Cay, it had only fourteen rooms, each of which could be rented for as little as twenty-five dollars a night. This was in part due to the modest nature of the accommodations, in part due to the location of the structure—not on the beach itself, but over on a commercial throughway, Ocean Boulevard.

The motel had no office. Persons who wished to check in merely looked around for someone to give them a key. The owner/manager/maid/desk clerk—the last white heavyweight boxing champion of the world—went to the room closest to the street and picked up a magazine.

The floor was covered with a worn orange carpet. The room was dominated by a large bed; this one had not been made. A half-full plate of doughnuts, left over from breakfast, sat on a shelf. Sunlight streamed through the window.

Ingemar Johansson read his magazine. At fifty he weighed more than he would have liked: 250 pounds. His close-cropped hair was gray. Today he wore a red T-shirt, a pair of madras Bermuda shorts, red socks, and frayed blue running shoes. There was a small swimming pool outside the door; only one guest reclined by its edge, his face turned up toward the sun. Johansson preferred to be indoors. He sat with his back to the window, flipping the pages.

"Ingo," they called him back in 1959. On the evening of June 26 that year they chanted the name: "Ingo, Ingo, Ingo." In Yankee Stadium he knocked Floyd Patterson to the canvas seven times in the third round. When the night was over he was heavyweight champ.

He had never lost a professional fight. Before the match with Patterson he had been mainly a curiosity: a challenger from Sweden, a handsome, barrel-chested young man with an easy smile and piercing blue eyes. After the fight his picture was seen in magazines and newspapers virtually every week. He appeared on television variety shows. He signed movie contracts. He was on his way to becoming a matinee idol.

It lasted one week short of a year. On June 20, 1960, in the rematch at New York's Polo Grounds, Patterson knocked him out in the fifth round. They fought one more time, in Miami

Beach on March 13, 1961. Patterson again won by a knockout, this time in the sixth round.

Johansson went back to Europe then. Sonny Liston took the heavyweight title from Patterson, and then Cassius Clay took it from Liston. The boxing world was changing. Clay became Muhammad Ali. Within five years after that night in Yankee Stadium, Ingemar Johansson was virtually forgotten.

Johansson opened the door of the motel room to let a visitor in. The visitor had heard that Johansson was running the Sea Cay; he had called the motel (the number is that of a pay phone next to the pool) and had asked if he could come by. Johansson had said yes.

Johansson walked to his chair. The mail carrier had just arrived; Johansson flipped through some bills. He was cordial, if not friendly; if the visitor wanted to talk, that was fine, but it was clear that Johansson would just as soon be working around the motel.

"The only boxing I follow anymore is on TV," he said in response to a question. "I don't go to matches."

His accent was still thick. He said that he had owned the motel for three years, and that it provided him with a living income.

"In my life I like to move around," he said. "Three, four, five years in one place, and then move to the next place. It's a good way to live. You can choose exactly the kind of weather you want."

He said that after he had been champion he had lived in Switzerland, in Majorca, and on the Spanish mainland before coming to the United States. He said he liked south Florida about as well as anyplace else.

"Pompano is nice," he said. "There aren't many people here, which I like. If I want to see people I drive over to Fort Lauderdale. There are older people here, and in a business like mine, the kind of people who come to the motel determines everything. Here if I rent a room to a person, I know who will be sleeping in the room. In Fort Lauderdale, with all the young kids, you rent to one person and you can be sure that ten will be sleeping in the room."

The visitor started to ask about the title fights with Patterson.

Johannson shrugged and looked away, as if he had heard the questions too many times before.

"A championship fight is not much different from a regular fight," he said. "If fighting is your business all the fights are the same, whether there are one thousand people watching or fifty thousand. Maybe there's a difference to the public. But to a fighter it's always the same thing. There's another guy in the other corner, and you have to knock him down.

"Boxing is not like any other sport. You train just as hard, but you risk everything every time you go into the ring. If you lose once, you're on the way out. If you lose again, you're considered out of the running. It's not like football, where you can lose one Sunday, and then win the next Sunday and be a hero again."

There were no trophies, photographs, or other memorabilia visible in the room. Johansson said that he preferred it that way: "Everything I won is stored in bags in Sweden." He said he used to have a big blowup of a picture of him hovering over Patterson, but he had not really liked it; he got rid of it long ago.

The visitor asked when it had occurred to Johansson that he might be the best boxer in the world.

"I never thought about it," he said. "You don't think about being the best in the world. You just think you have a chance of winning the next fight. I never thought I was going to lose, and I kept winning, and after I fought enough fights I was the champion. And then I lost and I wasn't the champion.

"That was okay, too. Just because I had become the champion didn't mean I was going to be the champion forever. About thirty guys in the whole world have ever been heavyweight champion, so if you are one of them then it's pretty good. It's not going to go on forever."

Johansson seemed vaguely uncomfortable talking about boxing. The visitor asked him if this was so, and Johansson said yes.

"The boxing has never been the main thing with me," he said. "I've never thought of my boxing career as my life. My life right now is living in Pompano and running my motel. I get up in the morning and I go for a run—that is part of my life. Everybody has something in their life that suits them. I'm fifty and I'm still looking for mine."

The door opened. A strikingly handsome blond man in swimming trunks came in. He talked to Johansson briefly in Swedish; then he went back outside, where he was applying a new coat of white paint to the Sea Cay's sign.

"That was my son, Thomas," Johansson said. "He's twenty-seven; he lives in Sweden, but he is here helping me this month." Johansson himself had been divorced twice; he was currently unmarried.

The visitor asked Johansson if he thought he would finally settle for good in Pompano Beach.

"No," he said. "As much as I like it, I always have to look for new places to stay. Small things make you feel good about a place. I was in California recently, and I went fishing. Here in Florida you catch tropical fish. But in California they had the same kind of fish we had in Sweden when I was growing up— mackerel, flounder, cod. I went out on a pier and bought a pole for one dollar. I threw the line in, and right away I caught three or four mackerel.

"It reminded me of home, fish-wise."

He said that some people recognize him, some don't. Usually they feel they have seen him someplace, but can't figure out where. "The more kilos I take off, the more they know who I am," he said.

Most of his evenings, he said, are spent watching television. "But there are no shows in the last two or three years that I'm really interested in. I don't like the family stuff. The show I really liked was 'The Untouchables.'

"Now even the detective shows are half detective and half funny. I don't like that. I like funny things, but either you're a tough show or you're a funny show. You shouldn't be both. This 'Magnum, P.I.' . . . it's for kids. He's not tough. He's more like a joke. Shit, let's face it."

He said that he thought Americans are brought up differently from people in other countries. "You always hear Americans say that America is the best country in the world. In Sweden children don't learn that in school. It just isn't something you are taught. I think it is a good thing about America; it makes American people try harder.

"But the kids today in this country are different. When I was growing up, a kid did what he was told. If you did something wrong, then the teacher was allowed to beat you up a little. Today, the kids wait outside the school and beat the teacher up. I could have done that, but I never would have."

The visitor asked Johansson if he recalled what it felt like to hit someone in the ring.

For the first time in the conversation, Johansson smiled widely. "Oh, that's the best feeling in the world," he said. He stood up. He clenched his right fist, and he slammed it into his left palm.

"When you hit someone the right way, the feeling runs right up your arm," he said. "It's . . . it's the best."

Johansson had some things to do around the motel. So the visitor walked out to the pool, where Thomas was fixing one of the chairs.

The visitor asked Thomas if he thought his dad had any bad feelings about having to run this place every day after having once had all the perquisites that come with being champion of the world.

"No, he really kind of likes it," Thomas said. "He doesn't want to live in the past. He knows that's over. He's a guy who wants to do everything by himself. If he sees a piece of furniture he likes in a store, he doesn't think about buying it. He says, 'I think I'll go home and make one like it.' "

Thomas said that one reason his father liked living in the United States was that, as time has gone by, he has stopped being constantly reminded of who he used to be.

"In Sweden, that would never happen," Thomas said. "I can't even explain to you what it is like to be Ingemar Johansson in Sweden. The night my father won the championship is the only thing in people's lives that they remember exactly where they were. It is like when President Kennedy died in America. In Sweden, every person who is old enough can tell you what he was doing when he heard my father had become the champion.

"Here . . . he doesn't have to live with that so much."

Johansson had talked with one of the motel's guests and had returned to the room next to the street.

The visitor stopped in to say goodbye and to wish him well.

"If I can be in good shape and stay away from sickness, that's all I want," Johansson said. "That's a lot."

The visitor asked him what a good day for him was.

"A good day?" he said. "When the motel is filled up, when I've been out running in the morning, when I've paid my bills. That makes me feel good."

And he really felt that he was still looking for a way to spend his life?

"It's true," Johansson said. "I'm sure if people will have anything to remember about me, they will see in a book what happened in nineteen-hundred-fifty-nine.

"That's for them, though, not for me. It doesn't matter so much to me if they remember me as champion. It doesn't mean so much to me if they remember me at all."

The Pleasure of Your Company

Boston—It's one of those nights. I've just come back from the bar on the first floor of the hotel, and now I'm in my room. The local eleven o'clock news is on the television set; strangers are telling me about the world. My plane tomorrow leaves at noon.

I like this work, but by definition it's solitary in nature; the reporting business has undergone rapid modernizing changes in the last century, but in a lot of very important ways it's still the same as when all you needed for a story were a man, a pencil, and a train ticket. Which is fine; there's a lot of romanticism to that, and in fact it's one of the main draws of the job.

Sometimes, though—it usually happens to me during the Christmas season—you ask yourself what the wisdom is in doing something that sends you off on your own so often, putting you in towns where you know no one, with the express purpose of delving into people's lives to extract a story, and then fleeing like the wind before a real human connection can be made. Most people wouldn't live like this.

The feeling goes away soon enough, but when it's there we all deal with it the best way we can. So tonight—back at the hotel from the story, having a final drink in the barroom before trying for sleep—I reached into my briefcase and pulled out the envelope I've been carrying around.

It had arrived back in my office, bearing a Tampa, Florida, postmark. When I opened it I had found another envelope inside; it was clearly a wedding invitation.

The invitation said that Kathryn Riley and Stephen Mark Smith were requesting my presence at their wedding. The location was the First Baptist Church in Tampa; a reception was to follow at the Holiday Inn Downtown.

I was puzzled; I didn't recall knowing anyone in that part of Florida. And then a handwritten note dropped out of the envelope, over the signature of Kathy Riley.

"I know it's a trifle unusual for you to receive a wedding invitation from two total strangers," the note said. "In attempting to explain myself, let me begin by saying that while we are strangers to you, you are not a stranger to us."

She went on to explain that she and her fiancé had been reading the column for the last several years in the *Tampa Tribune*. She said some very flattering things, the details of which are not necessary to go into here; the point was, some of the things I had been trying to say and do in the column had reached her, and had stayed with her. She seemed almost apologetic about sending the invitation; she assumed I would consider it an odd thing for her to do.

I guess she would consider it even odder if she knew that her invitation was now sitting on top of a hotel bar table in Boston, while I reread her note as the jukebox played. I hadn't realized why I had been carrying the invitation around, but I suppose it had something to do with instinctively knowing that it might come in handy at a moment like this—the inevitable moment when you find yourself wondering whether what you're doing has any value to anyone but yourself.

There's an unwritten contract when you do this kind of work. You go out and see things and put yourself in situations you probably have no business being in—all aimed at coming up with a story you can tell.

The unwritten contract says that there's someone at the other end. You always assume that; your various bosses can show you surveys and studies that can approximate just how many people you are reaching every day. But somehow none of the numbers ever seem real; they're too big, you can't think in terms of figures like that, and often it takes a voice on the phone or a letter in the mail—a letter like this wedding invitation—to remind you of why you do what you do.

I read through Kathy Riley's note again. Near the end, it said:

"And so while making out our guest list, we quickly realized there were people we felt close to even though we had never met them."

Her list made me smile; it was a short one, and I found myself in the company of Walter Cronkite, Bob Seger, Captain Kangaroo—"Each of you," Kathy Riley wrote, "during the course of our lives, has in your own way meant something special to us."

I listened to the music in the barroom, and thought about what an unusual thing it is to be a part of someone's life because you are somehow included in their media mix. Cronkite, Seger, the Captain . . . we had all ended up there because of twentieth-century communications, which seems a cold and bloodless thing.

And yet what can be less cold than the idea of a young man and woman, half a continent away, wanting you to be present on the afternoon they become man and wife? It's funny; when you do a job like this one it is with you all the time, day and night, weekends, too. It obsesses you, and yet you know that when you enter the lives of the people on the other end, you'll be lucky if they give you a couple of minutes a day.

Best not to ponder that, though; sometimes, apparently, those few minutes are enough. It is nearing midnight in Boston; in the next room, I can hear people talking. Time for sleep; there are places to go in the morning.